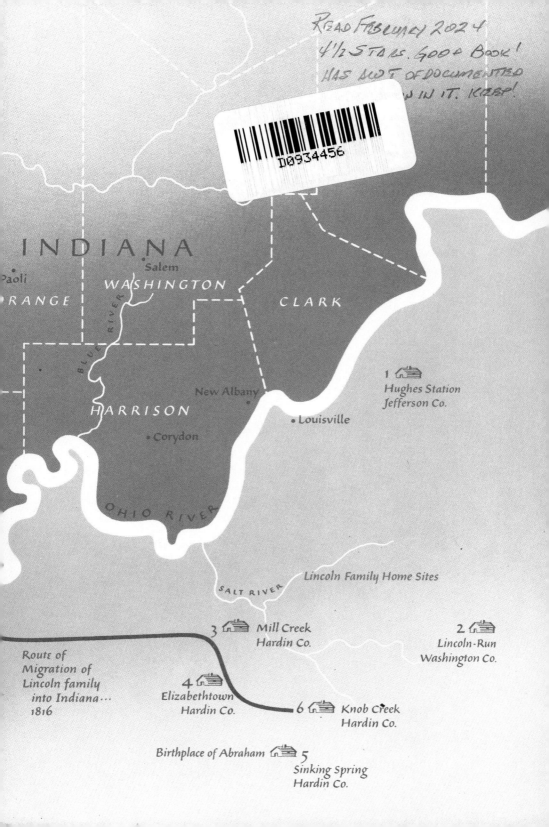

D0934456

INDIANA

Paoli

WASHINGTON

Salem

ORANGE

BLUE RIVER

CLARK

New Albany

HARRISON

• Corydon

• Louisville

1 Hughes Station
Jefferson Co.

OHIO RIVER

Lincoln Family Home Sites

SALT RIVER

3 Mill Creek
Hardin Co.

2 Lincoln-Run
Washington Co.

Route of
Migration of
Lincoln family
into Indiana…
1816

4 Elizabethtown
Hardin Co.

6 Knob Creek
Hardin Co.

Birthplace of Abraham 5

Sinking Spring
Hardin Co.

Lincoln's Youth
Indiana Years

Lincoln's Youth
Indiana Years
Seven to Twenty-one
1816-1830

by Louis A. Warren

INDIANA HISTORICAL SOCIETY

Indianapolis · 1991

Originally published in 1959 by the Indiana Historical Society, Indianapolis.

Printed in the United States of America.

The paper in this publication meets the minimum requirements of American National Standard for Information Sciences—Permanence of Paper for Printed Library Materials, ANSI Z39.48-1984. ∞

Library of Congress Cataloging-in-Publication Data

Warren, Louis Austin, 1885-1983
    Lincoln's youth : Indiana years, seven to twenty-one, 1816-1830 / by Louis A. Warren.
        p.   cm.
    Originally published: Indianapolis : Indiana Historical Society, 1959.
    Includes bibliographical references and index.
    ISBN 0-87195-062-6 (alk. paper)   ISBN 0-87195-063-4 (pbk. : alk. paper)
    1. Lincoln, Abraham, 1809-1865—Childhood and youth.
2. Presidents—United States—Biography.   I. Title.
E457.32.W284   1991
973.7'092—dc20
[B]   90-19784
                                                                         CIP

To my daughter
Evelyn
reared in Indiana

Acknowledgments

by the Author

UPON COMPLETION of the manuscript for *Lincoln's Parentage and Childhood* (The Century Co., New York, 1926) the author immediately began gathering source material for the book in hand. The policy for selecting supplemental data was influenced by a classroom axiom, "Be sure it is a fact," frequently expressed by Dr. Elmer Elsworth Snoddy, professor of philosophy at Transylvania College in Lexington, Kentucky. At the same institution Dr. William Clayton Bower's lectures on child psychology indirectly contributed to the pattern for developing the chronological sequence used in this biographical study.

The Southwestern Indiana Historical Society through "The Lincoln Inquiry" provided many worthy monographs, and one of its honored members, Mrs. Bess V. Ehrmann, also furnished valuable information. Personal interviews with descendants of the Lincolns' pioneer neighbors were helpful, and the identification of local historical sites by Ora V. Brown proved almost indispensable.

The opportunity to give undivided attention to the Lincoln theme was made possible in 1928 by the Lincoln National Life Insurance Company's sponsorship of a historical research foundation at Fort Wayne, with the author as its director. His successor, Dr. R. Gerald McMurtry, and staff have co-operated to the fullest extent. The recipients of *Lincoln Lore*, bulletin of the Foundation, should receive thanks for numerous historical contributions to the accumulation of evidence compiled.

Gratitude is expressed to the Library of Congress for making available microfilm copy of the Herndon-Weik Manuscripts in that library and in the Huntington Library in San Marino, California, which, used with circumspection, has contributed much to the text. The Indiana State Library and Historical Department, with which the author, as a member of the Library and Historical Board, was associated for many years, were especially anxious to make available their facilities. The title page of *The Arabian Nights* illustrated herein is from the copy in the American Antiquarian Society in Worcester, Massachusetts.

The author is under deep obligation to Arnold Gesell, M.D., for writing the Introduction. Dr. Gesell is director emeritus of the Clinic of Child Development, Yale University; research consultant of the Gesell Institute; author of studies in child development; nationally known authority on youth psychology.

The personal interest of Eli Lilly in having the book come out during the Lincoln sesquicentennial is sincerely appreciated. Without the support and co-operation of the Lilly Endowment, Inc., that objective could not have been attained.

These acknowledgments would be inadequate without recognizing the valuable assistance of the editorial staff of the Indiana Historical Society who have directed the progress of the manuscript and made it ready for the press.

Contents

Illustrations

Introduction

by Arnold Gesell, M.D.

ABRAHAM LINCOLN ranks as one of the most remarkable figures of modern times. His extensive writings assembled in chronological order, and a vast body of Lincoln literature which pertains to them, have created and continue to create a social heritage. In countless ways Lincoln's image has entered the folk consciousness of America. After thirty years of pioneering study of his life career, Ida Tarbell (in 1924) considered that "There's no man in American history with whom the people so desire intimate acquaintance as they do with Abraham Lincoln."

However, when Louis A. Warren, a native New Englander, came to Hodgenville, Kentucky, to edit the *Larue County Herald,* he found even the local folklore extremely unreliable and often contradictory. As a devoted friend of facts Warren resolved to search the public records for data which would supply documentary support for information. He gathered 550 court entries which bear the name of the Lincoln and Hanks families. In addition a thousand other documents were compiled which provided details of the activities of cognate families. A vast amount of source material was gained through personal papers, certificates, tombstone inscriptions, school and church records. The findings are reported in a richly factual volume, *Lincoln's Parentage and Childhood: A history of the Kentucky Lincolns supported by documentary evidence* (1926).

The concreteness and objectivity of this publication brought new light to many aspects of the Kentucky period (1809-16)—to the birthplace cabin on the Nolin Creek farm; the removal to the Knob Creek farm; the economic conditions of various trades and vocations as represented by millers, lawyers, doctors, social customs (including horse racing), religious influences; books, schools, and teachers. Ample documented evidence shows the historical Thomas to be a respected citizen of a growing community. The shiftless-father myth and likewise the myth of squalid poverty were proved to be unjust.

Church meetings and person-to-person discussions reveal the intense antislavery feeling and thought in this area of Kentucky. Thomas and Nancy Lincoln lived in the very center of slavery controversy. Abraham and Sarah heard the heated sermons of emancipator preachers. The little Lincoln family of four crossed the broad Ohio River in the autumn of 1816; the Indiana period extends from 1816 to 1830.

Dr. Warren completed his study of the Kentucky Lincolns in 1923. Immediately thereafter he turned his attention to the Indiana years. Indiana apparently made less general appeal than the Kentucky period. One writer permitted himself a statement to say laconically: "Kentucky gave Abraham Lincoln to Illinois; Illinois gave him to the nation; and the nation gave him to the ages." What was Indiana's role!

The Indiana field of Lincolniana had been greatly neglected. In a critical volume, *A Shelf of Lincoln Books* (1946), Paul M. Angle pointed to the value of the documentary type of investigation of the Kentucky years: "One of the crying needs of Lincoln literature is a survey like this for the years when the Lincoln family lived in Indiana." Dr. Warren made use of his well-tried methods of pursuing source material and continued his quest for objective data for over thirty-five years—fortunately in time to contribute to the sesquicentennial of the birth of Lincoln. The present volume is entitled *Lincoln's Youth—Indiana Years, Seven to Twenty-one, 1816–1830* (1959).

The fourteen Indiana years have a strategic position in the life cycle. They comprise one full fourth of Abraham Lincoln's allotted life span of fifty-six years. The Indiana years are highly formative, occupying as they do the long interval between early childhood and young manhood. At the age of twenty-eight years, Lincoln reaches exactly the mid-point of his career. He leaves rural Illinois for the practice of law in metropolitan Springfield. The preparatory Indiana years then bear their fruit.

The rate of development differs for different ages. For this reason chronology is an essential framework for biography, especially when the biography deals with the continuous yet changing phenomena of childhood and youth. In a documentary investigation, as in the present book, the chronological limits are respected. Each age represents a level or zone of maturity and the data appropriate to that age zone are brought together. Practically no dates beyond 1830 are used in order to protect the authenticity of the original date assigned. Dr. Warren's approach combines narrative, chronology and commentary. This means that the chronological sequence follows a straight-line continuity. The arrangement provides ample use of illustrative and other source material to suit the needs of the context. In other words, the method takes advantage of a flexibility which gives each age chapter its own individuality. The reader derives his own estimate of the changes which occur in the forward advance of the age chapters.

Growth is a key concept for understanding Lincoln as an exceptionally great man who was both simple and elusively complex. He came by his mind as he came by his body, through deep-seated mechanisms of growth. Such mechanisms operated throughout his life cycle from before birth to his final year. Although he was moved and moulded by the events of the world into which he was born, he was an end product of the vast universal forces of evolution which determine the primary growth potentials of each and every individual. Lincoln was uniquely endowed with patterns and capacities of growth which came to consistent and discernible manifestations in his public career. Were they not also present in the more private and limited career of his unrecorded childhood and youth?

We cannot now recapture the inner life of these early years in their primal essence; but by cautious deductions, we can hope to derive some of the developing traits which were precursors of the personality that has been so copiously delineated in biography, in history, poetry, and memorial art. Growth is a patterning process which psychologically manifests itself in sequences of behavior patterns which are governed by primarily internal individual timing factors. Every individual develops in accordance with a unique pattern of growth. The unique pattern is a variation of a ground plan of growth which is more or less characteristic of the human species.

Age accordingly is both a biological and a sociological concept. The annual revolution of the earth about the sun—the calendar year—has become a fundamental measure of time in ordinary appraisal and record of human affairs. The concept of the year is so firmly embedded in the ordinary orientations that it is incorporated in manifold regulatory laws, customs, and mores about life and language. It will serve a nontechnical but convenient function for the purpose of the present volume.

Time tends to keep pace with the development of language. Even in the cradle vocalizations take shape and assume pattern. Abraham had an extraordinary interest in words; spoken, self-written, and read. As an infant he listened to his mother's voice. We are told that she playfully intoned bits from the Bible while she was at work in the cabin with him near by. Abraham learned his letters from her at Knob Creek about the age of five. Here, too, he went to his first school at the age of six, accompanied by Sarah as a helpful companion. There is evidence that he was beginning to write letters soon after he arrived in Indiana. At eight years of age he read in the Bible and in Dilworth's Speller. At nine, *Æsop's Fables.* At ten, *Robinson Crusoe.*

All told, Dr. Warren assembled a group of about twenty-five different books all of which he placed in the appropriate age zones. These books make an impressive and varied course of study for Abraham's program of self-instruction. The sequence of the books is associated with stages in the maturing of his mind. Abraham was a book-loving boy. Warren presents many of the books with specimen excerpts, and with commentary and footnotes. (The reader will be rewarded with the wealth of information to be found in the footnotes.) There is ample room for empathy by sharing Abraham's reading.

At the age of twelve years Abraham was deeply stirred by reading the account of the Battle of Trenton in Parson Weems's *Life of George Washington.* Thirty years later (on February 21, 1861), in addressing the New Jersey Senate, he recalled his experience: "May I be pardoned if, upon this occasion, I mention that away back in my childhood, the earliest days of my being able to read, I got hold of a small book, such a one as few of the younger members have ever seen, 'Weem's Life of Washington.' I remember all the accounts there given of the battle fields and struggles for the liberties of the country. . . . I recollect thinking then, boy even though I was, that there must have been something more than common that those men struggled for. I am exceedingly anxious that that thing which they struggled for; that something even more than National Independence; that something that held out a great promise to all the people of the world to all time to come . . .

that this Union, the Constitution, and the liberties of the people shall be perpetuated. . . ."

A great universal idea thus had its germ in this boy at twelve years. Abraham at twelve was beginning to read at a level of conceptual thinking with a growing interest in broad principles of government. Later he sought for these principles and issues in the current newspapers as well. By one definition genius is an idea of youth developed in maturity. In Lincoln this was a slow and steady development. It took the form of recurring periods of sheer meditation. It was part of the process of growing up.

At twenty and twenty-one Abraham began to read and re-read a voluminous tome entitled *The Revised Laws of Indiana—to which are Prefixed, the Declaration of Independence, the Constitution of the United States, the Constitution of the State of Indiana, and Sundry other Documents, connected with the Political History of the Territory and the State of Indiana.*

This comprehensive volume makes a fitting climax for the remarkable series of books which document the direction and subject matter of Abraham's intellectual development.

"I grew up in Indiana." So said Abraham Lincoln, himself. He had laid many foundations of self-dependence in Kentucky and he was already a large boy for his age at seven years. Except for one brief flatboat trip to New Orleans, from seven to twenty-one years he was to remain in the Pigeon Creek settlement with pioneer people and pioneer ways. He attended three subscription schools for less than a year's time all told. Otherwise his education was concentrated in home, church, and community. He had a genius for getting and using knowledge, which trait Woodrow Wilson "regarded as more remarkable because it was free from morbid quality and slow, patient and equitable in its development. There was something native, natural rather than singular, and wholly inexhaustible about him."

But his life career tends to take on the dimensions and the design of a myth because there was a profound correspondence between his peculiar genius and the pioneer culture in which he grew.

Much of this correspondence is already foreshadowed in the illuminating Chapter One of Dr. Warren's monograph, which outlines the ancestral background and a fateful sequence of immigrations from England (1637) to Pigeon Creek, Indiana (1816). The Indiana Epoch of Fourteen Formative Years becomes a continuing test of potentials concealed and potentials revealed.

At first Abraham had very few close neighbors; but by age eleven the Lincoln family consisted of eight members. Combining three sets of orphans, it was a group of diverse origins and mixed personalities. By age thirteen within a mile radius of the Lincoln home were nine families with forty-nine children under seventeen years of age. As he grew the community grew and this served to stimulate his thinking and his observations.

What would we not give for a tape recording and film of young Lincoln in free play with his companions, or addressing them in an impersonation of a visiting preacher. He deserves more than a satirical portrayal as a backwoods rustic. It is possible to envisage him as a gentle boy, comely and healthy, with mobile expressiveness of his moods.

There are several personality traits which embrace his growing-up processes. It is the combination and distribution of these several traits in the person of one man that makes them significant. The traits are so fundamental that they must be considered from the standpoint of endowment as well as of experience. Dr. Warren's book gives abundant opportunity to suggest how these and associated traits came to their flowering in the culture which is so effectively portrayed.

First and foremost is Abraham's individual physique, if regarded in mental as well as bodily terms. At seven he was strong enough to wield an axe in the wilderness; his strength was the mainstay of his endurance, mental as well as physical, and the guardian of his self-confidence. His curiosity was for alertness, inquiry, and discovery—a veritable thirst for facts. With the aid of sympathy, curiosity led to understanding of human nature, and a tender awareness of animal life. Humor served to dissolve tension, to restore pliancy of the mind, to prevent it from over-stretching—and to entertain. Intelligence was one of the most significant of Abraham's traits. Reinforced by his tenacious memory and sagacity, it came to high uses during his presidential years. Friendliness stands out as the dominating personality trait in the sphere of emotions—it manifested itself in childhood and youth so naturally that it was acknowledged by everybody. Friendliness was to his emotions what curiosity was to his intellect, an engaging trait because it was his spontaneous language for expressing his respect for the dignity of the individual.

In an intimate vein the President spoke, with characteristic friendliness, to the 166th Ohio Regiment, passing through Washington a few weeks before the close of the war. Again he spoke of a great promise to all the people of the world, perhaps for all future time. The echoes of the Trenton address are heard: The continuance of popular government dependent on principles which Lincoln at the age of twelve began to see in their implications perhaps for all future time: "I beg you to remember this, not merely for my sake, but for yours. I happen, temporarily, to occupy this big White House. I am a living witness that any one of your children may look to come here as my father's child has."

Lincoln's Youth
Indiana Years

CHAPTER I

Ancestral Background

1637–1816

ABOUT THE TIME that the Mayflower landed at Plymouth, 1620, a child by the name of Samuel Lincoln was born at Hingham, England. Seventeen years later this boy joined his older brother Thomas, who had come to America in 1633 and was one of the six original settlers of Hingham, Massachusetts. Samuel became the progenitor of a number of distinguished men bearing the name Lincoln. Among them was an Attorney General of the United States; two brothers who served simultaneously as governors, one of Maine and one of Massachusetts; and still another statesman who became President of the nation.[1] One writer has listed the names of three hundred and fifty prominent men and women bearing names other than Lincoln who were descendants of Samuel through cognate families.[2] In 1937, on the three hundredth anniversary of his arrival, a memorial tablet was dedicated in Samuel's honor at the Old Ship Church in Hingham which he had helped build. A son of Samuel, Mordecai, remained in Massachusetts, and his substantial colonial home, still in good state of preservation, stands at near-by Scituate.

Two sons of Mordecai I, Mordecai II and Abraham, began a significant westerly migration, continued through succeeding generations, which kept the Lincolns in the vanguard of

3

the frontiersmen. They crossed the hill country, passed through the valley of the Shenandoah, then down the Wilderness Road, over Cumberland Gap, along the rivers and Indian trails, hewing their way through virgin forests and following the buffalo paths into the prairies of the West.

Mordecai, grandson of Samuel, was born in Massachusetts, married in New Jersey, and died in Pennsylvania; Mordecai's son John was born in New Jersey, married in Pennsylvania, and died in Virginia; and John's son Abraham was born in Pennsylvania, married in Virginia, and died in Kentucky. Abraham's son Thomas, of the sixth generation of the Lincoln family in America, was born in Virginia, married in Kentucky, and in keeping with the migratory tradition of his forebears, in 1816 contemplated a removal to Indiana.[3]

Thomas Lincoln came from Virginia to Jefferson County, Kentucky, with his father and mother, two sisters, and two brothers, when he was about five years old. He was the youngest son in the family. While the date of his birth seems to be January 6, 1778, his name appears on the Hardin County tax list in 1797 as a "white male twenty-one years or over." This would indicate the year of his birth as 1776 or earlier.[4] In 1786, four years after the family arrived in Kentucky, the father was killed by the Indians, and Thomas "by the early death of his father, and very narrow circumstances of his mother, even in childhood was a wandering laboring boy, and grew up litterally without education."[5] His mother had moved into the Beech Fork community in Washington County, and Thomas lived with her, working at odd jobs. About his eighteenth year he was in Hardin County where he found employment in Elizabethtown assisting Samuel Haycraft in building a mill and mill race. Thomas had steady work at this place for many weeks, as the account books of Haycraft show.[6]

There is no evidence that Thomas was living in Kentucky during 1798, which may have been the year that he was work-

4

ing in Tennessee: "Before he was grown, he passed one year as a hired hand with his Uncle Isaac on Wata[u]ga, a branch of the Holsteen [Holston] River."[7] However, he would have been at least twenty in 1798. His name appears on the tax book in Washington County in 1799 as the owner of two horses. He is also recorded as residing with his mother in 1800 and 1801.[8]

One of his brothers had married in 1792, and his other brother and two sisters were all married in 1801.[9] A year or two later the two daughters and their husbands, as well as Thomas, moved to Hardin County. The mother accompanied them, and lived with her daughter Nancy and her husband, William Brumfield, and Thomas on the Mill Creek farm which Thomas acquired in 1803.[10] By the purchase of land Thomas became a freeholder, and thereafter his name appears frequently in the public records as a taxpayer, petitioner, juryman, and patroller.[11]

On February 18, 1806, Thomas sold to Bleakley & Montgomery, merchants of Elizabethtown, "2400 pounds of pork at 15 pence [per pound] and 494 pounds of beef at 15 pence." This gave him credit at the store of "21 pounds, 14 shillings and 1½ pence."[12] This would indicate that he was engaged in farming. But he was also continuing his carpentry. He was hired by Bleakley & Montgomery to help construct a flatboat, and when it was finished, he was employed, along with Isaac Bush, to go down river to New Orleans with a load of goods. The boat left about the first of March in 1806, and Thomas was home again by the first of May.[13] After making a settlement with the merchants upon his return, he was credited on the ledger of Bleakley & Montgomery as follows:

Thomas Lincoln going to Orleans . . . Ł16.10.0
gold . . . . Ł13.14.7½ [14]

With the Ł21.14.1½ shown before he had a total drawing account of Ł50.38.9, a very respectable sum for a young man to have acquired by his own labor in the West in that day.[15]

5

What would the normal young man who owned a two hundred-acre farm, free from debt, and "with money in the bank" be thinking of at such a period in his life? Marriage, of course. The same ledger which carried his credits shows the purchases he made for his wedding. He bought cloth for his wedding suit—3½ yards of cashmere, 3 yards of coating, and almost 9 yards of material for lining, etc., also thread, tape, buttons, and other notions. He had already acquired a pair of suspenders, a new hat, and a calfskin to be made into boots. For his horse he purchased a "tipt" or decorated bridle.[16]

Thomas Lincoln's prospective bride was Nancy Hanks. She was the only daughter of James and Lucy (Shipley) Hanks. The date of her birth is supposed to have been February 5, 1784.[17] Her father had died some time before she and her mother moved from Virginia to Kentucky. Unfortunately the Hanks genealogy is not so easily traced as that of the Lincolns, since James Hanks, father of Nancy, cannot be positively identified. If it could be proved that he was the son of a Joseph Hanks who came into Kentucky about 1787 with his family, all the cousin relationship with Nancy claimed by this Joseph's children, would be confirmed.

The maternal line of Nancy Hanks can be more accurately traced. Nancy's earliest American Shipley progenitor was Adam Shipley who came to Ann Arundel County, Maryland, in February, 1668.[18] Adam and Lois (Howard) Shipley had a son Robert. This Robert and his wife Elizabeth had a son, Robert, Jr., who migrated first to Bedford County, Virginia, and then to Mecklenburg County, North Carolina. Robert, Jr., and Sarah (Dorsey) Shipley had a daughter Lucy who married James Hanks and by whom she had one daughter Nancy.[19] As we have said, after James's death Lucy and her daughter immigrated to Kentucky. Here Lucy married as her second husband Henry Sparrow. Lucy has been described as "shrewd, not very much of a talker, very religious and her disposition was very quiet." Three of her sons by Henry

6

Sparrow became ministers,[20] which would give support to her being "very religious." Lucy's daughter Nancy was a member of the fifth generation of American Shipleys.

It is through the Shipley family that the most dependable information about the girlhood of Nancy Hanks has come down to us. Lucy Shipley Hanks had four sisters. Their descendants' reminiscences of Lucy and her daughter Nancy are in agreement. Upon reaching Kentucky mother and child found a home with Lucy's eldest sister, Rachel Shipley Berry, wife of Richard Berry, Sr. Upon Lucy's marriage to Henry Sparrow, Nancy is said to have remained with her aged aunt and uncle.[21]

Nancy was very fortunate in having spent several years in this pleasant and comfortable home. Her uncle, Richard Berry, Sr., was a person of some standing in his community, and served for a while as constable of Washington County.[22] He seems to have been a successful and prosperous farmer. In 1792 he listed for taxation two slaves, ten horses, thirty-four head of cattle, and six hundred acres of land.[23] At his death in 1797 his will and the appraisal of his estate show the economic condition of these relatives with whom Nancy lived. Her Uncle Berry left a Negro boy, Fill, and a Negro woman, Nan, and her daughter Hannah, several horses, three cows and a calf, two yearling heifers, and ten steers; and household effects including three featherbeds, two spinning wheels, a reel, a chest, a table and seven chairs, a cupboard, basins, plates, dishes, pots, kettles, and a Dutch oven. The value of his personal property was estimated at £229.7, a sizable sum for that day. And it should be remembered that this did not include the value of his land holdings.[24]

Another niece of Richard Berry's wife Rachel also lived for a while in the household along with Nancy. This was Sarah Mitchell, daughter of Robert and Naomi (Shipley) Mitchell, born December 31, 1778. Sarah was an orphan. Her mother had been killed by Indians at a place called Defeated Camp

7

while the Mitchell family was migrating from North Carolina to Kentucky. Sarah herself had been carried off by the Indians, and, according to family tradition, her father was drowned in the Ohio River when he was attempting to cross it in search of his daughter. She was released after the Treaty of Greenville. One of the descendants of Sarah has made this statement with respect to their acquaintance: "Sarah Mitchell and Nancy Hanks were first cousins, both orphans, and were reared and educated by Uncle Richard Berry. These two girls grew up together, went to school together and became known as sister cousins." [25] Education for girls at that time was limited usually to instruction in spelling and reading.

Nancy would probably have tried to help Sarah make up for the years lost by her captivity. One family story goes that "Sarah Mitchell was the pupil of Nancy Hanks in learning to spin flax, the latter being adept in that now lost art. It was the custom in those days to have spinning parties, on which the wheels of the ladies were carried to the house designated to which the competitors, distaff in hand, came ready for the work of the day. At a given hour the wheels were put in motion and the flimsy fiber took the form of firmly lengthened strands. Tradition says that Nancy Hanks generally bore the palm, her spools yielding the longest and finest thread." [26]

A mile and a half from the Berry plantation was the home of Thomas Lincoln's widowed mother. The Lincolns and Berrys had been neighbors for seventeen years. Mordecai, Thomas' eldest brother, served as an appraiser of Richard Berry's estate. William Brumfield whom Nancy Lincoln, sister of Thomas, married, was a grandson of this Richard. Thomas Lincoln visited in the Berry home and formed an attachment for Nancy, which continued after he had moved with his family to the Mill Creek farm in Hardin County in 1803. The fact that both Thomas and Nancy had lived in the Beech Fork community since childhood, except for the past three years which Thomas spent in Hardin County, and that both young people came from sturdy, respectable pioneer families, would make their wedding of some significance.

Thomas Lincoln, dressed up in his wedding clothes, must have been the envy of the swains of the countryside as he rode over to the Beech Fork settlement in Washington County for his wedding. Nancy's attendant was her close friend and cousin, Sarah Mitchell, who had married John Thompson in 1799. Perhaps Mordecai, Thomas' eldest brother, attended him. Richard Berry, Jr., cousin to Nancy, signed the marriage bond as her guardian, and it would have been his office to have given the bride away. The Rev. Jesse Head performed the ceremony, and pronounced Thomas Lincoln and Nancy Hanks husband and wife on June 12, 1806.[27] This wedding united a sixth generation Lincoln with a fifth generation Shipley.

The ceremony was followed by a typical pioneer infare with such delicacies served to the guests as bear meat and barbecued sheep.[28] Apparently the Washington County Circuit Court, then in session, adjourned for the day in order to attend the wedding. This was just as well, for the minister, the best man, and the host at the festivities all had business with the court that term and might have been summoned on that day.[29]

After the ceremony the bride and groom occupied the new residence which the bridegroom had prepared in Elizabethtown. Thomas paid taxes that year on a cabin home and two house lots.[30] Two days after the wedding the couple made their first purchase at the Bleakley & Montgomery store, buying "½ set knives & forks" and "3 skanes silk."[31] Later they acquired at a sale "a dish and plates" for $2.68 and a "basin and spoons" which cost them $3.24.[32]

Sarah, Thomas and Nancy Lincoln's first child and a member of the seventh generation of Lincolns in America, was born in Elizabethtown on February 10, 1807. She was named for Sarah Mitchell Thompson, who had named her first daughter Nancy. It was here also in Elizabethtown that the prenatal life of the Lincoln's first son began in May, 1808. During this month there are many entries in the court records and store accounts that confirm the Lincolns' residence in the county seat town at this time. The Lincolns continued to live happily and prosperously in Elizabethtown until late in the year 1808. Then they moved to the farm on Nolin Creek, near Hodgen's Mill, in present Larue County, which Thomas purchased from Isaac Bush. Here in their new home by the Sinking Spring there was born to them, on February 12, 1809, a son named for his paternal grandfather, Abraham Lincoln.[33]

The Lincoln family lived at the Sinking Spring farm for only two years, then moved eight miles north, to a site on Knob Creek. A flaw in land title was responsible for the move.[34] At the Knob Creek farm a second son, named Thomas for his father, was born. He died in infancy.[35] It will be recalled that the first Lincoln to arrive in America was named Thomas and through the years it was a popular name with the family.

The Lincolns continued to live on Knob Creek, and Abe grew big and strong under the loving care of his parents. When he was five years old his mother was teaching him his letters. It has been claimed that by the time he was seven he was able to take his turn in the daily Bible readings of the family.[36] While Thomas and Nancy Lincoln had never had the privilege of a formal education, they were anxious that their children should take advantage of every opportunity that came their way to get instruction. Elizabethtown was the site of an academy, which had among its teachers at the time the Lincolns lived there Duff Green, who was to become the famous journalist-politician. He remarked at one of the school programs, "It must be most pleasing of all considerations to the parent, to be enabled to assist the minds of the rising family, to pursue virtue through the paths of literature." [37] These words, later published, may have reached the ears of Nancy and Thomas. Also it is very likely that they saw exhibi-

FIRST GENERATION

    Samuel, 1619–1690

    NO SIGNATURE AVAILABLE

SECOND GENERATION

    Mordecai, 1657–1727

THIRD GENERATION

    Mordecai, 1686–1736

FOURTH GENERATION

    John, 1716–1788

FIFTH GENERATION

    Abraham, 1744–1786

SIXTH GENERATION

    Thomas, 1776–1851

SEVENTH GENERATION

    Abraham, 1809–1865

Signatures of Abraham Lincoln and his American progenitors

tions of the academy students' work which contributed to their realization of the importance of education.

As soon as Sarah and Abraham were old enough they were sent to a subscription school. The schoolhouse was located about two miles north of their Knob Creek home on the same road on which they lived. An order in the Hardin County Court in 1800 locates the school when it mentions a point where the road from Rolling Fork intersects "the old road near a school house on Knob Creek." [38] Abraham was just six years old when he went to his first school. His teacher was Zachariah Riney. Spelling was probably his chief subject, as he had already learned his letters and could read a little. The textbook, which he shared with his sister and which will be examined later in detail, was Dilworth's Speller.

The next teacher who taught in this schoolhouse was Caleb Hazel. He happened to be the next door neighbor of the Lincolns; their cabin homes could not have been more than three hundred feet apart. [39] Not only were the Lincolns and Hazels neighbors, but the first Mrs. Hazel was related through marriage to Nancy Lincoln. Upon the death of his first wife Hazel married again, and Thomas Lincoln's name appears on his marriage bond. [40] The Lincolns and the Hazels were also members of the same church—the Little Mount Church, a Separate Baptist congregation.

Possibly Abraham's schooling—reading, writing, and spelling—continued after the regular session was over under the tutorship of Hazel. It takes no stretch of imagination to visualize the neighbor teacher, who, by the way, was a fine penman, taking a special interest in this eager, curious boy who lived next door. [41] In a community where there was much illiteracy the boy apparently surprised some of his neighbors: "He set everybody a-wonderin' to see how much he knowed and he not mor'n seven." [42]

After the Lincoln family had lived on the Knob Creek farm for five years or so, Thomas began to think of moving on.

11

Possibly his restlessness at this time might be construed as an inheritance from his Lincoln forebears that had moved westward with the advancing frontier. The Lincolns were not adventurers, explorers, or hunters, such as their distant kinsman Daniel Boone. They were tradesmen, farmers, and primarily homeseekers, who were hoping by each move to improve their economic condition. They should be associated with that substantial element of the pioneers who gave character and stability to the western movement. Two basic factors beside the lure of the frontier influenced Thomas Lincoln to seek a new home in 1816: insecurity of Kentucky land titles and slavery.

Virginia, the parent state of Kentucky, had required the holders of land warrants to provide at their own expense a survey of the tract that they proposed to claim, including a description of it. Since marked trees and movable stones were often used as corners, and meanders of creeks that ran dry as division lines, the descriptions of the surveys became vague and indefinite. As one historian put it, "In the unskillful hands of the hunters and pioneers of Kentucky, entries, surveys, and patents were piled upon each other, overlapping and crossing in endless perplexity." [43]

Thomas Lincoln was a victim of this antiquated method of surveying and recording. In 1803, when he was twenty-seven years old, he purchased 238 acres of land (the Mill Creek farm) for which he paid £118 in cash; but thirty-eight acres of this tract were lost to him because of an erroneous recording of the survey.[44] Five years later for $200 cash he acquired a farm (the Sinking Spring farm) of 348½ acres, but this tract was soon in litigation. Apparently he lost not only his $200 but also such improvements as he may have made. In 1811 he acquired title to a 230-acre farm (the Knob Creek farm).[45] But after he had lived on it for four years an ejectment suit was brought against him and nine of his neighbors by the Middleton heirs of Philadelphia, claiming prior title to a ten

12

thousand-acre tract which included the land Thomas had acquired by purchase.[46]

During a period of eight years Thomas had held 816½ acres of land but all he salvaged from these holdings was two hundred acres. He sold these in 1814 and took a loss of £18 under his original purchase price because of a faulty survey.[47]

In 1816, when Thomas Lincoln turned his eyes toward Indiana, it was not in the hope of acquiring large land holdings or more fertile fields, but it was a desire for security.[48] He wanted a place where land once purchased could be retained. Thomas Lincoln left Kentucky "chiefly on account of the difficulty in land titles"; however, "this removal was partly on account of slavery."[49] There is no valid reason to doubt this assertion, and much to confirm it. It should be given full consideration as an important factor in the final decisions of the Lincolns to migrate to a free state.[50]

A most disturbing and bitter controversy over the rights and wrongs of slavery was being waged in that part of Kentucky where the Lincolns lived. The record book of the South Fork Baptist Church, located within two miles of the Lincoln Sinking Spring home, shows that in 1808 fifteen members "went off from the church on account of slavery." At the time of Abraham Lincoln's birth this church had closed its doors because its members could not meet in peace. Among its congregation were friends of the Lincolns and relatives of Nancy Lincoln. As mentioned, Thomas and Nancy affiliated with the Little Mount Church, a Separate Baptist congregation located about three miles from the Knob Creek farm. Its members were antislavery in sentiment.[51]

The Ordinance of 1787 organizing the Northwest Territory provided that: "There shall be neither slavery nor involuntary servitude in the said territory." The Constitution of Indiana provided that "no alteration of this constitution shall ever take place so as to introduce slavery or involuntary servitude in the state." It was drafted in June, 1816. While its provisions may

13

not have reached the ears of Thomas Lincoln when he determined to leave Kentucky, it was generally understood that the institution of slavery would never cross the Ohio River.[52] In fact, it would be safe to conclude that in the case of most of the migrating Kentuckians, and in that of Thomas Lincoln, in particular, the guarantees of land boundaries and the advantages of a free state over a slave state were primary factors in the change of location.[53]

In the year 1816 the Lincoln family moved across the Ohio where the drama of "Lincoln's Youth—Indiana Years" was to be enacted.

CHAPTER II

7

Wonder

1816

JAMES MADISON, the fourth President of the United States of America, issued a proclamation on May 1, 1816, announcing that "certain lands in the Indiana territory" would be offered for sale to the highest bidder. The procedure was in keeping with former disposition of government property in the West. An auction was held at Vincennes beginning on the second Monday in September and continuing three weeks. Altogether 906 tracts comprising 144,960 acres, averaging $3.00 per acre,[1] were sold, an indication of the flourishing character and bright prospects of the new state that was coming into being. Even the Eastern cities were impressed with this expansion, and the Boston *Gazette*, as quoted by the Vincennes *Western Sun* for June 20, 1816, stated: "Probably no country ever progressed so rapidly in population and improvement as our own western states and territories have in the last fifteen years. . . . Even Indiana, which we had hardly learnt to consider anything but a pathless wilderness, has risen to the magnitude of a state, her population having increased from 30 to 60,000."

At this time Indiana Territory was approaching statehood. The enabling act was passed the preceding April, a constitution for the new state was drafted in June, and the first election was held in August. On December 11, 1816, Indiana

15

became the nineteenth state of the Union. Those who observed with most interest the establishment of the new commonwealth were the Kentuckians to the south who lived in the counties bordering the Ohio River. It is accepted generally that the earliest Anglo-Saxon settlements in Indiana were made by them. They established what might be termed a "Kentucky Colony" in the adjacent wilderness to the north. One of the participants in this mass migration was Thomas Lincoln who brought his family across the river to found his Indiana home just about the time the new state was received into the Union.

Earlier that fall Thomas Lincoln made a preliminary trip of inspection into Indiana to select a homesite. He decided that a quarter section of land in Hurricane Township, Perry County, would answer his needs. When he had made his choice, he followed the practice of marking his tract by piling up brush at the four corners and erecting some kind of modest improvement, such as a hunter's half-face camp, near the place where the cabin was to be built. Such a structure would provide a temporary shelter upon the arrival of the family. The distance from the Knob Creek farm to the Indiana site selected by Thomas Lincoln was less than a hundred miles. It took him about a week to make the round trip.[2]

After the location for the new home had been established, the problem of moving had to be faced. It is not known for sure what type of conveyance was used by the Lincolns to move their goods to Indiana. Thomas listed four horses for taxation in 1815, and so we may assume that he had horses either for riding or for drawing a wagon.[3] For several years the family had lived on a much traveled road and they would have had ample opportunity to observe the various types of wagons used by immigrants coming into Kentucky. Thomas, who by trade was a carpenter, would have had no difficulty in making some kind of horse-drawn vehicle sufficiently strong to convey their personal belongings and household

16

Lincoln Family Migrations
and homesites,
1637–1816

THE STATES AS OF 1816, WITH THE DATES OF THEIR ENTRANCE
INTO THE UNION
(*Louisiana, admitted April 30, 1812, is not shown on the map.*)

1. Delaware, December 7, 1787
2. Pennsylvania, December 12, 1787
3. New Jersey, December 18, 1787
4. Georgia, January 2, 1788
5. Connecticut, January 9, 1788
6. Massachusetts, February 6, 1788
7. Maryland, April 28, 1788
8. South Carolina, May 23, 1788
9. New Hampshire, June 21, 1788
10. Virginia, June 26, 1788
11. New York, July 26, 1788
12. North Carolina, November 21, 1789
13. Rhode Island, May 29, 1790
14. Vermont, March 4, 1791
15. Kentucky, June 1, 1792
16. Tennessee, June 1, 1796
17. Ohio, March 1, 1803
18. Louisiana, April 30, 1812
19. Indiana, December 11, 1816

effects for the comparatively short distance that they would have to travel.[4]

Thomas and Nancy had been married ten years and had accumulated the usual amount of plunder, so-called, customarily found in the one-room log cabins of that period. They made no attempt to move furniture such as tables, chairs, or cupboards, because these and even a bedstead could be built by Thomas after their arrival. They did take their good feather bed and such other bed coverings as would make them comfortable, a spinning wheel, and utensils for cooking.[5] Among the important items which would have been included were an axe and other wood-clearing implements, a steel point for a plow, and, of course, Thomas' carpenter's tools, his primary means of making a living.

Provisions and provender for the winter were an important consideration. Wild game would be available in abundance at the new home, but such cured meats as they had prepared during the recent hog-killing season undoubtedly would have been added to their food supply. Corn, both shelled and ground, and especially seed corn for the spring planting, would be included. They had to leave behind in the loft of a neighbor's cabin a surplus of forty bushels of corn.[6] At least one cow would be taken along, possibly the one which Thomas had purchased at auction two years earlier, as a heifer, for $9.42.[7]

There was one sad mission to perform just before leaving for Indiana, a visit to the grave of little Thomas. This was in a cemetery on a hilltop just south of the Lincoln farm. The spot had been marked with a small field stone on which the initials T. L. were cut.[8]

Once started on their grand adventure the most exciting experience anticipated by the children was their first sight of the Ohio River, of whose broad expanse and shiny splendor they had heard so much. They were assured it would look "some different" from the tiny Knob Creek by which they had

18

lived. Long before they came near it, as they reached elevated places on the trail, they strained their eyes for a glimpse of the bright winding waterway. The family's first destination was the ferry operated on the Ohio from a point on the Kentucky side opposite the mouth of Anderson River by Hugh Thompson.[9] This was the ferry that would put them down closest to their future homesite. Abraham probably received a real thrill out of the ferry ride—a sensation which his mother and little Sarah may not have shared. The charges as prescribed by law about this time for ferrying were: $1.00 for a horse and wagon; 25 cents for a man and horse; 12½ cents for great cattle; 12½ for foot passengers. Children under ten years of age—which would include Sarah and Abraham—were usually carried free.[10]

It is hardly possible that the children would have seen a steamboat on the Ohio, although earlier in the month the *Washington* and the *Pike* descended the rivers to New Orleans,[11] and the *Aetna* and the *Enterprise* were also making regular trips to the Gulf. By the end of 1816 seven had been launched on the western waters, but at least one of these had been destroyed at New Orleans and another was operating around the city.[12] But what a sight it would have been for them! Perhaps they did see flatboats and barges, like of which they had never before beheld.

The exact day on which the Lincolns stepped onto Indiana soil is not known, but, as mentioned, it was close to the day that Indiana came into the Union—December 11, 1816—sometime between the present Thanksgiving Day and Christmas.[13] The editor of the Vincennes *Western Sun*, anticipating Indiana's statehood, wrote enthusiastically on August 31, 1816: "What a sublime spectacle will your country present to the world, if your union can be preserved! and preserved we trust it will be." The most difficult part of the journey still lay ahead of the Lincoln family, although they had only sixteen more miles to go. The Perry County Court, in October, 1815, had ordered the road overseers "to open a road from Troy [on the Ohio River] to the Hurricane, 12 feet wide, in such manner that carriages can conveniently pass and that they have the same completed by next November court." [14]

The road followed a very early trail to Polk Patch in Warrick County, where a blockhouse was built a few years before, and it passed within four miles of the Lincoln homesite. How much had been done on this road to meet the specifications of the court by the time the Lincolns came is not known. Undoubtedly they would have encountered their greatest difficulties when they had to leave it and pick up a township trail. One of Lincoln's new neighbors related that Thomas Lincoln "came in a horse wagon, cut his way to his farm with an ax felling the trees as he went." [15] And this seems to coincide with family tradition. This toilsome journey through the almost impenetrably entangled grapevines made a deep impression on the little seven-year-old boy, who in early years "never passed through a harder experience than he did in going from Thompson's Ferry" to their homesite. [16] One of the early settlers of Indiana observed that the lowlands were so thick with underbrush that "one could scarcely get through." The pioneers called the thickets "roughs."

It is interesting to speculate on what factors influenced Thomas Lincoln in selecting his land. A salt lick near by which attracted wild game in abundance would have been a contributing feature. [17] The field notes of David Sanford, deputy surveyor, made in March, 1805, reveal the condition of the land as he moved along the southern boundary of what later became Carter Township. Starting on the east with Section 31 he observed that the land was level barrens, open and wet with some oak and hickory. Section 32, where the Lincoln land was located, he described as "land level, oak and hickory, medium growth is hazel and other brush very thick. The timber on this mile is chiefly destroyed by fire." Section 33 was described as mostly level, chiefly creek bottom, over-

flowed by high water. The three following sections in the
township consisted of broken or uneven land mostly poor, of
second- or third-rate quality.[18] Certainly the discovery of "a
living spring of water" was important in determining where
the cabin would be located. "Springs furnishing water suitable
for drinking purposes existed on the west side of Lincoln's
eighty acres. . . . Such water was an asset to any tract of
land. . . . On the south line of Lincoln's eighty there was a
brook ten links wide running north-west."[19] The immediate
site of the cabin was a knoll which, because of the elevation,
would be dry and healthy. Furthermore, their cabin would
face the township trace over which they had hewn their way.

Just how the family had protected themselves from the
weather during their stops along the way is not known.
Naturally their first thoughts upon arrival would be a perma-
nent shelter. The crude half-face camp which Thomas had
thrown together when he had selected his land would have
provided some security. Or perhaps the mother and the children found a temporary lodging in a neighbor's house, while
their own cabin was being put up.[20]

The harvest season was now past and the settlers were free
to help in the home-building project. Thomas Lincoln was
experienced in cabin building, having assisted in erecting
many in Kentucky, including two or three of his own, and had
once contracted for supplying the timber for a mill.[21] The
construction of a cabin was not a time-consuming enterprise.
One family reaching southern Indiana about the same time
as the Lincolns reported: "Arrived on Tuesday, cut logs for
the cabin on Wednesday, raised the cabin on Thursday, clapboards from an old sugar camp put on Friday and on Saturday
made the crude furniture to go to housekeeping."[22]

The routine in building a cabin was as follows: the trees to
be felled were carefully selected to provide logs a foot in
diameter and twenty feet long. Sixteen of these logs were
needed, eight for the front and eight for the back wall. Sixteen

21

logs, eighteen feet long were cut for the two end walls, and in addition, a few shorter ones of proper length were cut to fill the gables. This would mean that approximately forty logs, one foot in diameter, would have to be prepared. They would then be rolled to the cabinsite or pulled there by oxen or horses. Four large stones would be laid at the corners for the foundation, and, with an axeman at each corner to notch the logs properly for a close fit as they were put in place, construction would get under way.

Smaller logs for the loft floor would be laid, then others reaching from gable to gable, to serve as joists for the roof, and finally the ridge pole would be set in position. Clapboards, a half-inch thick, would be set in their proper courses on these joists to make the roof waterproof, and over the clapboards poles would be laid to keep them in place. After this the openings for the door, window, and fireplace would be cut out and a stick chimney would be constructed on the outside of the cabin to connect with the place that had been cut for it. The construction of such a home with the help of neighbors was not a difficult task. It should not have taken more than four days to have the structure ready for occupancy.

Now the chinking on the outside could begin, and this is where the children could be of real help. Abraham could split thin slabs of wood and drive them between the logs, up as high as he could reach, where there were open places, wedging them in one by one. Sarah could then daub moistened clay between the logs where the wedges had not completely filled the cracks. It must have been a fascinating experience for a boy and girl of their ages to assist in building the home in which they were to live. In a very special sense they could refer to the cabin as "our home." It could be said, quite literally, that the Lincoln family had cut their house out of the wilderness.

When the cabin had been made fairly wind and moisture proof on the outside, the process of chinking and daubing would be continued on the inside, but with a little more care, so as to give the cabin interior walls a more even surface. Later a floor made of puncheons could be put down, but for the time being the hard clay was allowed to serve. In one of the corners there was an opening into the loft and pegs were driven into the logs to serve as a ladder.[23]

Once the cabin itself had been completed, Thomas turned his attention to building a pole bedstead in one of the corners opposite the fireplace. At the proper height from the floor holes were made between the logs to receive the side poles, and a corner post set out on the floor to which these poles could be attached. Slats were then laid across the side poles to hold the mattress made of corn husks or leaves. On top of this Nancy laid the feather bed brought from Kentucky. The next piece of furniture was a table. This Thomas handily constructed, as well as chairs, benches, or stools, or possibly all three. A corner cupboard, which took more time to make, rounded out the furnishings.

The Lincolns had brought with them a spinning wheel, a skillet or spider, a Dutch oven, a large kettle, and small pans. A few wooden bowls, pewter dishes, knives and forks, and a few simple utensils completed their cooking and dining equipment. Besides the light from the fireplace, they may have had candles or a simple lamp made by lighting a wick which was placed in a cup of bear's grease.

There is a tendency to visualize the pioneer cabins in Kentucky and Indiana as they appear in photographs taken many years after they had been deserted and used for purposes other than dwellings. Usually they present a delapidated condition and repulsive surroundings. As an experienced builder Thomas erected a house that was adequate for the family's needs and similar to the other cabin homes of that era. It was new and clean, with the aroma of newly cut timber both within and without the walls. We hope that they were able to get the new home ready to occupy by December 16, as on that day "a shock of earthquake was very sensibly felt" in southern Indiana, according to the Vincennes newspaper.[24] Also the family would have wanted to spend their first Indiana Christmas in their new home.

More important than the material surroundings of the children in the wilderness was the cultural environment created in the home. The two principal actors in the children's world, which evolved around the open hearth, were the parents. They had no rivals for the esteem of their children now so often experienced. The occasional preacher was a "come and go" circuit rider, the schoolteacher an itinerant, a trained youth leader was unheard of, and a director of any kind of organized recreation was unknown in the wilderness and on the prairies.

Especially where the homes were in sparsely settled communities with no opportunity for daily intercourse of the people, the family became a close-knit institution. Upon the parents rested the responsibilities for the religious, educational, and social activities of their children, as well as the legal responsibility for their vocational guidance. The binding out of children to learn a trade in which they had no special interest or qualification was by no means an exception. Fortunate indeed were the Lincoln children not only in having parents who were capable of directing their childhood activities but who through both the Lincoln paternal ancestry and the Shipley maternal forebears provided a rich heritage that contributed much to their native ability.

When Abraham and his sister arrived in Indiana, she was nine years old and he was but seven. Abraham was endowed with two very unusual accomplishments for a boy so young, especially one brought up on the frontier. He could both read and write. One author, whose information comes firsthand, states with reference to Abraham's penmanship: "For this acquirement he manifested a great fondness. It was his custom to form letters, to write words and sentences wherever he

24

found suitable material. He scrawled them with charcoal, he scored them in the dust, in the sand, in the snow—anywhere and everywhere that lines could be drawn, there he improved his capacity for writing." [25]

This statement, well authenticated, sets before us the unusual role which Abraham played as a scribe. "Upon the arrival of the family in Indiana the friends who were left behind were to be written to. The elder Lincoln could do nothing more in the way of writing than to bunglingly sign his name. The mother, though a ready reader, had not been taught the accomplishment of writing. In this emergency Abraham's skill as a penman was put into requisition, and with highly satisfactory results. From that time on he conducted the family correspondence. This fact soon became public, little Abraham was considered a marvel of learning and wisdom by the simple-minded settlers. . . ." [26]

Letter writing by an adult living on the frontier was an accomplishment, but for a lad of seven years almost unbelievable. It is impossible to evaluate the significance of this early way of expression by the boy Abraham. Possibly we have living in this newly built Indiana cabin of Thomas and Nancy Hanks Lincoln one whom some psychologists would call a gifted child. [27]

CHAPTER III

8

Imagination

1817

ABRAHAM'S INTELLECTUAL ACCOMPLISHMENTS when but a young boy may not have impressed the neighbors quite so much as his unusual physical development. Upon reaching Indiana Abraham, then being in his eighth year, "was large for his age, and had an axe put in his hands at once; . . . he was almost constantly handling that most useful instrument." The Lincolns "settled in an unbroken forest; and the clearing away of surplus wood was the great task ahead!" [1] How inadequate for the undertaking the father and son must have felt as they surveyed the acres of standing timber that must be felled and burned. The vast, almost invincible army of giant trees and dense thickets which confronted them were a more formidable foe than the Indians who menaced their Kentucky forebears.

Southern Indiana in that day was described by an Eastern visitor as "covered with heavy timber—comprising oaks, beeches, ash, three kinds of nut trees, three to four feet in diameter with trunks fifty to sixty feet high—splendid material for all kinds of cabinet work. Gum trees, hackberry, sycamore, persimmons, wild cherries, apples and plums, also wild grape vines of enormous diameter and heights. . . .

"There are also a large number of maple and sugar trees from two to three feet in diameter, and a kind of poplar. . . ." [2]

The first task of the settler after his home had been constructed was the clearing of the land. One traveler referred to Indiana as "a vast forest larger than New England." It is difficult for us to visualize the size of some of the trees then standing in the wilderness. In Harrison County, Indiana, near the place where Josiah Lincoln, brother of Thomas, had settled when migrating from Kentucky, there was a gigantic sycamore tree that was eighteen feet in diameter and sixty-five feet in circumference.[3]

However, it was not especially the largeness of the trees which characterized the Indiana wilderness, but the almost impenetrable thickness of the growth so well described in this sketch: "Tall trees covered the whole country with their wide-spreading branches, depending to the ground, and the shrubbery below arose and united with the branches of the trees. Huge grapevines, scorning to associate with the humble shrubs, like great serpents ascended and festooned the trees to the topmost branches, and thence, spreading in every direction, crept from tree to tree, tying and uniting the tops of a dozen together into an indistinguishable net-work of vegetation. . . ."[4]

To young Abe fell the task of chopping out the undergrowth while his father felled the trees. The usual procedure in making a clearing was to leave standing any trees over eighteen inches in diameter. All the smaller ones were chopped down, trimmed, and the brush and logs piled around the trees left standing. The undergrowth was grubbed out and piled with the cut timber. When the weather conditions were right, the great piles were set afire and burned. The big trees were thus deadened and later felled. All this was hard work, but the great fires were a thrilling sight. When the clearing was made, the first crop was planted.[5]

About 1810 a hurricane swept over the country not far from the site of the Lincoln home, cutting a swath through the forest and felling the heavy trees. It devastated a stretch of

27

country five miles long, and thereafter a dense growth of young timber sprang up making a favorite retreat for wild animals.[6] Young Abe heard about the roaring winds and saw the mark they had left on the landscape. He must have marveled at the wild force of nature.

After their long working hours, Abraham and Sarah resumed their schoolwork. During the winter evenings the boy and girl continued through their textbook started in Kentucky—Dilworth's Speller.[7] Fortunately Dilworth's was an excellent book, for it was more than just a list of words. It contained sentences for practice in reading and also a section entitled "Of Grammar." Equally important to the impressionable little boy was the prevailingly high literary quality of the excerpts in the book. They were of a moral or religious nature, comprising largely selections from Proverbs and the Psalms, with an occasional preachment about behavior.

The first schoolbook published by Thomas Dilworth appeared in England in the year 1740, entitled *A New Guide to the English Tongue*. Testimonies of more than one hundred clergymen and schoolteachers united in declaring it "the best of its kind that hath been made public." The book, by the year 1795, had appeared in eighteen editions. In 1796 John McCulloch of Philadelphia published a volume which he called *Dilworth's Spelling-Book, Improved. . . . A New American edition; with many Additions and Alterations*.

We are not certain just what edition of the book the Lincoln children used. The copy in hand is the one published by McCulloch mentioned above. Out of this book the student first learned both Roman and italic letters of lower and upper case, as well as Arabic and Roman numerals. Then the student progressed from monosyllables of two letters, to those of three letters, and finally of four. With these simple sounds and words mastered, he was ready for sentences, composed of monosyllabic words.

The following are some examples of sentences showing the

moral and religious content of the lessons and consisting of words not exceeding three letters:

> "No man may put off the law of God."
> "The way of God is no ill way."
> "My joy is in God all the day."
> "A bad man is a foe to God." [8]

An interesting diversion from the usual method of using lesson sentences is found in the illustration for one-syllable words of not more than six letters. The paraphrase of Psalms 4:8, "I will lay me down in peace and take my rest" is followed by this familiar children's prayer:

> Now I lay me down to sleep,
> I pray the Lord my soul to keep;
> If I should die before I wake,
> I pray the Lord my soul to take.[9]

When words of two syllables were reached, those with the accent on the first syllable were separated from those with the accent on the last, and so on, as the syllables increased.

Part One of the book concluded by naming the fifteen states comprising the Union at the time of publication, with their respective capitals. Two territories are also mentioned, the Northwest and the Southwest, with Marietta and Knoxville given as their respective seats of government.[10] Featured in Part Two are a table of words, "The same in sound, but different in spelling and signification"; also four pages of "difficult Words, according to their Spelling and Pronunciation." This latter list must have been especially helpful to those entering spelling bees. Also in Part Two is a table of numbers, Arabic and Roman, with their proper spelling.[11]

"Of Grammar" is the title of Part Three. A statement "To the Public" at the front of the little volume says that "This Grammar has been taught in this city [Philadelphia], and received the approbation of good judges, as a plain and easy system for beginners." The twenty-seven pages in this section are divided under these captions: Orthography, Prosody, Et[y]mology, and Syntax.

Part Four presents selections in both prose and verse for reading, mostly of a religious nature. A few paragraphs to encourage self-education were chosen, such as the following: "It is a commendable thing for a boy to apply his mind to the study of good letters; they will be always useful to him: they will procure him the love and favor of good men, which those that are wise value more than riches and pleasures."[12]

The concluding section of the book was probably the most interesting for Abraham, for it contained a dozen "Select Fables," each supplied with an interpretation. An important feature of these fables was the fact that they were illustrated with crude woodcuts, or as the author states "with sculptures." These may have been the first pictures that Abraham ever saw. It is difficult today to conceive of a boy growing up in a world with almost no printed pictures; and when one occasionally did appear in some book, it was usually a simple line drawing without detail. But even at that, it left an indelible impression on the reader's mind.

Along with studying Dilworth, the children continued their Bible reading. The Bible was their "First Book," not only the first book which they read, but the first in importance in their daily living.[13] This was true generally in the cabins on the frontier where often it was the only book. "It was . . . [Nancy Hanks Lincoln's] custom on the Sabbath, when there was no religious worship in the neighborhood—a thing of frequent occurrence—to employ a portion of the day in reading the Scriptures aloud to her family. After Abraham and his sister had learned to read, they shared by turn in the duty of Sunday reading."[14]

The Lincoln family Bible, fortunately, has been preserved.[15] On the inside of the back cover is the signature of Thomas Lincoln, and on the back of the front cover the name of Abraham Lincoln. Other notations reveal that the book once sold for $5.00, and also that the original price was "27 shillings," later changed to "30 shillings." The title page of this old Bible reveals that it was published in 1799, "with arguments prefixed to the different books and moral and theological observations illustrating each chapter." These commentaries were "composed by the Reverend Mr. Ostervald, professor of divinity and one of the ministers at Neufchatel in Switzerland."

There are some notes in the Preface, apparently by the Rev. Mr. Ostervald, under the heading: "The Preliminary Discourse Giving Some Direction Concerning the Reading of The Holy Scripture." Then follow these observations: "That great numbers neglect the reading of the Holy Scripture is evident as it is deplorable. . . .

"Christians there are innumerable who are almost entirely ignorant of the Bible because those that have the rule over them suffer it to be read only by particular persons, and with the greatest precaution, as if it were a dangerous thing to put the work of God indifferently into the hands of all men. . . . Many, it is true, for want of learning, may not be in capacity to read the Scriptures which is a great misfortune and a shame to Christians, that the number of those who cannot read should still be so great among them.

"The Scriptures therefore are the most valuable blessings God ever bestowed upon us except the sending of his son into the World. They are a treasury containing everything that can make us truly rich and truly happy. . . ."

After these comments appear some general statements with reference to the value of the Bible. The Rev. Mr. Ostervald then goes into a lengthy and detailed discussion about the history of the Bible, touching upon the difference between the historical, doctrinal, and moral books. His statement with regard to the New Testament as compared with the Old Testament is worthy of note: "The New Testament is that part of the Scriptures which it most concerns us to be acquainted with. If the Old Testament and the New Testament be compared together the latter is certainly the clearest and most perfect." Between the Old and New Testament in this edition of the Bible there appeared also the Apocrypha which must have greatly interested Abraham.

The last and possibly the most important section of the Preface has to do with the proper method of reading the Bible. The author clearly marks five rules which should be followed and discusses each thoroughly. Abraham may have studied these sound rules and applied them in his reading of other books. The five rules are presented under the following captions: 1. Attention and Deliberation. 2. Fervently and Diligently. 3. Judgment and Directness. 4. Submission and Obedience. 5. Piety and Devotion.

The Bible made a remarkable contribution of pure and simple language to those who had but little in the way of education and very few books to read. Passages of Scripture memorized and recited and others read over and over again, inculcated a simplicity of diction that contributed greatly to the ability of the frontiersman to express himself clearly and with dignity.[16]

Abraham's mother "interested him in Bible stories before he had learned to read." [17] There unfolded before him in his early youth a panorama of characters from both the Old and New Testament—men, women, and children, who became imaginary tenants of the cabin home, almost real people brought alive by the lively imagination of a young lad thirsting for knowledge.

The storytelling of an evening in the cabins where there were few books would not be entirely confined to tales from the Bible. Next in popularity in early Kentucky and Indiana were Indian stories. Those of most interest to Sarah and Abraham related to the tragic experiences of their own ancestors at the hands of the red men. Among the stories which Abraham heard told by his father was one which

concerned the murder of his own grandfather, Abraham,
". . . and Uncle Mordecai, then fourteen years old, killing
one of the Indians. . . ."[18] This oft-told tale was imprinted
on his mind and memory more strongly than all others. There
are many versions of the story differing only in minor details.
What perhaps is the most dependable account states that the
pioneer Lincoln was "sowing hemp seed near the fort [Hughes
Station] . . . and while thus engaged an Indian slipped up
and shot him dead. Thomas [Abe's father] . . . then 6 years
old was with his father in the hemp patch and at the crack of
the gun broke for the fort. The Indian, anxious to capture the
boy, gave chase, and caught him near the fort and started to
run with the boy in his arms, when Mordecai Lincoln,
Thomas's oldest brother, shot the Indian from the fort, and
killed him. When the Indian dropped, he fell foremost upon
the little fellow. The boy made a terrible struggle and got from
under the dead body of the savage, and ran into the fort."[19]

Possibly Thomas' own father had told him before his tragic
death about his first visit to Kentucky in 1780 when he was
captured by the Indians and made to "run the gauntlet."[20]

Nancy Lincoln also had an Indian story to tell which would
be heard with intense interest by Sarah because she was
named for the heroine. It was the story of the captivity of a
little girl by the Indians when she was about Sarah Lincoln's
age. It was the same story Nancy Lincoln had heard repeated
by the captive herself, Sarah Mitchell, Nancy's cousin, with
whom, as we have seen, she lived for four years. An account
by a descendant of Sarah's follows:

"Sarah Mitchell was captured when a girl, in 1790, by the
Indians, twenty-five miles beyond Crab Orchard, Kentucky,
at a place called Defeated Camp. Walter Caruth was leading
the expedition. He had led parties into Kentucky before. The
Indians rushed upon them with wild whoops and commenced
tomahawking. Naomi Mitchell [Sarah's mother] was struck
down. Her husband, Robert Mitchell, stood by with a spear

33

and carried her into Crab Orchard Fort. She died the next day. Sarah Mitchell's oldest brother seized her by the hand and ran away pursued by several savages. He was about to lead her over a log over a deep stream when her courage failed her and she stood petrified with fear. Her brother dashed across the log and escaped. Sarah was carried into Canada and remained in captivity five years with the Pottawatamies. She was also carried about the lakes in the vicinity of Detroit, and heard the guns of St. Clair's defeat and saw the Indians come in with their booty and prisoners. Robert Mitchell went in search of his daughter and was drowned. . . . Sarah Mitchell was surrendered under Wayne's Treaty." [21]

Thomas Lincoln, when a youth, enlisted to protect the borders of Washington County, Kentucky, where he lived, against the Indians. He had many thrilling stories to tell, not only about his own experiences but about those told by his fellow patrollers.[22] Thomas was an excellent storyteller and had a stock of pioneer lore which he loved to relate.

Although the Indians had departed from southern Indiana when the Lincolns arrived, the very name of the state itself would arouse the curiosity of the children. Around Little Pigeon Creek, as in every community, there were stories about the Indians. There was an old Indian trace which ran from the Yellow Banks on the Ohio River to the headwaters of Little Pigeon Creek where the deer licks were located, and on to Honey Spring, northwest of the Lincolns. The area around the Lincolns had been an important Indian hunting ground.[23]

While no evidence of prehistoric habitation of any significance has been discovered near the Lincoln home, several sites showing intensity of occupation have been located along the Ohio River in Spencer County. Abraham and Sarah may have heard of axes and arrowheads and other artifacts being found along the banks and streams and turned up by the farmer's plow.[24]

34

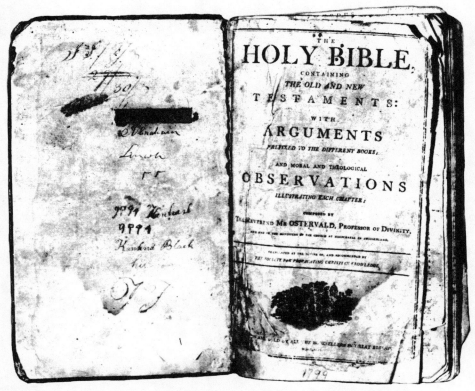

The Lincoln family Bible and fragments of family records written therein

Thos. Lincoln was born
Jan. the 6th A.D. 1778 and
was married June 12th 1806
to Nancy Hanks who was born
Feb. 5th 1784.

       Sarah Lincoln,
Daughter of Thos. and

*Portion set in type above
believed to be lost fragment*

The last Indians who are known to have lived near the Lincoln cabinsite was the family of a subchief of the Shawnee, an old Indian named Setteedown, who tended his traps along Little Pigeon Creek after the white man began settling the neighborhood. He resented the encroachment on his hunting ground, and took his revenge on the Meeks family who had settled on the creek.

Early one morning in May, 1811, Setteedown and his son, aged about seventeen, and another Indian, Big Bones, stationed themselves outside the Meeks cabin. When the son of the family, Atha, Jr., stepped out to go to the spring for water, one of the Indians fired on him, wounding him in the knee. When Atha, Sr., came to the door, Big Bones shot him dead, while Setteedown and his son attacked Atha, Jr., with tomahawks. The boy, though severely wounded, fought them off until his uncle, William Meeks, who lived in a near-by cabin, had time to seize his rifle and fire at the Indians. Big Bones was wounded fatally, and Setteedown and his son fled. William Meeks gave the alarm in the neighborhood and a party of white men pursued them. They captured, in all, Setteedown, his squaw, the son who had been with him, and two or three children, and confined them in the cabin of Uriah Lamar, a justice of the peace, near Grandview. Three men, including William Meeks, kept guard at the cabin, and during the night the old chief was shot. It was generally believed that William had taken justice into his own hands and revenged his brother's death. The remaining Indians were ordered to depart.[25]

The story's sequel is gruesome indeed. Setteedown was buried in his Indian blanket in a shallow grave close to the Lamar cabin. Mischievous boys were reported to have pushed sticks down through the soil until they pierced the old blanket. And for many years old Setteedown's ghost was supposed to be visible at times in the vicinity.[26] The Lincoln children were sure to hear this whole story, and more like it.

On the Ohio, in Anderson Township, Perry County, was a locally famous "pirates' retreat." Here was a stone wall about four feet high in the shape of a letter U, called Troxel's Horseshoe and supposed once to have been a place of refuge for a Spanish pirate of that name who operated on the Ohio and Mississippi. There were tales of treasure buried here to excite the children's imagination, but no treasure is known to have been found.[27]

The stories of Indians were supplemented by hunters' tales of thrilling encounters with cunning wolves and giant bears. "Abraham and his sister often sat at . . . [their mother's] feet to hear of scenes and deeds that roused their young imaginations, and fed their hungry minds."[28]

As mentioned before, the almost total absence of pictures meant that pioneer children were forced to cultivate their imagination. They drew their own visions of persons, places, and objects that they read about and were told about. They were surrounded by a vividly colored wilderness which would help stimulate the fancy of a sensitive, observant child. Nature ran riot in southern Indiana with the great variety of birds in the trees and on the waters, animals in prairies and forests, and rodents and reptiles that went creeping and slithering across the paths. The air often appeared to be alive with colorful insects, and there were bees to lead the children on a merry chase to find their honey-laden storehouses.

One of Abe's earliest recollections of Indiana was of a flock of wild turkeys that approached the new cabin. His father was not at home, and he asked his mother if he might use his father's gun. Permission granted, standing inside the cabin he "shot through a crack and killed one of them." The consequences were not what might have been expected. Apparently he was impressed not by his own marksmanship but by the beauty of the bird he had brought down. His "early start as a hunter was never much improved afterward." In fact, he never again "pulled a trigger on any larger game."[29]

The wild turkey Abe shot was the same as illustrated by John James Audubon as Plate I in his *Birds of America,* perhaps Audubon's most famous drawing.[30] Upon studying it, one can understand how a sensitive boy might feel upon realizing he had so thoughtlessly taken its life.

It is interesting to reflect that at this same time Audubon was living at Henderson, Kentucky, on the Ohio, about forty miles from the Lincoln cabin. The artist-naturalist had come to Henderson about 1810, and it remained his headquarters until about 1820, though during most of the time he was on expeditions. It is possible that Audubon might have visited the headwaters of Little Pigeon Creek and the deer licks near the Lincoln home which were favorite haunts of the birds and animals. But if Abe ever saw a man with a dog and gun, carrying a strange box on his back containing pencils and colors and drawings, no account of it has been preserved.[31]

Carolina parakeets (illustrated as Plate No. XXVI in *Birds of America*) were found in profusion in southern Indiana while Abe was growing up, and he must have observed these colorful birds with great delight. They measured thirteen inches from bill to tip of tail. Their bodies were a combination of green and yellow, the head and throat a vivid yellow, with the forehead an orange red and the beak ivory white. When Maximilian, Prince of Wied-Neuwied, visited New Harmony, Indiana, in 1832–33, he noted that "paroquets abound and remain here during the winter. I saw large flocks of parrots in the forest of which we often shot many with great ease. . . . with a shrill cry they flew from tree to tree, where their beautiful bright green color was seen to advantage. . . . if we did not disturb them they sat in a row close together."[32]

The Carolina parakeet has disappeared, as has also the passenger pigeon. The latter has been said in its day to have numbered into the millions and to have been the most abundant of any bird in America. The passenger pigeons "literally formed clouds, and floated through the air in a frequent succession of these as far as the eye could reach, sometimes causing a sensible gust of wind, and a considerable motion of the trees over which they flew." [33] Audubon observed, "Multitudes are seen, sometimes, in groups, at the estimate of a hundred and sixty-three flocks in twenty-one minutes. The noonday light is then darkened as by an eclipse, and the air filled with the dreamy buzzing of their wings." [34]

Southern Indiana was a feeding and breeding ground for these pigeons, and Little Pigeon Creek is supposed to have been one of the great pigeon roosts. The Englishman William Cobbett, going down the Ohio in June, 1817, noted thousands of pigeons near that creek. [35]

Shooting pigeons under such conditions would not have been much of a sport, but Thomas Lincoln undoubtedly shot some of them and other game birds and animals in order to supply his table. There is no evidence that he was an inveterate hunter, though this often has been alleged. [36] Certainly he imparted no such inclination to his son. Thomas Lincoln had to hunt to get fresh meat, particularly in the early years in Indiana, but this would not have been time consuming.

Abe "loved animals generally and treated them kindly." [37] All the creatures of nature that stir the imagination of a boy were present in Indiana in that day. A traveler passing through the region about the time that the Lincolns arrived, wrote: "The forest is full of deer, antelope, bear, wolves, ground-hogs, hares, wild-cats, squirrels . . . ," [38] and he might have added that mink, weasels, skunks, raccoons, and opossums were also in abundance.

Hunting certainly was a sport and diversion indulged in by the pioneers. And though it does not seem to have appealed to Abe or his father to any extent, they did occasionally join the community bear hunts. Bears were a real threat to a farmer, for they took a heavy toll of his livestock and were a menace to human beings. Bear hunts were usually organized after some of these beasts had devastated farmers' stock. In what may have been the last such hunt on Pigeon Creek nine beasts were killed. The most famous hunter in the region was Peter Brooner who lived near the Lincolns.[39] The hunts were wild affairs and made a deep and lasting impression on Abe. An excellent description of an actual bear hunt in the Little Pigeon community while the Lincolns lived there has been preserved:

> A wild-bear chace, didst never see?
>   Then hast thou lived in vain.
> Thy richest bump of glorious glee,
>   Lies desert in thy brain.
>
> When first my father settled here,
>   'Twas then the frontier line:
> The panther's scream, filled night with fear
>   And bears preyed on the swine.
>
> But wo for Bruin's short lived fun,
>   When rose the squealing cry;
> Now man and horse, with dog and gun,
>   For vengeance, at him fly.
>
> A sound of danger strikes his ear;
>   He gives the breeze a snuff:
> Away he bounds, with little fear,
>   And seeks the tangled *rough*.
>
> On press his foes, and reach the ground,
>   Where's left his half munched meal;
> The dogs, in circles, scent around,
>   And find his fresh made trail.
>
> With instant cry, away they dash,
>   And men as fast pursue;
> O'er logs they leap, through water splash,
>   And shout the brisk halloo.

Now to elude the eager pack,
  Bear shuns the open ground;
Th[r]ough matted vines, he shapes his track
  And runs it, round and round.

The tall fleet cur, with deep-mouthed voice,
  Now speeds him, as the wind;
While half-grown pup, and short-legged fice,
  Are yelping far behind.

And fresh recruits are dropping in
  To join the merry *corps:*
With yelp and yell,—a mingled din—
  The woods are in a roar.

And round, and round the chace now goes,
  The world's alive with fun;
Nick Carter's horse, his rider throws,
  And more, Hill drops his gun.

Now sorely pressed, bear glances back,
  And lolls his tired tongue;
When as, to force him from his track,
  An ambush on him sprung.

Across the glade he sweeps for flight,
  And fully is in view.
The dogs, new-fired, by the sight,
  Their cry, and speed, renew.

The foremost ones, now reach his rear,
  He turns, they dash away;
And circling now, the wrathful bear,
  They have him full at bay.

At top of speed, the horse-men come,
  All screaming in a row.
"Whoop! Take him Tiger. Seize him Drum."
  Bang,—bang—the rifles go.

And furious now, the dogs he tears,
    And crushes in his ire.
Wheels right and left, and upward rears,
    With eyes of burning fire.

But leaden death is at his heart,
    Vain all the strength he plies.
And, spouting blood from every part,
    He reels, and sinks, and dies.[40]

The howling of the wolves as well as the panthers' screams that filled the darkness must have been chilling to the little boy and girl huddled under their blankets on a cold night. The shocking story of the two children, a little older than Abraham and his sister, who were attacked by a panther in Perry County some years earlier, may have been told to them. Mary and Joseph Bowers were a short distance from home picking grapes when they saw a panther coming towards them. The only weapon the boy had was a tomahawk. The panther first attacked Mary, who had tripped over a vine as she started to run, and the animal quickly clawed her to death. Joseph was successful in driving his tomahawk into the beast's skull but could not pull it out in time to deliver another blow. Before the panther died, it clawed the flesh from the boy's legs and he was unable to walk for many months.[41]

After Thomas Lincoln had made his first clearing and planted and harvested his first crop, he decided that it was time to secure the title to the land. Several of the pioneers who had come to the Little Pigeon community during that year had visited the United States Land Office at Vincennes to make their initial payments on the lands on which they had settled. It was a round-trip journey of one hundred and twenty miles. William Whitman and Noah Gordon, Thomas' nearest neighbors, went with him, and all three entered land on the same day, October 15, 1817.[42]

Thomas Lincoln's two tracts were of eighty acres each, comprising the southwest quarter of Section 32, T 4 S, R 5 W.[43] Thomas made the required initial payment of $16.00 to secure his right to the land, and two months later he paid an additional $64.00, making a total of $80.00 or one fourth of the purchase price of $320.00.[44]

This property was well located on an east-west trace separating Congressional townships 4 and 5. Following along this joint township line from west to east were the following landholders, all of whom had entered their lands in 1817 or before: in Section 31, John Jones, and David Casebier; in Section 32, Thomas Lincoln and Thomas Barrett; in Section 33, Thomas Carter; in Section 34, Noah Gordon.

Within a year after his arrival in Indiana, Thomas Lincoln had achieved the primary objective of his move to Indiana: he had an undisputed title to a hundred and sixty-acre tract of land and had paid the required one quarter of the total purchase price. For the first time in his life he had the satisfaction of being secure in his landholding. Also he was living in a state in which slavery was prohibited. His family was sheltered in a cabin, simple but adequate. He found wild game plentiful and had raised his first crop and his family's food supply was assured. The children, likewise, were contented, and although they shared in the hard work of life in the wilderness, in that very wilderness they found excitement and beauty far beyond any they had imagined. It was virtually a boy's paradise.

CHAPTER IV

9

Sympathy

1818

ENTERING THE SECOND YEAR of their residence in the Indiana wilderness the Lincolns were pleased to notice the increasing number of immigrants coming into the sparsely settled part of the state where they lived. Although we have observed that Thomas Lincoln established his home in Hurricane Township of Perry County, by 1818 the General Assembly of the state voted to divide the counties of Perry and Warrick and create a new county to be called Spencer after Spier Spencer who had lost his life at the Battle of Tippecanoe. The county seat was established at Rockport. The Lincoln farm now lay within the bounds of Spencer County, in Carter Township.[1]

Most of the letters sent from Indiana to Kentucky were carried by friends visiting back and forth. There were, however, mail facilities available at this early date. The closest mail route for the Lincolns passed through Troy where they did their trading. The carrier left Louisville on Monday at 6 A.M. every week and arrived at Harmonie on Thursday by 10 A.M. The return trip was started by 1 P.M. the same day and terminated at Louisville by 7 P.M. Sunday. The towns on the route were: Louisville, Corydon, then the state capital of Indiana, Shoemaker, Troy, Mt. Pleasant in Perry County, Darlington, Evansville, and Harmonie later New Harmony. There was also a mail route from Corydon to Elizabethtown,

43

Kentucky. This schedule gave Troy two mails each week, one east and one west, and the Little Pigeon Creek settlers could reach their Hardin County friends and relatives by mail via Corydon.[2]

Nancy Hanks Lincoln had at least one relative living in Perry County two years before the Lincolns arrived. Joseph Hanks, who had resided at Elizabethtown, is listed as serving on a jury in Perry County as early as July 4, 1815. This is the youngest son of Joseph Hanks, Sr., of Nelson County, Kentucky, and a cousin of Nancy. Other members of this Hanks family remained in Nelson and Hardin counties.[3]

Thomas had relatives in Indiana, but none lived close enough to be called a neighbor. His brother Josiah had migrated into the Blue River country, Harrison County, in 1812. A little over a year before Thomas came to Indiana, Austin and Davis Lincoln, sons of Hannaniah Lincoln, cousin of the pioneer Abraham, settled in Perry County. Thomas had known them in Elizabethtown, Kentucky, when he went there to work, and had lived in their home for a while. Austin served on a jury in Perry County in 1815. Undoubtedly, Thomas visited them when he made his prospecting trip to Indiana and the site he chose was not more than six miles from their farms. Austin lived on the northwest quarter of section 31, T 5 S, R 3 W. Davis Lincoln served as a justice of the peace in Spencer County from 1823 to 1825.[4]

One of the ways young Abraham was able to see what was happening in the surrounding country was by going on the periodic treks that had to be made to the nearest gristmill. "Going to mill" was an essential part of pioneer life. As soon as a boy was big enough to ride a horse, which would be at a fairly early age, he would go with his father or some other older man. Then when he had learned the proper paths to take and could manage the heavy sack of corn and the unwieldy bag of meal, he would be sent alone. The only alternative to going to mill was to grind the corn at home, Indian fashion, by pestle

44

and mortar, and it is supposed the Lincolns had to resort to this method sometimes during their first years in Indiana.

Troy on the Ohio River, in Perry County, was their nearest trading center and it had a gristmill. Somewhat closer was a mill which was operated by George Huffman on Anderson River ten miles north of Troy and almost directly west of the Lincoln farm. The spot eventually became known as Huffman's Mill. It was "a tub-wheel mill with wooden gearing," and buhrs fashioned from "flinty rocks from the surrounding country." It was housed in an unhewed log structure.[5]

Abraham may have accompanied his father to the mill at Troy, and Henry Brooner, a neighbor boy four years older than Abraham, often went with him "on horseback to Huffman's Mills, on Anderson Creek, a distance of sixteen miles." These expeditions, escapes from the monotony and confines of the farm, were treats greatly anticipated and thoroughly enjoyed. They meant new faces, news, and chances for the boy to hear stories and tell his own. Henry Brooner marveled at Abraham's great memory and how well he could relate what he had read while they rode along.[6]

Noah Gordon, who lived less than two miles from the Lincolns, built a horse mill—the customers supplying their own horses—about 1818, and this was also patronized by Thomas Lincoln. It was at this mill that Abraham was "kicked by a horse, and apparently killed for a time."[7] There were others ahead of him and he had to wait his turn while the horses went round and round providing the power for grinding the grain. Watching the slow process, Abraham remarked that "his dog could eat the meal as fast as the mill could grind it." When his turn came, the boy hitched his horse to the end of the beam and followed the well-beaten circular path. Time was passing and Abraham was urging the beast on with a few strokes of the switch and "clucking" in the usual manner. Suddenly the animal let loose with a swift kick which sent the boy sprawling flat on the ground in a coma. Just how long he remained unconscious is not certain. One account indicates it was but a short time: "With the first instant of returning consciousness he finished the cluck, which he had commenced when he received the kick, (a fact for the psychologist) and with the next he probably thought about getting home, where he arrived at last, battered, but ready for further service."[8] There are several different versions of this incident.[9]

A man traveling through Indiana in 1819, the year after the above accident happened, came across a horse mill of a different type. In this instance the animal kept in the same position, making no advance, but continually walking on a circular movable platform which was geared to the machinery of the mill and turned the stones. The most interesting part of the story was the description of the millwright in charge at the time—a nine-year-old boy, the same age as Abraham.[10]

What were the tales with which Abraham entertained his companions on the road and with which he helped pass the time for the cluster of farmers' boys while they waited their turns to grind their grain? The Bible and Dilworth's Speller provided some stories, but how his fund of tales was increased when a copy of *Æsop's Fables* came into his hands.[11] One of the playmates of Abraham stated, "He kept the Bible and Æsop's always within reach, and read them over and over again."[12]

In an early and rather scarce American edition of the *Fables,* there was a biographical sketch of Æsop which depicted him as having been a slave in his youth and then through wisdom and virtue finally rising to gain the esteem of his fellowmen. In a prefatory statement the purpose of a fable is set forth and the following, from Joseph Addison, is quoted: "Reading is to the mind, what exercise is to the body, and by the one health is preserved, strengthened, and invigorated; by the other, virtue is kept alive and confirmed."

After criticizing one of the European editions of Æsop, the American editor, in his preface, lamenting the political and religious concepts placed before European children, expressed the hope that such teachings will not be placed before the children of America, and continues: "For they are born with free blood in their veins and suck in liberty with their very milk. This they should be taught to love and cherish above all things, and upon occasion, to defend and vindicate it, as it is the glory of their country, the greatest blessing of their lives, and the peculiar happy privilege in which they excel all the world besides. . . . But let the minds of our charming youth be forever educated and improved in that spirit of truth and liberty for the support of which their ancestors have bravely exhausted so much blood and treasure."

One of the features of the American edition is the preachments which follow each fable. These morals may have influenced the growing child more than the *Fables* themselves. To illustrate this, one of the subjects "Æsop at play" or "The Unstrung Bow" is used as an example. After stating the parable this conclusion is drawn: "If you keep a bow always bent, it will break presently; but if you let it go back, it will be fitter for use when you want it." This is the moral drawn: "Sports and diversions soothe and slaken it [the mind] and keep it in condition to be exerted to the best advantage upon occasion." [13]

A few of the other fables of Æsop are herewith presented with merely the title of the fable noted and the moral drawn:

THE OLD MAN AND HIS SONS—"Nothing is more necessary towards completing and continuing the well-being of mankind than their entering into and preserving friendships and alliances. The safety of government depends chiefly upon this; and therefore it is weakened and exposed to its enemies, in proportion as it is divided by parties. A kingdom divided against itself is brought to desolation. And the same holds good among all societies and corporations of men, from the great constitution of the nation, down to every little parochial vestry."

47

THE CAT AND THE MICE—"Prudent folks never trust those a second time who have deceived them once."

THE LION AND THE FOUR BULLS—"A kingdom divided against itself cannot stand and as undisputed a maxim as it is, it was however thought necessary to be urged to the attention of mankind by the best man that ever lived."

THE CROW AND THE PITCHER—"A man of sagacity and penetration upon encountering a difficulty or two does not immediately despair, but if he cannot succeed one way, employs his wit and ingenuity another, and to avoid or get over an impediment makes no scruple of stepping out of the path of his forefathers."

THE MULE—"As a man truly great shines sufficiently bright of himself without wanting to be emblazoned by a splendid ancestry; so they whose lives are eclipsed by foulness of obscurity of showing to advantage, look but the darker for being placed in the same light with their illustrious forefathers."

THE APE AND THE FOX—"A weak man should not aspire to be a king. To be qualified for such an office, an office of the last importance to mankind, the person should be of a distinguished, prudent, and of most unblemished integrity, too honest to impose upon others, and too penetrating to be imposed upon. Thoroughly acquainted with the laws and genius of the realm he is to govern; grave but not passionate; good natured but not soft, aspiring at just esteem; despising vain glory; without superstition; without hypocrisy." [14] One author in a pensive mood wrote, "The incomparable Æsop, reducing the sublimest principles of morality, political economy and aesthetics, even to the slender comprehension of a little child." [15]

John Bunyan's *The Pilgrim's Progress* was the fourth book which came into Abraham's hands, and it proved to be a significant acquisition. His father is supposed to have noticed an old copy at a friend's house, and immediately thought how

Abraham would enjoy it. He acquired it for the boy who was so delighted that "his eyes sparkled, and that day he could not eat, and that night he could not sleep." [16]

It is difficult for us in this day to appreciate fully how religious themes dominated the conversation and the reading of the pioneers. If books were found in a pioneer home, they could be expected to include first the Bible, and then very likely *The Pilgrim's Progress*. The story it related had a special appeal to children, its theme found approval among parents, and its high literary quality made it a good volume for youngsters to read. One Illinois boy, born in 1811, stated, "Pilgrim's Progress I read in my tenth year as a veritable history." [17]

The first edition of *The Pilgrim's Progress*, bearing the imprint London, 1678, carries the subtitle "Wherein is Discovered, the manner of his setting out, His Dangerous Journay. And Safe Arrival at the Desired Countrey." It was "Printed for Nath. Ponder at the Peacock in the Poultrey near Cornhill." The copy which is being used by the author as a basis of study was printed at Philadelphia in 1817. [18]

The concluding paragraph of the Preface to the American edition similar to the one Lincoln must have read makes this suggestion: "It is also submitted to the consideration of heads of families, whether the PILGRIM, in this form, may not be well adapted for the purpose of reading to their children and servants on the Lord's day evening." [19] This suggestion was probably followed on week-day evenings as well as on Sunday in the frontier cabins.

Possibly Abraham's introduction to biography, aside from the account of Æsop in the *Fables*, was in the twenty-page sketch of John Bunyan in the preliminary pages of this volume. The first sentence excites the reader's interest by introducing Bunyan as "a man converted from singular depravity of manners, to eminent piety; and raised from the deepest obscurity, to be an author celebrated for genius, and uncommonly useful to mankind." [20]

Abraham, during this period of his boyhood when his sympathies were easily aroused, would be especially interested in the near tragedies which Pilgrim experienced while struggling against the forces that would try to destroy him. There would be little in Pilgrim's religious experiences that would seem inconsistent with the reactions of the people who lived in pioneer Kentucky and southern Indiana.

Abraham would find Bunyan's "Author's Apology," an arrangement in verse, of interest. This "Apology" was probably the first rhyming poem of any length which the youth had seen. It was developed by couplets, and the unique way in which Bunyan expressed his thoughts in order to bring about the ending of the lines with words corresponding in sound would be intriguing. Here is an example, telling how Bunyan happened to write *The Pilgrim's Progress*:

> Thus I set pen to paper with delight,
> And quickly had my thoughts in black and white.
> For having now my method by the end,
> Still as I pull'd, it came; and so I penn'd
> It down, until it came at last to be
> For length and breadth, the bigness which you see.

Possibly of more interest to a boy would be these lines in the same "Apology" which set forth his procedure:

> You see the ways the fisherman doth take
> To catch the fish; what engines doth he make?
> Behold! how he engageth all his wits;
> Also his snares, lines, angles, hooks and nets:
> Yet fish there be, that neither hook, nor line,
> Nor snare, nor net, nor engine can make thine;
> They must be grop'd for, and be tickled too,
> Or they will not be catch'd, what e're you do.[21]

While these introductory pages presented much that was novel, the text of the book itself would initiate the Lincoln children into the allegorical form of literature. Whether read to them by their mother, or read out loud to each other, they

50

Site of Nancy Hanks Lincoln grave at crest of hill

Elm tree that stood near cabin home during her lifetime

Poison snakeroot that indirectly caused her death

would never forget the Slough of Despond, the Wicket Gate, the Cross, Hill Difficulty, Death, Delectable Mountain, Enchanted Ground, Beulah Land, and finally The City of God. The many striking characters they read about, whom Abraham and Sarah would tend to associate with people they knew, would stay with them throughout their lives.

It cannot be known for sure that Abraham had read *Æsop's Fables* and *The Pilgrim's Progress* by the fall of 1818. We hope that he had, because the story of Pilgrim and the wise philosophy of Æsop would have stood the boy in good stead that fall. For in October he went down into his own "slough of despond."

In the fall of 1817 the Lincoln family was joined by an aunt of Nancy's, Elizabeth Sparrow, and her husband Thomas who was a brother of Nancy's stepfather, and their ward, nephew to Elizabeth Sparrow, Dennis Hanks. This family had been driven from their Kentucky home by an ejectment suit[22] similar to the one that had caused Thomas Lincoln to migrate to the new state north of the Ohio River. The Sparrows and young Hanks, counting on the hospitality of Thomas and Nancy Lincoln, came to their farm and were given refuge in the old half-face camp put up by Thomas Lincoln when he came to Indiana to select his land. Thomas Sparrow was apparently averse to work, and during the short time he lived at the Lincoln farm he did nothing much in the way of helping to improve the land.[23]

When Thomas Lincoln selected his land, he may have failed to make the proper inquiries about the healthfulness of the region. Probably he was unaware that malaria was prevalent and that ague and intermittent fevers paid an annual visit. But even more devastating than these diseases was one that struck southern Indiana as soon as milk cattle were brought into the wilderness. This mysterious and deadly malady called "milk sickness" by the settlers ravaged whole communities. An account in an Evansville paper shows the great fear and near panic which the affliction caused on the frontier:

"There is no announcement which strikes the members of a western community with so much dread as the report of a case of milk sickness. The uncertainty and mystery which envelopes its origin, and its fearful and terrible effects upon the victims, and the ruinous consequences upon the valuable property, which follows in its train, makes it in the eyes of the inhabitants of a district the worst looking foe which can beset their neighborhood. No immigrant enters a region of Southern Indiana, Illinois, or Western Kentucky to locate himself without first making the inquiry if the milk sickness was ever known there, and if he has any suspicions that the causes of the disease exist in the vegetable or mineral productions of the earth, he speedily quits it. . . . I have passed many a deserted farm where the labors of the emigrant had prepared for himself and family a comfortable home, surrounded with an ample corn and wheat field, and inquired the reason of its abandonment and learned that the milk sickness had frightened away its tenants and depopulated the neighborhood. I saw this season a number of farms in Perry County, Indiana, lying uncultivated and the houses tenantless which last autumn were covered with corn fields whose gigantic and thrifty stalks overtopped a man's head on horseback." [24]

In the late summer, after a hot dry season, the cattle seeking forage in the woods, were attracted to a plant called poison snakeroot, already in bloom, putting forth clusters of chalk-white flowers. Its matted fibrous roots were able to secure enough moisture in the shadiest places to send up stems waist high.[25] It flourished in the dark shade, and its fatal enemy, the woodsman, had not yet come in sufficient numbers to clear the forests and in so doing check the growth of the plant. The hungry cattle fed upon its stems and leaves ravenously. After devouring a certain quantity, they were stricken with what the pioneer called "the trembles," and usually they were dead within three days thereafter.

52

The appearance of the "trembles" in the cows was a fore-warning that the people in a community should be on the alert. It had been determined that persons who had drunk milk from an affected cow would be stricken with the milk sickness. The pioneers were aware that the cattle were in some way responsible, but they did not know what caused the trembles. No one in that day supposed that the plant with the white flowers supplied "tremetol," which contained the fatal poison.[26] The water supply of the cattle was suspected of being contaminated in some way. It was thought that perhaps arsenic, cobalt, copper, or even lead were somehow poisoning the streams and springs. Still clinging to the moisture theory the people surmised that minerals through evaporation in the night contaminated the morning dew.

While its cause was unknown, the symptoms of the disease were easily recognized. Dizziness, nausea, vomiting, stomach pains, intense thirst, and a sickening odor of the breath were positive indications. The realization that it was almost certain to prove fatal to its victim, produced panic in the community. If a case ran true to form, the respiration of the patient became irregular, the pulse showed variations, temperature was subnormal, and eventually prostration was followed by a semi- to complete coma. The malady ran its course in a week or even less.[27]

In the fall of 1818 it was discovered that one of Thomas Lincoln's cows had the trembles. Then Thomas Sparrow was stricken with the dread disease. He failed very rapidly. On September 21 he made his will, bequeathing all his property to his wife, an indication that she was still living. One of the witnesses was Nancy Lincoln which would imply that she was in good health at that time. One week later Thomas Sparrow was dead, as the appointed executor of his estate, Thomas Carter, made oath on September 28 that he was "a by stander and heard . . . [the will] acknowledged."[28] Shortly after Thomas Sparrow died, his wife followed, a victim of the same sickness.

Another was the Lincolns' neighbor, Mrs. Peter Brooner. Nancy Lincoln nursed and comforted the Sparrows and visited Mrs. Brooner, and did what she could to ease their last days.[29] But the resources at her command to assuage their suffering were meager indeed. The community was without a physician, but no doctor in that day could have saved the victims. By the time Mrs. Brooner succumbed Nancy herself was showing the symptoms of the disease. It became evident to Thomas Lincoln and Abraham and Sarah that she, too, was going to die. Dennis Hanks related the pathetic scene many years later: ". . . She [Nancy] knew she was going to die & called up the children to her dying side and told them to be good & kind to their father—to one another and to the world, expressing a hope that they might live as they had been taught by her to live . . . love—reverence and worship God." No doubt she impressed upon Sarah the great measure of responsibility that would now rest upon her shoulders, and the care and attention she should give to her young brother. Her talk with Abraham centered primarily on his character. Her final admonition was reported as "I am going away from you, Abraham, and I shall not return. I know that you will be a good boy that you will be kind to Sarah and to your father. I want you to live as I have taught you, and to love your Heavenly Father." [30]

On October 5, just one week after Thomas Sparrow's death, Nancy died.[31] Death in a one-room cabin in the wilderness was a grim experience for the survivors. The body was prepared for burial in the very room in which the family lived. For the three lonely Lincolns there was no near relative to offer sympathetic help and to assume responsibility. After the death of the Sparrows, Thomas Lincoln had whipsawed logs into planks, then planed them, and with wooden pegs which young Abe had fashioned, he fastened the boards together into rude coffins. When Mrs. Brooner died he made hers. "Tom was always making a coffin for some one" that fall, one of his neighbors recalled. And with Nancy's death he again fell to the task. Perhaps he found some solace in the physical labor. After the body of "the angel mother" [32] was properly prepared and dressed by the neighbor women, it was lowered into the casket and the cover put in place. The wooden pegs which Abe had whittled were placed in the auger holes of the cover and driven gently in, to secure the lid. The coffin was then put on a primitive sled and drawn by the family's old farm horse to the burial plot on a crest of a hill fifteen hundred feet south of the cabinsite. Nancy's grave had been dug next to the ones prepared for the Sparrows such a short time before. [33] Close by was Mrs. Brooner's grave. Her son recalled years later: "I remember very distinctly that when Mrs. Lincoln's grave was filled, my father, Peter Brooner, extended his hand to Thomas Lincoln and said, 'We are brothers now,' meaning that they were brothers in the same kind of sorrow." [34] Young Lamar, an elder of the Little Pigeon Baptist Church, was present and conducted the simple interment rites. Following a custom used in Kentucky, Thomas probably placed field stones at the head and foot of the grave and carved the letters N. L. in the head-stone. [35]

The autumnal frost had already colored the foliage of the huge trees of oak, maple, and walnut into a brilliantly painted canopy, which soon would gently drop its patchwork creation, piece by piece, to cover the unlovely mounds of earth with a beauty and warmth suitable for those who were to rest there through that winter and other winters to come. But the Lincoln family would not be satisfied until David Elkin, pastor of the Little Mount Church in Kentucky, of which Nancy was a member, came to Indiana and at Nancy's grave spoke of her staunch Christian faith and the virtues she exemplified as a faithful wife and revered mother.

There is a tradition that Abraham, who at that time could already write a good hand, sent a letter to the Rev. Mr. Elkin asking him to come and preach at his mother's grave. [36] The

Baptist preacher did deliver a sermon at Nancy's grave. In fact his grandson recalled, "Grandfather Elkin went to visit his sons [Hodgen and Warren] who had moved to Indiana, and on the way he stopped at Thomas Lincoln's, whom he had known when Thomas lived in Kentucky. While there he preached the funeral service of Nancy Hanks. He then went on and spent some time with his sons before returning." [37]

An eye-witness account of the little ceremony recalled: "As the appointed day approached notice was given the entire neighborhood. On a bright sabbath morning the settlers of the neighborhood gathered in. Some came in carts of the rudest construction, their wheels consisting of huge boles of forest trees and the product of axe and auger; some came on horseback, two or three upon a horse, others came in wagons drawn by oxen, and still others came on foot. Taking his stand at the foot of the grave Parson Elkin lifted his voice in prayer and sacred song and then preached a sermon. He spoke of the precious Christian woman who had gone, with the warm praise which she had deserved, and held her up as an example of true womanhood." [38]

Whatever the Rev. Mr. Elkin may have said of Nancy Hanks Lincoln, it could not have been more laudatory of her character than the testimonies of others who, also, were in a position to speak with assurance. According to one: "She was a woman of deep religious feeling, of the most exemplary character, and most tenderly and affectionately devoted to her family. Her home indicated a degree of taste and a love of beauty exceptional in the wild settlement in which she lived. . . ." [39] A close neighbor of the Lincolns observed: "Mrs. Lincoln was a very smart, intelligent, and intellectual woman; she was naturally strong-minded; and a gentle, kind, and tender woman, a Christian of the Baptist persuasion she was a remarkable woman truly and indeed." [40]

A member of the Grigsby family into which her daughter Sarah was to marry commented: "Mrs. Lincoln . . . was a woman known for the extraordinary strength of her mind among the family and all who knew her: she was superior to her husband in every way. She was a brilliant woman, a woman of great good sense and morality. Those who knew her best, with whom I have talked, say she was a woman of pale complexion, dark hair, sharp features, high forehead, bright, keen gray or hazel eyes. Thomas Lincoln and his wife were really happy in each others presence, loved one another." [41]

Dennis Hanks it will be recalled came to Indiana with the Sparrow family and saw Nancy Lincoln several times a day during the year before her death. He gives this description of her, "Mrs. Lincoln . . . was 5-8 in high[t], spare made—affectionate—the most affectionate I ever saw—never knew her to be out of temper, and thought strong of it. She seemed to be unmovably calm; she was keen, shrewd, smart, & I do say highly intellectual by nature. Her memory was strong, her perception was quick, her judgment was acute almost. She was spiritually and ideally inclined, not dull, not material, not heavy in thought feeling or action. Her hair was dark, eyes were bluish green—keen and loving. Her weight was one hundred thirty. . . . She was one of the very best women in the whole race known for kindness, tenderness, charity, and love to the world. Mrs. Lincoln always taught Abe, goodness, kindness, read the good Bible to him, taught him to read and to spell, taught him sweetness and benevolence as well." [42]

The practice of the pioneers of burying their loved ones in a family plot near their home had a tendency to keep alive vivid memories of those who had passed away. Each morning as the members of the Lincoln household stepped out of the cabin door, they faced the knoll that must have appeared to be a huge burial mound. If the departed mother could have listened, she would have been able to distinguish the voices of those she had loved and cherished as they called to each other in the near-by clearing.

CHAPTER V

10

Loyalty

1819

AFTER THE RAVAGES of the milk sickness had passed, only four persons remained in the Lincoln home—Thomas, the father; Sarah, Abraham, and Dennis Hanks. It is impossible to imagine what great change this tragedy had worked in the lives of the husband and children—in loneliness and grief, in hardship and labor, in the daily routine of living.

Our greatest sympathy goes to the young brother and sister who were so close to their mother. After her death, as was perhaps only natural, Abraham idealized and even idolized her memory, until she became to him a truly saintlike character to which he clung and which came to have a strong spiritual influence on him. He is said to have resembled his mother physically and intellectually.[1] Nancy herself was more Shipley than Hanks, and Abraham's tall, strong physique marked him a Shipley descendant.[2]

Possibly it was Sarah who suffered the loss of her mother most deeply. While Abraham would have his father to console him, Thomas could not have been so close to his daughter, and there were no loving aunts or other relatives in whom she could confide. Dennis Hanks recalled, "Sairy was a little gal, only 'leven, and she'd git so lonesome, missin' her mother, she'd set by the fire an' cry. Me 'n' Abe got 'er a baby coon an' a turtle, an' tried to get a fawn but we couldn't ketch any."[3]

On February 10, following Nancy's death, Sarah became twelve years of age and two days later Abraham became ten. The mother's birthday was also in February on the sixth day of the month. These three anniversaries, all falling within seven days, had made the second week in February a festive season in the Lincoln home. Now all was changed. When Sarah had started to school, while the family was living on the Knob Creek farm, she had taken Abraham with her, and had probably helped him learn his letters and numbers. In Indiana they were necessarily together for companionship since there were no other children close by; and when Nancy died, it seems only natural that Sarah would feel a deep sense of responsibility for her younger brother. Those who have commented about the relationship of Sarah and Abraham have emphasized the deep affection that they had for each other.

No doubt the tasks which Sarah now performed—cooking, cleaning, keeping their simple clothing in as good order as she could—kept her occupied and helped assuage her grief. But in ". . . the lonely months after her mother's death . . . the Bible, she had read, had taught him [Abraham] to read, was the greatest comfort he and his sister had. . . ." [4] There was also *The Pilgrim's Progress* to read over and over. Now some of the sections, such as those on "The Cross," "Death," "Beulah Land," and "The Eternal City," would be more real than they had appeared before. *Æsop's Fables,* too, offered a kind of escape and diversion.

A year and two months after Nancy's death Thomas Lincoln, unable to stand the loneliness of the dreary cabin any longer, returned to Kentucky seeking a wife and mother for his children. His choice was Sally Bush Johnston, widow of Daniel Johnston. Thomas and Nancy Lincoln had known the Johnstons in Elizabethtown. Nancy and Sally had become good friends. They had become mothers of baby girls about the same time.

The great-grandfather of Sally Bush Johnston came from

Rotterdam to New York. Christopher, the father of Sally, migrated to Kentucky about 1780, and settled at Hardin Station, later Elizabethtown. A brother who came with him was killed by the Indians. In 1781 Christopher Bush entered two hundred acres of land on Hardin Creek including a mill-site. He continued to purchase property, and by 1793, when his daughter Sally was five years old, he listed for taxation 495 acres of land, three horses, and seven head of cattle.[5] By the time Sally was fifteen he was in possession of 1,020 acres of land in Hardin County and a thousand acres in Breckinridge County.

Thomas Lincoln probably saw Sally for the first time when he came to Elizabethtown to work as a young man of about twenty and lived in the home of Hannaniah Lincoln. Sally was only eight years old at that time. The tradition that Thomas Lincoln and Sally Bush had been sweethearts before either was married seems most unlikely because of the difference in their ages. When Thomas Lincoln became a patroller for Hardin County in 1803, Sally's father was a captain of the group.[6] Thomas and Sally probably saw each other occasionally over the years, and as we have seen, after both were married, were friends in Elizabethtown.

Sally came from a flourishing family. Her father ". . . was a stirring, industrious man, and had a large family of sons and daughters. The sons were stalwart men, of great muscular power; there was no backout in them; never shunned a fight where they considered it necessary to engage in it, and nobody ever heard one cry 'enough.'" On one occasion one of the sons, Isaac, was shot in the back. As was the custom, the doctors prepared to tie him while the bullet was extracted, since there were no anaesthetics. He refused to be tied but lay "down on a bench with a musket ball in his mouth, which he chewed to pieces as the surgeons cut nine inches in length, and one in depth, before they got the bullet, Bush never wincing during the operation."[7]

60

Sally Bush had, in all, six brothers and two sisters: William, Samuel, Isaac, Elijah, Christopher, and John; and Hannah and Rachel. Hannah married a Yankee schoolteacher, Ichabod Radley, and Rachel married Samuel Smallwood of Elizabethtown. Thomas Lincoln also knew Sally's brothers, and with one of them, Isaac, he made the flatboat trip to New Orleans. It was while they were on this trip that Sally married Daniel Johnston, and upon their return each one bought a wedding gift for the bride.[8]

The marriage took place on March 13, 1806, the ceremony being performed by the Rev. Benjamin Ogden, a Methodist preacher. Perhaps Sally's marriage did not have her father's blessing. Where one usually finds the parent's name on the marriage bond, the name of Sally's brother Elijah appears, Elijah signing by making his mark.[9] Very little is known of Daniel Johnston whom Sally married, and unfortunately what can be gleaned from the records is not to his credit. Within three months after his marriage he was borrowing money from his brother-in-law Isaac Bush, and from Robert Bleakley and William Montgomery, the Elizabethtown merchants. During the first year of his marriage his name appears on the delinquent tax list for Hardin County. He gave a note for $82.00 to George Newman on August 8, 1809, endorsed by his brother-in-law Samuel Bush. It was to be paid between the fifteenth and twenty-fifth of December, 1810, but Johnston failed to meet the obligation and suit was brought for collection. A note on the record states "Without funds."[10]

While still under obligation to Newman, Johnston signed another note on August 10, 1810, with his father-in-law as his security, to be paid the following January 1. This note also went unpaid and suit was brought and the notation "Without funds" set down.[11] Johnston opened an account at the Bleakley and Montgomery store, and under his unpaid balance on the ledger someone jotted, "An empty vessel makes the most noise."[12]

In 1809, in the Hardin County Commissioners record book, Daniel Johnston is listed as having five hundred acres of land in Breckinridge County. This was Sally's portion of the land owned by her father in that county. Johnston is not credited with the land in later records.[13] In 1814, however, he was in possession of a half acre in Grayson County. Johnston apparently earned some money in 1812 on a construction job in Elizabethtown, but we have only the account of the balance due him—$7.60.[14]

All this indicates that Daniel Johnston was far from successful in his finances. It is hoped, for Sally's sake, that he had certain compensating qualities which would have helped make up for his failure as a provider of his family's needs. A kind of salvation came in his appointment on November 14, 1814, as jailor of Hardin County, to succeed Frederick Tull who had died of cholera. While but one or two men were usually sufficient to put up a thousand dollar bond for a jailor, Johnston was forced to secure no less than six signatures before the required amount of security was guaranteed. None of the six were members of the Bush family.[15]

A stone jail had been built in Elizabethtown in 1806, forty-two by twenty-one feet with a dungeon underneath. Living quarters for the jailor's family were provided in one part of the building.[16] The jailor's wife cooked for the prisoners and kept the premises clean. Sally Johnston thus had a job cut out for her, beside taking care of her own family of three children. A jail with a grim dungeon in the basement and whipping posts in the jail yard would not have provided a very good environment in which to raise a family, and Sally may have endured unhappy times during her year and a half residence there. Then sometime in June or July, 1816, Daniel Johnston died.[17] Sally was left to provide for herself and her three children, Elizabeth, John D., and Matilda, aged as near as can be estimated, nine, seven, and five. The settlement of Johnston's estate confirms that he was an economic failure and had dissipated his wife's inheritance. Sally declared in open court that she refused to take upon herself the burden of administering the meager estate of her husband, and Matthew W. Culley qualified as administrator, posting only a hundred dollar bond.[18] If Sally Bush previously had an opportunity to choose between Thomas Lincoln and Daniel Johnston as suitor, which is unlikely, she made a most unfortunate mistake in selecting Johnston.

Sally Johnston moved her three children into a cabin home belonging to Samuel Haycraft. On February 12, 1817, she entered into an agreement to buy the cabin.[19] Apparently she was able to complete her payment by March 17, 1818, as on that date Samuel Haycraft and his wife Peggy conveyed to her "one undivided moiety of half part of a certain lot or piece of ground containing one and one quarter acres lying near Elizabethtown . . . it being the same lot on which Sarah Johnston holds a bond on the said Samuel Haycraft dated the 12th day of February 1817."[20] This same Samuel Haycraft referred to Sally in a *History of Elizabethtown* as "an honest poor widow."

No doubt Thomas Lincoln had heard of Daniel Johnston's death before he left Kentucky for Indiana in 1816, and it was Johnston's "honest poor widow" that he set out to see in November, 1819. Not only was he seeking a wife for himself, but was on a magnanimous mission which would provide a mother for his own children and a home and security for Sally's. There are several versions of the story of the approach Thomas Lincoln made to the Widow Johnston on the subject of matrimony. The one which appears most likely to be true was given to the author by Squire Bush, last surviving nephew of Sally. According to him, Thomas Lincoln arrived at Sally's cabin one day unannounced, and informed her that he had been a widower for more than a year. He soon added "that they had known each other for a long time and had both lost their partners, and asked her to marry him. She told him that she could not just then, and when asked the reason why, replied that she owed a few small debts which she must pay. Thomas Lincoln asked her how much they were, and after learning, went out and paid off each of them and they were married." [21] Probably it was not as quickly and smoothly accomplished as this account indicates, but the matter was settled pretty promptly. The marriage bond was obtained, Christopher Bush signing on behalf of his sister, her father having died. The signatures of both Christopher Bush and Thomas Lincoln are well written. On December 2, 1819, the Rev. George L. Rogers, a Methodist minister who lived next door to Sally, pronounced Thomas Lincoln, aged forty-one, and Sally Bush Johnston, aged thirty-one, husband and wife. [22]

This wedding was a fortunate and commendable union for all parties. To Sally it brought security. Her willingness to leave her relatives and friends and the town where she had been born and go into the wilderness of Indiana, indicates that she must have had both courage and an implicit trust in the man she married and under whose care she was placing herself and her children. It was a fine testimonial to the good character and high standing of Thomas that he could return to Hardin County where he had lived with his first wife for ten years and to Elizabethtown where he had brought her as a bride, and claim another in marriage. That Sally was a fine woman is well established, but she did not marry below the intellectual, moral, or economic level of the Bush family when Thomas Lincoln became her husband. [23]

Now three years after his first move to Indiana, Thomas Lincoln prepared to transport another family there. Ralph Crume, who had married Thomas' sister Mary, helped him with preparations and furnished a wagon which they loaded with Sally's belongings. Into it went a bureau, a table, a set of chairs, a clothespress, bedclothes, and kitchenware. Clothing for her and the children would be included. Thus the second Lincoln caravan bound for Indiana set out—Thomas riding on horseback and Sally and the children crowded into the already loaded wagon.

One can imagine with what mingled eagerness and anxiety Sarah and Abraham waited for their father to return. He had told them the import of his mission, and their curiosity about the new mother and new sisters and brother that he might bring to them, must have been running high. The horses and wagon finally pulled up at the cabin and their father dismounted, Sally climbed down from the wagon, and the three children came tumbling out. Then there was a general getting-acquainted session. Sally saw her new children; Abe and Sarah their new mother; and, perhaps most exciting for all, the lonely brother and sister saw three new playmates and companions.

Without casting any reflection on Nancy Lincoln as a house-keeper or on the domestic efforts of the twelve-year-old Sarah, it can be said that there was plenty of work for Sally to do in the cabin. She had lived in a settled community all her life, and years later she recalled her arrival in Indiana: "When we landed in Indiana Mr. Lincoln had erected a good log cabin, tolerably comfortable. . . . The country was wild and desolate."[24] Among Sally's innovations in the cabin life were improved facilities for "cleaning up." The habit of cleanliness is at low ebb in a boy of ten and no doubt Abraham needed considerable inducement to make use of the washstand and basin and gourd of soap which she set near the cabin door.[25] Sally then took an inventory of the clothing of the various members of the household. Sarah's and Abraham's garments were in need of repairs or replacement, and her ministrations to them must have warmed their hearts. "She soaped, rubbed, and washed the children clean, so that they looked pretty, neat, well & clean. She sewed and mended their clothes & the children once more looked human as their own good mother left them."[26]

Sally also stirred up Thomas Lincoln to make some repairs

and improvements in the cabin. The roof was fixed so that snow did not blow into the loft and cover the boys' beds. Lumber was whipsawed for a cabin floor, and a bed built in one corner for the three girls. With a total of eight mouths to feed, Thomas, in addition to his carpentry work, had to clear more land on which to raise crops.[27]

Sally's coming meant the re-establishment of two broken families into one congenial unit. A story is told of two families brought together during pioneer days in much the same manner as the Lincolns and Johnstons. One of the children stated: "When father and mother married he had children and we went there to live with her, and she took the children and mixed us all up together like hasty pudding, and has not known us apart since."[28] That is just what Sally Lincoln did in the cabin in Spencer County, and a new family loyalty was created.

Abraham's new mother not only provided a refreshing new home life for him, but through her his world of books reached exciting new dimensions. Tucked among the furniture in the wagon from Kentucky were three volumes which the boy eagerly seized upon and soon he had made their contents his own. One of these was Webster's Speller.[29]

Although it follows much the same pattern as Dilworth's, Webster's has some important supplementary features. It does not contain as many Biblical quotations or religious sentiments, but pays more attention to behavior and education in general. Two pages were utilized for "Precepts Concerning Social Relations," containing advice to both young men and young women on how to proceed in selecting a partner for life. Furthermore, the relationships which should exist between husband and wife, parents and children, brother and sister, are discussed. The concluding paragraph of this section emphasizes the reverence one should have for one's father and mother.

There are many preachments in the book, including a very

Know all men by these presents that we Thomas Lincoln & Christopher Bush are held & firmly bound unto the Commonwealth of Kentucky in the just & full sum of fifty pounds United States currency which payment well & truly to be made & done we bind ourselves our heirs &c. jointly severally & firmly by these presents sealed with our seals and dated this 9th day of December 1819

The condition of the above Obligation, that if there should be no legal Marriage shortly to be solemnized between the above bound Thomas Lincoln and Miss Sarah Johnston

for which a license was this day issued. Then the above Obligation to be Void else to remain in full force & virtue in law

Thomas Lincoln (Seal)

Christopher Bush (Seal)

Marriage bond of Thomas Lincoln and Sarah Bush Johnston

Log house, built 1806, in which
Thomas and Sarah were married.
From photograph taken in 1922
at the time it was being razed

impressive essay on temperance. The section embracing the last twelve pages is called "A Moral Catechism." A few of the questions and answers presented are noted under their respective heads:

HUMILITY—Q. *What are the advantages of humility?* A. . . . The humble man has few or no enemies. Every one loves him and is ready to do him good. . . .

MERCY—Q. *Should not beasts as well as men be treated with mercy?* A. . . . It is wrong to give needless pain even to a beast. . . .

PEACE-MAKERS—Q. *Who are peace-makers?* A. All who endeavor to prevent quarrels and disputes among men; or to reconcile those who are separated by strife.

REVENGE—Q. *Is this justifiable?* A. Never, in any possible case. . . .

JUSTICE—Q. *Is it always easy to know what is just?* A. . . . where there is any difficulty in determining, consult the golden rule.

GENEROSITY—Q. *Is this a virtue?* A. . . . To do justice, is well; but to do more than justice is still better, and may proceed from more noble motives.

AVARICE—Q. *Can an avaricious man be an honest man?* A. . . . the lust for gain is almost always accompanied with a disposition to take mean and undue advantages of others.

FRUGALITY AND ECONOMY—Q. *How far does true economy extend?* A. To the saving of every thing which is not necessary to spend for comfort and convenience; and the keeping one's expenses within his income or earnings.

INDUSTRY—Q. *Is labor a curse or a blessing?* A. . . . constant moderate labor is the greatest of blessings.

CHEERFULNESS—Q. *What are the effects of cheerfulness on ourselves?* A. Cheerfulness is a great preservative of health. . . . We have no right to sacrifice our health by the indulgence of a gloomy state of mind. . . .

Another book which is said to have been brought from Kentucky by Sally Lincoln was *Robinson Crusoe*.[30] Abraham must have known about this book and looked forward to the time when he could secure a copy. Now that he had an opportunity to read the book, he would be thrilled with its exciting story: the wrecking of the vessel with Crusoe the only survivor; his being cast on the beach of a lonely island and making trips back to the wreck, first bringing with him the only living things on the boat, a dog and two cats; then by the use of rafts transporting to shore all that he could salvage from the ship.

Abraham would be interested in how Crusoe went about building his home, first using the ship's sails as a tent put up in front of a small cave, and later enlarging the cave. Reading about taming of a wild goat and teaching a parrot how to talk may have made Abraham want to try the same thing. Out of the skins of animals, Abraham read, Crusoe made a cap and a suit of clothes, and also a huge umbrella. His observing a man's footprint in the sand, the discovery of a tribe of cannibals that came to the island for a banquet, and the capture from among them of "his man Friday" highlighted the story that Abe eagerly devoured. Then came the final rescue of Crusoe by a sea captain whose crew had mutinied and brought their captain to the island prepared to desert him. In the closing pages, before Crusoe returns to his home, a picture is drawn of an attack by bears and over fifty wolves. That would surpass the wildest stories that Abraham had heard in Indiana.

All through the book Crusoe preaches to his readers by quoting Scripture and drawing morals from the incidents of his life.[31] The book is in some respects like *The Pilgrim's Progress*. The preface states: "The story is told with modesty, with seriousness, and with a religious application of events to the uses to which wise men always apply them . . . and to justify and honour the wisdom of Providence in all the variety of our circumstances, let them happen how they will." At one point Crusoe says, "I ought to leave them to the justice of God, who is the Governor of Nations, and knows how, by national punishments to make a just retribution for the national offenses and to bring public judgments upon those who offend in a public manner by such ways as best please him." [32]

Abraham had been somewhat prepared for the reading of his next book, *The Arabian Nights,* by the pattern of *Æsop's Fables,* in which he had found animals and birds impersonating people and carrying on conversation. In this exciting new volume he was transported into a realm of Arabian enchantment. Among the episodes Abraham enjoyed most was undoubtedly "The Seven Voyages of Sinbad the Sailor." These are brief and not so complicated as some of the longer legends. Living in a land where there were many birds, Abraham must have been intrigued by the Roc, a white bird so large that when it was in flight it darkened the sun. One leg of the bird was as big as the trunk of a tree and the egg it laid was fifty yards in circumference. Once when an elephant and rhinoceros were fighting, a Roc came and snatched them up with her talons and carried them to her nest to feed her young.

Among other monstrosities encountered by Sinbad was a prodigious fish so large that it was taken for an island and men landed upon it, only to learn that it was alive and moved. Serpents of all kinds and sizes, some capable of swallowing an elephant, made the voyages of Sinbad better daytime than nighttime reading. [33]

"Aladdin and his Wonderful Lamp" would not be soon forgotten. It would seem like another story of Sinbad, since, in the end, it was the request that a Roc's egg be brought from the top of Mt. Caucasus, that was responsible for the loss to Aladdin of his wonderful lamp. The bronze horse that galloped through the skies, the diminutive cannibals covered all over with red hair, and "The Old Man of the Sea" would give Abraham's imagination a good stretching.

Dennis Hanks upbraided Abraham for his interest in *The Arabian Nights* which Dennis called "a pack of lies." Abraham's retort was, "Mighty fine lies." Dennis said that the book had "a lot o' yarns in it. One I ricollect was about a feller

69

that got near some darn fool rocks 'at drawed all the nails out o' his boat an' he got a duckin." [34] The tale Dennis recalled is in the series on "The Story of the Three Calendars, Sons of Kings, and of Five Ladies of Bagdad." The incident alluded to is experienced by the "Third Calendar" who describes "a mountain which is a rock of adamant . . . . and that they would approach so near that the iron and nails shall be drawn out of the ship which of course must fall to pieces."

Dennis Hanks recalled that "Abe'd lay on his stummick by the fire, and read [*The Arabian Nights*] out loud to me 'n' Aunt Sairy, an' we'd laugh when he did . . . . I reckon Abe read the book a dozen times, an' knowed them yarns by heart." [35]

Samuel Taylor Coleridge, who was still living at the time Abraham was reading *The Arabian Nights*, was presented with a copy of this book when he was a small child. He said it "filled him with a strange mixture of obscure dread and intense desire . . . . My whole being was with eyes closed to every object of present sense, to crumple myself up in a sunny corner, and read, read, read." [36]

CHAPTER VI

11

Ambition

1820

THE LEGENDARY CHARACTERS such as Aladdin, Sinbad, and Robinson Crusoe introduced to Abraham by books presumably brought to Indiana by the new Mrs. Lincoln, found a welcome place in the recesses of the youth's imagination. The three children in flesh and blood, one boy and two girls, who came with her, were now dwelling under the same roof with the Lincoln offspring, and they also played a significant roll in the unfolding drama of the cabin home. The Lincoln family now consisted of Thomas Lincoln, forty-two years old, Sally Johnston Lincoln, thirty-two, Dennis Hanks, twenty-one, Sarah Lincoln, thirteen, Elizabeth Johnston, thirteen, Abraham Lincoln, eleven, John D. Johnston, ten, and Matilda Johnston, nine.

Comprised of three sets of orphans it was a group of diverse backgrounds and mixed personalities. But apparently Sally Lincoln, with her talents of homemaker and mother, welded them into a harmonious group. Certainly things were more cheerful for Abraham and Sarah. Their dismal cabin was being repaired and refurnished with the exciting new furniture which Sally had brought. And they had new playmates. Whereas they had been sad and dejected after their mother's death, now they joined in fun and laughter.

For Sarah there was Elizabeth, about her own age, and

Matilda three or four years younger, with whom she could establish a true sisterly companionship and for whom she could develop affection. The eleven-year-old Abraham had for the first time since coming to Indiana a companion of about his own age in John Johnston. How he reacted to the addition of two girls into the family we do not know. He was of a retiring disposition and at times he may have felt that there were too many people in the cabin, particularly when he was trying to read. But it was good for him to be caught up in the fun and frolic, and no doubt he played his part in the monkeyshines and tomfoolery which would be inevitable in a family that was obliged to provide its own recreation and amusement.

One wonders if the Johnston children did not have some trouble adjusting to their new life in the woods. They had been, with little ceremony, lifted out of a busy county seat town with many children of their own age, and set down in a wilderness. They gave up their own cabin home to move into another already occupied by four people. Moreover, they were obliged to share their mother's attention with two others. On the other hand, they acquired a new father and a sense of security that they probably never would have known with their own father, Daniel Johnston.

While Sarah Lincoln had been born in Elizabethtown, both she and her brother Abraham had been brought up on a farm. Abraham's birthplace was in the country, and he had always lived there. The Johnston children, however, had for the last three years resided within a block of the Hardin County Courthouse, a center of much coming and going, and before that they had lived in quarters in the county jail.

There was one thing certain, both groups had much to tell and teach each other. The young Johnstons informed Sarah and Abraham about town life, and their mother joined in, bringing Thomas up to date on everything that had happened in Hardin County since he had moved away. Sally had a stock of fresh stories for the Lincoln children, and her own children enjoyed prompting her and correcting her if she slipped up on any details. Sarah and Abe loved hearing about the traveling shows that visited Elizabethtown on their swings about the countryside. Recently there had been an exhibition of an elephant and other wild and exotic animals. The Lincoln children had read about such creatures but had never seen them.

Just a month before the Johnston family left Elizabethtown a rope dancer named Welsh announced he would perform there. Whereupon the trustees of the town concluded that inasmuch as his was a performance "which neither improves the morals nor understanding of the citizens and only has a tendency to draw their cash which might be better applied," a tax of three dollars should be leveled on Mr. Welsh.[1] No doubt Sally made a good story out of this, and it is too bad we do not know whether she and her children witnessed the performance.

When city children visit the country, they are usually the ones who are intrigued by what they see and hear. Abraham and Sarah would have plenty of interesting things to show the Johnston youngsters, especially when the springtime allowed them to be out-of-doors most of the time. The good things to eat which they could find for themselves without having to buy them at a store would be especially welcomed by the town juveniles.

The pioneer's harvest began in the early spring when the maple sap began to run, and at this time candy bars for the whole year were provided. The gathering at the sugar camp was a social event of supreme importance to all, and offered about the only opportunity during the year for the younger element to sit up at night. The fire under the giant kettle had to be kept burning steadily; however, there were plenty of volunteers to watch the fire. Here the stock of candy molded in the form of sugar hearts, diamonds, or little scalloped pies was stored in great jars at no cost except the fun of boiling down the sap.

The sassafras bush was one of the children's favorite shrubs, and in the spring of the year its roots were dug up and the sassafras tea made from them was a drink not to be despised, either as a beverage or spring tonic. The bark and root of the sassafras throughout the year was always within reach of the children of the forest.

Not even the children of today have the variety of berries which the pioneer youth harvested as their taste prompted. First came the June berry, and shortly after the mulberry, and also the wild strawberries which were so plentiful in some places that an early traveler stated that in riding through some localities "his horse's hoofs were red with their juice." The large black dewberry also grew in great abundance and was equally enjoyed. For both stimulant and medicine the blackberry was a more welcome gift of nature, but not so tasty as the red raspberry which was not only harvested for immediate consumption, but with its cousin the blackberry, found its way into cordials.[2]

It was in the fall of the year that nature made her best gifts to the pioneers. It seems as if the fun of gathering harvests, especially fruits and nuts, must have been of innate origin; certainly it was not work to the average pioneer lad. The pawpaw and the persimmons, which are unknown to most American boys and girls, were plentiful in southern Indiana. The wild grape crop was abundant and the clusters of two varieties, October and fox, were gathered for jellies and beverages. The fox grapes were often found hanging on the vines until Christmas time. Nature usually provided some low tree as a grape basket into which the pioneer child could reach and satisfy his appetite without price. Along with the grapes should be mentioned red and black haws, also the wild plum and the crab apple which were often made into marmalade or fruit butter. Thomas Lincoln also set out several apple trees which provided winter fruit.

Possibly it was the gathering of the nut crop which offered

74

THE

PILGRIM'S PROGRESS

FROM

THIS WORLD

TO THAT WHICH IS TO COME.

DELIVERED

UNDER THE SIMILITUDE OF

A DREAM.

BY JOHN BUNYAN.

IN THREE PARTS.

A NEW EDITION, DIVIDED INTO CHAPTERS.

TO WHICH ARE ADDED,

EXPLANATORY AND PRACTICAL NOTES.

BY MESSRS. MASON, SCOTT, AND BURDER.

EMBELLISHED WITH ELEGANT ENGRAVINGS.

PHILADELPHIA:

PUBLISHED BY JONATHAN POUNDER, 134 N. FOURTH STREET
AND WILLIAM W. WOODWARD 52 S. SECOND STREET

Griggs & Co. Printers.

1817.

FABULÆ ÆSOPI Selectæ,

OR

Select FABLES of ÆSOP;

WITH

AN ENGLISH TRANSLATION AS LITERAL AS POSSIBLE,
ANSWERING LINE FOR LINE THROUGHOUT, THE *ROMAN*
AND *ITALIC* CHARACTERS BEING ALTERNATELY
USED; SO THAT IT IS NEXT TO AN IMPOSSIBI-
LITY FOR THE STUDENT TO MISTAKE.

A NEW EDITION wherein the errors in the Latin text
of the best and latest European copies of Mr. Clarke's selection are corrected : some antiquated English words and
modes of construction are expunged, and their places supplied by those which are more proper.

ALSO.

The signs of quantity to assist the pronunciation are added.

By JAMES ROSS,

PROFESSOR OF THE LATIN AND GREEK LANGUAGES IN
FRANKLIN COLLEGE, BOROUGH OF LANCASTER.

LANCASTER:

PRINTED BY BURNSIDE AND SMITH, NORTH
QUEEN-STREET.

1804.

THE

LIFE

AND MOST

SURPRISING ADVENTURES

OF

ROBINSON CRUSOE,

OF YORK, MARINER,

WHO LIVED EIGHT AND TWENTY YEARS

IN AN

UNINHABITED ISLAND,

ON THE COAST OF AMERICA, NEAR THE MOUTH OF THE
Great River Oroonoque.

WITH AN

ACCOUNT OF HIS DELIVERANCE THENCE

AND HIS AFTER

SURPRISING ADVENTURES

A New Edition, complete in One Volume.

WITH PLATES, DESCRIPTIVE OF THE SUBJECT

London

PUBLISHED AND SOLD BY THE BOOKSELLERS
AND BY T. WILSON AND SON, PRINTERS
HIGH-OUSEGATE, YORK.

1810.

THE

ORIENTAL

MORALIST,

OR

THE BEAUTIES

OF THE

ARABIAN NIGHTS

ENTERTAINMENTS.

TRANSLATED FROM THE ORIGINAL,

AND

ACCOMPANIED WITH SUITABLE REFLECTIONS

ADAPTED TO EACH STORY.

BY THE REVEREND MR. COOPER.

Author of the History of England, &c. &c. &c.

THE FIRST AMERICAN EDITION.

DOVER:

PRINTED BY SAMUEL BRAGG, JR. FOR
WM. T. CLAP, BOSTON.

1797.

Literary classics read by Abraham

the boys, especially, as much real fun as the harvesting of any other crop which nature provided. The shell- or shagbark was the favorite nut, and the hazelnuts contributed to a mixed nut bowl to be brought out on winter evenings.[3]

All the goodies which the children could snatch between meals were supplemental to the food for the table which would be picked up almost as easily. The woods provided the main dishes for the regular meals. Venison, rabbits, squirrels, turkeys, quail, pigeons, and wild ducks were plentiful. It is safe to conclude that Sally Johnston's youngsters never had had such a variety of good eating as they did after reaching their Indiana home.

The cabin arrangements were adjusted to the new family's needs. Abraham now shared the loft not only with Dennis Hanks but also with John Johnston. The three girls—Sarah, Elizabeth, and Matilda—slept in the new bed Thomas built in the one room of the cabin. Sally provided linen pants and shirts for the boys in the summer, buckskin pants and linsey-woolsey jackets in the winter. Abraham grew so fast that one of his schoolmates recalled that "there was bare and naked, six or more inches of Abe's shin bone." [4] The girl's garments were equally simple and plain, but it required considerable effort on Sally's part to keep them all warm and clean.

The children were largely dependent on their own resources for their fun. They made their own balls for the game of "bull pen" by wrapping yarn around a pebble and then covering it with a piece of buckskin. Other games included hare and hounds, wet and dry stones, prisoner's base, hide-and-seek, and in the winter when the snow fell, fox and geese. Hoops were made of hickory saplings wrapped with raw hide. Grapevines provided jumping ropes. In this family of five children all about the same age we can understand how Abraham "had a jolly time. . . . It was a rough life, of course, and without luxuries, but it was not a life of exceptional privations. . . . he had a joyous, cheerful comfortable time." [5]

Sally Bush Lincoln is supposed to have brought from Kentucky one other book, *Lessons in Elocution,* by William Scott. There was a copy of the book in the Bush family, for on May 27, 1806, Isaac Bush purchased at the Bleakley and Montgomery store in Elizabethtown, "Dictionary, Scott's Lessons in Elocution and Introduction." [6] This may have been the very volume that eventually came into Abraham's hands. It was by far the most important of the four books Sally Lincoln brought.

An edition was published in Philadelphia in 1801. [7] As the title indicates, this is primarily a book on public speaking. Thirty-six pages are devoted to "Elements of Gesture." Included under this heading are sections "On speaking of speeches at school," "On the acting of plays at school," and finally "Rules for expressing with propriety, the principal passions and humours, which occur in reading or public speaking." In this last, eighty-one "passions and humours" are considered, each with its own particular manner of expression. The first is "tranquility or apathy" and the last is "mixed passions and emotions." "*Mixed* passions and emotions of the mind, require a mixed expression. *Pity,* for example, is composed of grief and love. It is therefore evident, that a correct speaker must, by his looks and gestures, and by the tone and pitch of his voice, express both grief and love, in expressing pity, and so of the rest."

One pities the student who was obliged to twist his head, body, and limbs, as well as maneuver his mouth, eyes, and eyebrows in the manner prescribed by William Scott to interpret properly each of these eighty-one emotions. There are four drawings showing the correct positions of the body in speaking, with special attention to the hands and feet when gesturing. Since Abe was now at the age when he "wanted to be the center of the stage," probably he studied these rules carefully, and attempted to apply them in his first efforts at speechmaking.

The remainder of the volume was divided into two parts.

Part I was called "Lessons in Reading," and Part II "Lessons in Speaking." Included here were selections from the world's great literature, a real treasure trove of readings. Short pithy sayings, "select sentences," came first, with a strong religious and moral emphasis, followed by longer prose pieces and poetry. The extracts given below, taken from complete poems included in the volume, give a cross section of the selections:

> And still they gaz'd, and still the wonder grew,
>   That one small head could carry all he knew.
> "Character of a Country Schoolmaster," GOLDSMITH

> Now came still evening on, and twilight gray
>   Had in her sober livery all things clad.
>   "Evening in Paradise Described," MILTON

> The curfew tolls the knell of parting day;
>   The lowing herds wind slowly o'er the lea:
> The ploughman homeward plods his weary way,
>   And leaves the world to darkness and to me.
>   · · · · · · · · · · · · · · · ·
> Let not ambition mock their useful toil,
>   Their homely joys and destiny obscure:
> Nor grandeur hear, with a disdainful smile,
>   The short and simple annals of the poor.[8]
> "Elegy Written in a Country Church Yard," GRAY

> Shut, shut the door, good John!—fatigu'd, I said:
>   Tie up the knocker; say, I'm sick, I'm dead.
> "Humourous Complaint to Dr. Arbuthnot on the
>   Impertinence of Scribblers," POPE

> Hail, holy light! offspring of heaven first born!
>   Or, of th' Eternal, coeternal beam!
>   "Lamentation for the Loss of his Sight," MILTON

> Hence, loathed Melancholy;
>   Of Cerberus and blackest midnight born. . . .
>   "L'Allegro, or the Merry Man," MILTON

All are but parts of one stupendous whole,
  Whose body Nature is, and God the soul. . . .
                    "The Order of Nature," POPE

She is the fancy's midwife: and she comes
In shape no bigger than an agate stone
On the fore-finger of an alderman. . . .
"Description of Mab, Queen of the Fairies,"
                                    SHAKESPEARE

Honor and shame from no condition rise;
Act well your part—there all the honor lies.
                    "Pursuits of Mankind," POPE

Now let us sing—"long live the king;"
  And Gilpin long live he:
And when he next does ride abroad,
  May I be there to see!
            "Facetious History of John Gilpin," COWPER

This volume may have been Abraham's introduction to
Shakespeare. It included such famous pieces as the following:
  Tragedy of Hamlet: Hamlet's advice to the players; soliloquy of Hamlet's Uncle on the murder of his brother; soliloquy
of Hamlet on death.
  Tragedy of Julius Caesar: Cassius instigating Brutus to join
the conspiracy against Caesar; Brutus' harangue on the death
of Caesar; Antony's oration over Caesar's body.
  Tragedy of Henry IV: Hotspur's account of the Fop;
Hotspur's soliloquy on the contents of a letter; Henry's solilo-
quy on sleep; Falstaff's encomiums on sack; Falstaff's soliloquy
on honor.
  Tragedy of Richard III: part of Richard III's soliloquy the
night preceding the battle of Bosworth.
  From *As You Like It*, there is Jacques's speech beginning
"All the world's a stage . . ."
  Among the other speeches and soliloquies there were
Douglas' account of himself, and Douglas' account of the

hermit, from John Home's *Tragedy of Douglas;* and Sempronious' speech for war, Lucius' speech for peace, and Cato's soliloquy on the immortality of the soul, from the *Tragedy of Cato,* by Joseph Addison.

In the 1811 edition there is a section entitled "Rules Respecting Elocution."[9] Here are eight requirements for a polished speaker. If Abraham saw this edition, he may have memorized these and put them into immediate practice:

I. Let your articulation be Distinct and Deliberate.
II. Let your pronunciation be Bold and Forcible.
III. Acquire a compass and variety in the Height of your voice.
IV. Pronounce your words with propriety and elegance.
V. Pronounce every word consisting of more than one syllable with its proper accent.
VI. In every Sentence distinguish the more significant words by a natural, forcible and varied emphasis.
VII. Acquire a just variety of Pause and Cadence.
VIII. Accompany the Emotions and Passions which your words express by correspondent tone, looks, and gestures.

Among the "Selected Sentences" in the 1811 edition were the following: "... there is nothing truly valuable which can be purchased without pains and labor." *Tattler*

"A man acquainted with history may, in some respect, be said to have lived from the beginning of the world...." HUME

"Never sport with pain and distress in any of your amusements, nor treat even the meanest insect with wanton cruelty." BLAIR

"You must love learning, if you would possess it." KNOX

"Good manners are, to particular societies, what morals are to society in general—their cement and their security." CHESTERFIELD

"Whatever you pursue, be emulous to excel." BLAIR

Abe may have adopted this last as his own particular motto. Even in his youth "he was ambitious and determined and when he attempted to excel man or boy his whole soul and energies were bent on doing it."[10] His stepmother recalled that he "could easily learn and long remember, and when he did learn anything he learned it well and thoroughly. What he learned he stored away in his memory which was extremely good. What he learned and stored away was well defined in his own mind, [he] repeated it over and over again until it was so defined and fixed permanently in his memory." [11]

Lincoln's retentiveness must have been exceptional. John Romine, one of his neighbors, recalled that "while but a boy [he] had the best memory of any person I ever knew." [12] Henry Brooner claimed that when Lincoln came to his home, they would sit around and "for hours he would tell me what he had read." He commented on Lincoln's fine memory. [13] All seemed agreed that everything Abe had once learned "was always at his command."

Dilworth gave Abraham a good vocabulary and illustrated by example how words should be put together. Scott made available a tremendous amount of well-written prose and poetry designed for practice pieces. Having studied his lessons, Abraham sought to expound them. He did not want for listeners. They were right under his own roof. He grew so fast that by this time he was towering over the other four children and he made them his "captive" audience. They sat quietly before him, not interrupting his orations. In the summer months he held these sessions out-of-doors, mounting a stump and addressing Sarah and the three Johnstons as they sat on a fallen tree. Sometimes his father and Sally and Dennis Hanks and visiting neighbors would stop to listen. John Hanks, a cousin of Dennis' who visited the Lincolns in 1823, recalled observing Abraham making speeches "to his step-brother, his sister, his stepsisters and youngsters that would come in to see the family." [14] His stepmother stated that "he made speeches such as interested him and the children. . . . His father had to make him quit sometimes as he quit his own work to speak and made the other children as well as the men quit their work." [15]

The additional children in the Lincoln family may have hastened the opening of the first school in the Little Pigeon community. Four years had passed since Sarah and Abraham had attended their last class in Kentucky. Tradition has it that Thomas Lincoln "had suffered greatly for want of an education and that he determined early that Abraham should be well educated." [16] The stepmother was sympathetic toward education but had not been able, because of her financial circumstances, to do much for her own children in Kentucky.

The early subscription schools of Spencer County, while following no specific pattern, did not usually keep more than two or three months, and the customary fee was $1.50 or $2.00 per pupil. It was seldom that teachers were available in the remote districts more than once in every two years. Of course, schools were only in session during seasons when the children could be spared from work on the farm. It is known definitely that Abe attended schools in Indiana taught by Andrew Crawford, James Swaney, and Azel W. Dorsey. [17]

The earliest schoolhouse in the Little Pigeon community stood on the Noah Gordon farm in Clay Township, adjacent to Carter Township on the south. [18] There was an excellent spring of water here. This was a mile and a half south of the Lincoln home in about the center of the scattered population then living near the headwaters of Little Pigeon Creek. It was a one-room building erected by the subscribers to the school. The teacher was Andrew Crawford. The first record of his living in Spencer County is his commission as a justice of the peace, dated May 8, 1818. [19] On December 19, 1818, the Vincennes *Western Sun* carried this notice: "Taken up by Jesse Hoskins in Spencer County, Carter Township, a horse valued by George Lee and William Hoskins at $40.00. A true copy from my estray book. A. Crawford, Justice of the Peace." Jesse Hoskins was a neighbor of Thomas Lincoln and this would indicate that Andrew Crawford was probably living in the Lincoln neighborhood as early as 1818.

Crawford was a man about thirty-five years of age. In the 1820 census [20] he was listed as between twenty-six and forty-five years, with a wife between eighteen and twenty and a son and daughter under ten. Curiously the marriage register of Warrick County, adjacent to Spencer County on the west, records the marriage of Andrew Crawford and Elizabeth Hargrove on November 2, 1820.[21] Crawford is firmly established in the Pigeon Creek neighborhood by marriages which he performed as justice of the peace. The names of the young people he joined in marriage show that they were from Little Pigeon families and may have been his pupils.[22]

It is impossible to determine whether it was in the winter of 1818–19 or 1819–20 that Andrew Crawford held a school attended by the children of the Lincoln household.[23] That he was in the county early enough to have held one in the winter of 1818–19 is true. But that was the winter after the heavy scourge of milk sickness and it seems probable that the parents did not have the heart to organize a school. The arrival of the three Johnston children in time for the 1819–20 term, thus increasing the number of pupils, makes it seem this was the more likely time for securing an instructor.

In the Pigeon Creek schools nothing "was ever required of a teacher, beyond *readin'*, *writin'*, and *cipherin'*,' to the Rule of Three. If a straggler supposed to understand latin, happened to sojourn in the neighborhood, he was looked upon as a wizzard. There was absolutely nothing to excite ambition for education." [24] A report of one interesting feature of Crawford's school which has come down to us is that he tried to teach the children good manners. If he taught his pupils the art of receiving and introducing guests properly, as seems to have been the case, it is likely he also strove to impart to them other forms of etiquette.[25]

Nathaniel Grigsby, a pupil at the school, who is responsible for the report that Crawford emphasized etiquette, is also the source of the well-known story of how Abraham Lincoln helped out Ann Roby in a spelling contest. Crawford usually held a spelling match every Friday. On this particular Friday Ann was given the word "defied" to spell. She started bravely "d e f", then paused, not knowing whether to say "y" or "i." She looked at Abe and saw that he was pointing his finger to his eye. She took the hint and spelled the word correctly.[26]

Apparently it was customary for the students to take turns reading out loud from the Bible. On one occasion the story of Nebuchadnezzar and the Golden Image from the third chapter of Daniel was being read. One of the members of the class was an undersized boy called Bud, who had not progressed very far in the art of reading. To him fell verse number 12 which contained the names Shadrach, Meshach, and Abednego, the Israelites who were thrown into the fiery furnace. These names appear repeatedly throughout the chapter. The story of the boy's struggle with these three difficult words was related as follows:

"Little Bud stumbled on Shadrach, floundered on Meshach, and went all to pieces on Abed-nego. Instantly the hand of the master dealt him a cuff on the side of the head and left him wailing and blubbering as the next boy in line took up the reading. But before the girl at the end of the line had done reading he had subsided into sniffles and finally became quiet. His blunder and disgrace were forgotten by the others of the class until his turn was approaching to read again. Then, like a thunderclap out of a clear sky, he set up a wail which even alarmed the master, who with rather unusual gentleness inquired, 'What's the matter now?'

"Pointing with a shaking finger at the verse which a few moments later would fall to him to read, Bud managed to quaver out the answer:

"'Look there marster,' he cried, 'there comes them same damn three fellers again.'"[27]

CHAPTER VII

12

Admiration

1821

ACCORDING TO CHILD PSYCHOLOGISTS, when a boy is about twelve years old he enters into a period of "hero worship." In a sparsely settled community, such as the one in which Abraham was growing up, there were few persons who ranked as champions in the eyes of a young boy. There were no grandfathers, uncles, or older brothers close by, in fact no immediate relatives to admire. There was, of course, Dennis Hanks, nine years Abe's senior, who lived with the Lincolns, but he does not seem to have excited esteem in the youth. And he was soon to leave. On June 14, 1821, Dennis Hanks and Elizabeth Johnston, daughter of Sally Lincoln, were married, and moved into their own cabin about a mile east of the Lincolns.[1] Abe was, therefore, drawn to his father who was his constant companion at work, at mealtime, and in the evening hours as well. Thomas having no rival for his son's admiration and affection played a heroic role in the boy's life at this time.

Thomas Lincoln was a worthy parent. There is not recorded a single factual incident in which he brought discredit upon his family or himself. The death of Abraham's mother tended to draw him closer to his father. It is not difficult to visualize a congenial filial relationship between a father who was good-humored, "loving everybody and everything," and a son who

84

was "kind to everybody and to everything."[2] Certainly these parallel characteristics should have created an ideal father and son companionship.

Furthermore, Thomas was the type of man to invite a boy's admiration. He was noted in the community for his unusual physical power, which must have brought pride to his son. He approached six feet in height and weighed almost two hundred pounds. Dennis Hanks described him as "a man of great strength and courage and not one bit of cowardice about him. He could carry fatigue for any length of time, was a man of uncommon endurance." Hanks also claimed that once in Kentucky Thomas was matched in a fight with a man by the name of Hardin to see which was the best man—Hardin or Lincoln. The fight was prompted by no anger or malice; it was simply a contest to see who was the stronger. Lincoln, according to Hanks, won without a scratch.[3]

For all his superior strength Thomas was not overbearing or quarrelsome. ". . . his desire was to be on terms of amity and sociability with everybody." One of his Indiana neighbors affirmed that "Thomas Lincoln was a man of good morals, good health, and exceedingly good humor."[4]

His friendly good nature was supplemented, as might have been anticipated, with a flair for storytelling. "He had a great stock of border anecdotes and professed a marvelous proclivity to entertain by 'spinning yarns' and narrating his youthful experiences."[5] John Hanks, who had good opportunity to observe him, remembered him as "a good-humored man, a strong brave man, a very stout man, loved fun, jokes, and equalled Abe in telling stories."[6]

One member of the Johnston family into which Thomas Lincoln married declared that he "was one of the best men that ever lived. A sturdy, honest, God fearing man whom all the neighbors respected."[7] Another added, "Uncle Abe got his honesty, and his clean notions of living and his kind heart from his father. Maybe the Hanks family was smarter, but some of them couldn't hold a candle to Grandfather Lincoln, when it came to morals." [8]

Abraham would have no reason to be ashamed of his father's personal appearance. Thomas Lincoln was clean shaven. He had "a high forehead, straight nose, green or light blue eyes, rather a broad face and black hair." His manner in combing his hair is said to have given him a picturesque appearance. The fact that he rarely used intoxicants and was free from profanity is commendable.[9]

In 1821 Thomas Lincoln was chosen to supervise the construction of the Little Pigeon meetinghouse. This was the most important job that he is known to have undertaken in Indiana. Up to this time there had been no church building in that part of the county. The Little Pigeon Baptist Church had been organized in 1816 in Warrick County, but it was not until March 13, 1819, that consideration was given to building a house of worship. There was the usual difference of opinion as to where it should be built and the decision was postponed until there was more of a "oneness of mind concerning the seat." In July of the same year a committee of five was appointed to view three different locations which had been suggested for the churchsite. On December 11, 1819, it was decided that "the meeting house be built at Brother [Noah] Gordon's." This was about a mile and a half south of the Lincoln cabin. The selection was largely influenced by the spring of water near by belonging to Samuel Howell.

On February 12, 1820, the congregation accepted plans for their church edifice and determined to "build their walls of hewed logs in the following form to wit: The height one story and six feet, and the size twenty-four feet wide by thirty-two feet long with outlets in back and front of six feet square, three doors, five windows and covered with clapboards." Construction was again postponed, and on September 9, the plans were altered. Eventually, on March 10, 1821, a committee of five was appointed with final authority to agree upon a plan for the structure both as to form and size. They determined that the meetinghouse should be "30 x 26 feet, hewed logs, 8 feet in the under story and 6 feet above the joists."

The committee had also been empowered "to employ workmen to perform the said work," and chose Thomas Lincoln to direct the construction and also to perform some of the labor. He may have suggested some of the alterations in the plans. He was responsible for the pulpit, window casings, and other cabinetwork. There was a ladder to a loft which was used for sleeping quarters by those who came from a long distance to attend services and association meetings.[10]

Abraham assisted his father and the other workers in the building of the church and there were many tasks which he could perform acceptably. For the normal boy of twelve it would be a great privilege to work beside his father and to share in any task that they could perform together, especially when his father was the boss carpenter.

On the frontier there were few personal contacts outside the family circle so the biographies of eminent men became helpful sources of inspiration. When about twelve Abe read two books of great importance, the first books by Americans about America and her people that he acquired. They came to him at a good time, for he had reached the age when he could take pride in the history of his country and in the achievements of its leaders. The volumes were the autobiography of Benjamin Franklin and Parson Weems's *Life of Washington*. Wesley Hall, a young friend of Abe's, remembered that one evening while he was staying with the Lincolns, Thomas asked his son to read aloud to them for awhile. The book from which the boy chose to read was Franklin's autobiography.[11]

In 1947 a committee of the Grolier Club, devoted to the promotion of literature on book collecting and the art of book making, made a selection of one hundred influential American books printed before 1900. In the published catalogue the selections are arranged chronologically by date of publication. Number 21 concerns the earliest editions of Franklin's autobiography: "The most widely read of all American autobiographies, the gift to adolescents of countless parents, godparents and well-wishers, this book holds the essence of the American way of life." [12]

The part of the autobiography available in print when Lincoln read it covered only the first years of Franklin's life—1706–1731—which he wrote at Twyford in England in 1771. This had been published in France in 1791 and then published in translation in London in 1793.[13] *The Life of Dr. Benjamin Franklin*[14] which Abe probably read is really a book of three parts. In it the autobiographical section, based on the 1793 London version and requiring 122 pages, ends abruptly, and the narrative of Franklin's life is continued by Dr. Henry Stuber, a close friend of Franklin, who in seventy-odd pages brings the story to a close with an epitaph written by Franklin many years before his death. The concluding ten pages contain extracts from the last will and testament of Franklin which in itself is a unique and interesting document.

Franklin advised a friend that in writing of his life he strove to "omit all facts and transactions that may not have a tendency to benefit the young reader, by showing him, from example, and my success in emerging from poverty, and acquiring some degree of wealth, power, and reputation, the advantages of certain modes of conduct which I observed, and of avoiding the errors which were prejudicial to me." [15]

In the first twenty pages Franklin tells what he knows of his forebears and immediate family, and gives a description and penetrating analysis of his father. Franklin was the thirteenth child in a family of seventeen. Skipping over his first years, he proceeded to describe the education he received and his training for his trade as a printer in Boston. Like Abe young Franklin was an avid reader. He said that he did not remember learning to read, in fact he could not remember when he could not read. When he was eight years old, he attended a grammar school for less than a year and made rapid advancement, but, for financial reasons his father removed him from that school, and placed him in one devoted to teaching writing and arithmetic. Here he acquired a good hand in the former, but made little progress in the latter. At ten years he was assisting his father, a soapmaker and chandler, in cutting wicks, filling moulds, keeping shop, and running messages. Two years later he began serving an apprenticeship in his brother John's printing shop. He often spent a great part of the night reading, possibly a borrowed book that was to be returned to its owner the next morning. He was determined to become a successful writer of the English language and put himself through rigorous exercises to train himself to express his ideas clearly and in good literary style.

When Franklin was seventeen he left Boston for Philadelphia where he worked as a printer. In 1724 he made a trip to London, but two years later he returned to Philadelphia where he resumed his trade. Here he began publishing the *Pennsylvania Gazette* in 1730, and launched his many other successful enterprises and projects. The autobiography, as read by Abe, ended with the account of the organization by Franklin and some friends of a subscription library, the first such library in America.

Abe must have been completely absorbed by this personal account of a famous American's youth. Like Franklin, Abe loved books, and like him he wanted to learn to use the English language correctly and effectively. Also, his family, like Franklin's, was in modest circumstances, and he had to work hard during his youth, and indulge in his reading and writing only after his tasks were finished. Franklin demonstrated that industry, economy, self-discipline, and temperance had been in large measure responsible for his rise to success. Self-improvement is the ever-recurring theme in the autobiography. Franklin also carefully noted what he considered the

89

"errata" of his life in the hope, as he said, that they would serve as lessons to his young readers.

Having finished the autobiographical section Abe read the continuation of Franklin's life by his friend Dr. Stuber. Here he found accounts of Franklin's inventions and his experiments with electricity. The story of the kite made with two crossbars covered with a silk handkerchief, the upright bar pointed with iron, a key within reach on the string, and the remarkable discovery resulting from this experiment would be noted with wonderment. Here also Abe acquired a good background for understanding the American Revolution. Franklin served as agent of Pennsylvania and later of other colonies to represent them before His Majesty's government. His examination before the House of Commons during the debates on the repeal of the Stamp Act won him great renown at home. He liked living in England, but his love of America and the liberty and justice that she represented caused him gradually to accept the idea of revolution. Abe then read of Franklin's return to Philadelphia and his service in the Continental Congress with membership on the committee which drafted the Declaration of Independence. The next nine years of his life were spent in performing various diplomatic assignments in France where he won completely the love and respect of her people. Though old and ill he served as a member of the Constitutional Convention, adding much to that assemblage by his prestige and personality. Finally, Abe read that in 1788 Franklin was elected president of the Pennsylvania Society for Promoting the Abolition of Slavery, and that his last public act was signing a memorial from that organization to the United States House of Representatives "praying them to exert the full extent of power vested in the constitution, in discouraging the traffic of the human species." [16]

This book offered a completely new reading experience for Abe. It must have made a deep impression on him, as it has on

THE

·LIFE

OF

DR. BENJAMIN FRANKLIN.

WRITTEN BY HIMSELF.

MONTPELIER:
PRINTED BY SAMUEL GOSS,
FOR JOSIAH PARKS.
1809.

THE LIFE

OF

GEORGE WASHINGTON

WITH

CURIOUS ANECDOTES,

EQUALLY HONOURABLE TO HIMSELF AND
EXEMPLARY TO HIS YOUNG COUNTRYMEN.

A life how useful to his country led!
How loved! while living!—how revered! now dead.
Lisp! lisp! his name, ye children yet unborn!
And with like deeds your own great names adorn.

EIGHTH EDITION—GREATLY IMPROVED.

EMBELLISHED WITH SEVEN ENGRAVINGS.

BY M. L. WEEMS,

FORMERLY RECTOR OF MOUNT-VERNON PARISH.

PHILADELPHIA:
PRINTED FOR THE AUTHOR.
1809.

THE LIFE

OF

GEN. FRANCIS MARION,

A CELEBRATED

PARTISAN OFFICER

IN THE

REVOLUTIONARY WAR,

AGAINST THE

BRITISH AND TORIES

IN SOUTH CAROLINA AND GEORGIA.

By Brig. Gen. P. HORRY, of Marion's Brigade : and
M. L. WEEMS.

"On VERNON's CHIEF, why lavish all our lays?
"Come, honest Muse, and sing great Marion's praise."

EIGHTH EDITION.

PHILADELPHIA :
M. CAREY & SONS– CHESNUT STREET.
1822.

AUTHENTIC NARRATIVE

OF THE LOSS OF THE

AMERICAN BRIG COMMERCE,

WRECKED ON THE WESTERN COAST OF AFRICA, IN THE MONTH
OF AUGUST, 1815.

WITH

AN ACCOUNT OF THE SUFFERINGS

OF HER

SURVIVING OFFICERS AND CREW,

WHO WERE ENSLAVED BY THE WANDERING ARABS ON THE GREAT

AFRICAN DESART, OR ZAHAHRAH,

AND

OBSERVATIONS HISTORICAL, GEOGRAPHICAL, &c.

MADE DURING THE TRAVELS OF THE AUTHOR, WHILE A SLAVE TO
THE ARABS, AND IN THE EMPIRE OF MOROCCO.

BY JAMES RILEY,

LATE MASTER AND SUPERCARGO.

PRECEDED BY A BRIEF SKETCH OF THE AUTHOR'S LIFE ; AND CONCLUDED BY
A DESCRIPTION OF THE FAMOUS CITY OF TOMBUCTOO, ON THE RIVER NIGER,
AND OF ANOTHER LARGE CITY, FAR SOUTH OF IT, ON THE SAME RIVER, CALL-
ED WASSANAH ; NARRATED TO THE AUTHOR AT MOGADORE, BY SIDI HA-
MET, THE ARABIAN MERCHANT.

WITH AN ARABIC AND ENGLISH VOCABULARY.

ILLUSTRATED AND EMBELLISHED WITH TEN HAND-
SOME COPPERPLATE ENGRAVINGS.

NEW-YORK:
PRINTED AND PUBLISHED FOR THE AUTHOR.
E. T. & W. MERCEIN, No. 93 Gold-street.
1817.

Abraham's literary heroes

thousands of American boys and girls of succeeding generations.

More popular than the *Life of Dr. Benjamin Franklin* was Mason Locke Weems's *The Life of Washington* which Abe probably read shortly thereafter. This volume influenced him more than any other early book except the Bible. Weems gave him a hero to challenge his very best endeavors. It presented to him the American way of life as revealed by the founding fathers. It impressed him with the great sacrifices which were made for freedom and it became the outstanding inspirational volume of his boyhood days. It, too, was selected by the Grolier Club as one of the influential American books published before 1900.[17] The first edition which appeared in 1800 was essentially biography. Then in 1806 Weems rewrote his book and enriched it "with a number of very curious anecdotes" including the famous cherry tree story. In this form it went through twenty-eight editions during Weems's life (he died in 1825), and was reprinted as recently as 1927. The edition of 1809 is selected since it bears the same date as the Franklin volume. It is not known who presented the book to Abraham, but it seems to be in some way associated with his schoolteacher, Andrew Crawford, whose classes he had been attending. Undoubtedly Abe read an edition which included the "curious anecdotes," and was illustrated with crude woodcuts, one a portrait of Washington, another "The Defeat of General Braddock" showing the General in a two-wheeled cart by which Washington is standing and Indians and soldiers fighting in the background. The other five, all relating to the Revolution, were: "Death of Gen'l Montgomery," "The Battle of Lexington," "Battle of Bunker's Hill & Death of Gen'l Warren," "Capture of Major Andre," and the "Surrender of Lord Cornwallis." [18] Some of the early editions also contained a map of the United States locating the battlegrounds.

While Abraham read the lives of both Franklin and Washington "with zest," [19] it was Washington that became his hero. Young George's athletic prowess caught the boy's admiration. According to John Fitzhugh, as quoted by Weems: "EGAD! he ran wonderfully. . . . he had nobody here-abouts, that could come near him." Col. Lewis Willis, a childhood play-mate of Washington's, was quoted as saying that he had often seen George throw a stone across the Rappahannock, at the lower ferry of Fredericksburg. "It would be no easy matter," commented Weems, "to find a man, now a-days, who could do it." ". . . when his daily toils of surveying were ended, George, like a young Greek training for the Olympic games, used to turn out with his sturdy young companions, 'to see,' as they termed it, 'which was the best man,' at running, jump-ing, and wrestling." [20] Abe had approached the time when he, too, was beginning to compete with boys of his own age in such contests, and his unusual strength was catching the attention of the Little Pigeon Creek neighborhood.

Many of those who today are inclined to ridicule the cherry tree story have never read it in its original context. "NEVER," wrote Weems, "did the wise Ulysses take more pains with his beloved Telemachus, than did Mr. Washington with George, to inspire him with an *early love of truth.* 'Truth, George,' said he, 'is the loveliest quality of youth. I would ride fifty miles, my son, to see the little boy whose heart is so *honest* and his lips so *pure,* that we may depend on every word he says. . . .

". . . whenever by accident, you do anything wrong, which must often be the case, as you are but a poor little boy yet, without *experience* or *knowledge,* you must never tell a false-hood to conceal it; but come *bravely* up, my son, like a *little man,* and tell me of it: and, instead of beating you, George, I will but the more honour and love you for it, my dear."

"When George . . . was about six years old," the story continues, "he was made the wealthy master of a *hatchet!* of which, like most little boys, he was immoderately fond; and was constantly going about chopping every thing that came his way. One day, in the garden, where he often amused himself hacking his mother's pea-sticks, he unluckily tried the edge of the hatchet on the body of a beautiful young English cherry-tree, which he barked so terribly, that I don't believe the tree ever got the better of it. The next morning the old gentleman finding out what had befallen his tree, which, by the by, was a great favourite, came into the house; and with much warmth asked for the mischievous author, declaring at the same time, that he would not have taken five guineas for his tree. Nobody could tell him any thing about it. Presently George and his hatchet made their appearance. *George,* said his father, *do you know who killed that beautiful little cherry-tree yonder in the garden?* This was a *tough question;* and George staggered under it for a moment; but quickly recovered himself: and looking at his father, with the sweet face of youth brightened with the inexpressible charm of all-conquering truth, he bravely cried out, *I can't tell a lie, Pa: you know I can't tell a lie. I did cut it with my hatchet. Run to my arms, you dearest boy,* cried his father in transport, *run to my arms; glad am I, George, that you killed my tree; for you have paid me for it a thousand fold. Such an act of heroism in my son, is more worth than a thousand trees, though blossomed with silver, and their fruits of purest gold."* [21]

Throughout the book, of course, Washington is portrayed as the perfect example for youth to follow. His policy was "the *divine policy of doing good for evil.* It melted down his iron enemies into golden friends." [22]

The episodes, tragedies, and triumphs of the Revolution are dramatically described by Weems. Here, for example, is his account of the Battle of Trenton: ". . . Washington and his little *forlorn hope,* pressed on through the darksome night, pelted by an incessant storm of hail and snow. On approaching the river, nine miles above Trenton, they heard the unwelcome roar of ice, loud crashing along the angry flood. But the object before them was too *vast* to allow one thought about difficulties. The troops were instantly embarked, and after five hours of infinite toil and danger, landed, some of them frost-bitten, on the same shores with the enemy. Forming a line they renewed their march. . . .

"The Sun had just tipt with gold the adjacent hills, when snowy Trenton, with the wide-tented fields of the foe, hove in sight. To the young in arms this was an awful scene, and nature called a short-liv'd terror to their hearts. But not unseen of Washington was their fear. He marked the sudden paleness of their cheeks, when first they beheld the enemy, and quick, with half-stifled sighs, turned on him their wistful looks. . . . Thus stately and terrible rode *Columbia's first and greatest son,* along the front of his halting troops. The eager wish for battle flushed over his burning face, as, rising on his stirrups, he raised his sword towards the hostile camp, and exclaimed *'there! my brave friends! there are the enemies of your country! and now, all I ask of you, is, just to remember what you are about to fight for. March!'* His looks and voice rekindled all their fire, and drove them undaunted to the charge. . . . the Americans led on by Washington, advanced upon them in a stream of lightning, which soon decided the contest." [23]

Weems's glorification of the Revolution and the founding of the nation made Abraham aware "that there must have been something more than common that these men struggled for. . . that something even more than National Independence; that something that held out a great promise to all the people of the world to all time to come. . . ." [24] That something Weems personified as the "Genius of Liberty," [25] and under Washington's leadership the struggle for liberty was victorious.

So successfully did Weems portray his subject as the great American hero, that he became in fact, as Gen. Henry Lee eulogized him, "first in war, first in peace, and first in the hearts of his countrymen." Abe did not find in Washington's youth many similarities to his own situation. From Benjamin

94

Franklin he received practical instruction in self-improvement and self-discipline. In Washington, as depicted by Weems, he found an ideal, to serve as an inspiration and challenge, a personification of the hopes and inspiration of those who had fought for independence and founded the new nation conceived in liberty and dedicated to justice.[26]

Elias Nason, one-time editor of the *New England Historical and Genealogical Review*, pays this tribute to Mason Weems: "The patriotic Weems, by the vivacity and glowing fervor of his style, inspiring as no other man a love for country in the breast of youth." [27]

CHAPTER VIII

13

Selection

1822

CAPTIVATED BY STORIES of Franklin, Washington, and the soldiers of the Revolution, Lincoln, in 1822, entered the ranks of the teenagers. He may have had some difficulty now in his speechmaking, as his voice was changing and he could not always control its modulations. Although already tall, he was still growing, and no doubt his father at times wondered if he would ever stop. He was a robust, healthy lad. "He would always come to school. . . ," one of his friends recalled, "good humoredly and laughing. He was always in good health, never was sick, had an excellent constitution and took care of it." [1] His stepmother stated many years later that "Abe was a moderate eater and I now have no remembrance of his special dish; he sat down and ate what was set before him, making no complaint, he seemed careless about this. He always had good health and was never sick." [2]

John Hanks who had many meals at the Lincoln table is witness that both Nancy Hanks Lincoln and Sally Bush Lincoln were good cooks. [3] Another relative commented that Thomas Lincoln "made a good living, and I reckon he would have got something ahead if he hadn't been so generous. He had the old Virginia notion of hospitality—liked to see people sit up to the table and eat hearty. . . ." [4]

Besides the wide range of game and fish, fruit, nuts, honey,

96

and maple sugar available to the pioneer for the taking, there
were such home-grown vegetables as potatoes, turnips, cab-
bage, beets, roasting ears, pumpkins and squash, and one
Spencer County citizen wrote in August, 1822, "There are
plenty of cucumbers, egg plant and I have pulled the large
water melon." [5]

That the Lincolns had a garden is evident in the story of the
cow getting into it "and making and committing depredation."
Abraham discovered her one day standing meekly at the gate
and to her great surprise "leaped upon her back, digging his
bare heels into her side, the astonished animal broke away
down the road in a gallop, Abe swinging his hat and shouting
at the top of his voice." [6]

Once some neighbor boys raided the Lincoln melon patch,
and one of them recalled: "We got the melons, went through
the corn to the fence, got over. All at once to our surprise and
mortification Lincoln came among us, on us, goodnaturedly
said: 'Boys, now I've got you.' Sat down with us, cracked jokes,
told stories, helped eat the melons." [7]

It was when he reached his teens that Abraham's neighbors
began to play a larger part in his daily life. Actually the Little
Pigeon community had not developed very rapidly, and at
that time there was still no village or anything resembling a
community center, unless the newly built church could be so
designated. But one should not have the impression that the
Lincolns were living in an uninhabited area. Their farm was
located just one mile east of the junction point of Carter, Clay,
and Jackson townships, Spencer County, and Pigeon Township in Warrick County. The people who were living in these
four townships might be said to constitute the Little Pigeon
neighborhood. Usually not more than two or three families
settled on a single section of the Congressional surveys comprising six hundred and forty acres, and, of course, some
sections were entirely vacant. An attempt is made here to visualize this population, using the Lincoln home as a center.

The early land records reveal the names of the persons entering land and the 1820 census gives the names of heads of families and the number of children in each household under eighteen years of age. From these we can determine the families with their number of children who were the Lincoln neighbors.[8] Not knowing the exact location of the cabin homes on the tracts of land entered, the section boundary closest to the Lincoln home is used in determining the distance of their neighbors.

Within a mile radius of the Lincolns there lived Thomas Barrett, with four children; Thomas Turnham with three; Thomas Carter with six; John Carter with eight; Samuel Howell with seven; David Casebier with eight; John Jones with four; and probably John Romine with four. Adding to these Thomas Lincoln and his five, we have a total of nine families with forty-nine children, fifteen boys and thirteen girls under seven years of age, twelve boys and nine girls between the ages of seven and seventeen.

Beyond the one-mile radius but within two miles of the Lincolns were Joseph Wright with four children; William Wright with seven; Noah Gordon with seven; James Gentry with seven; William Whittinghill with four; and William Wood with five. Between the two and three miles radius were James Blair with three children; Reuben Grigsby with eight; William Jones with three; and Peter Brooner with eight. Those who were residing about four miles from the Lincolns were Lawrence Jones with five children; William Smith with one; Henry Gunterman with five; John Hoskins with two; Jacob Hoskins with four; William Stark with one; David Winkler with four; and Joseph Hoskins with one. The total number of children within the four-mile radius were forty-five boys and forty-five girls under seven, and twenty-three boys and twenty-five girls between seven and seventeen.

Other heads of families who were living in Carter, Clay, Jackson, and Pigeon townships, but more distant neighbors of

98

the Lincolns, were Thomas Medcalf, Isaac Johnston, John Dutton, Samuel Moore, Lewis Allen, Berry Williams, Josiah Sullivan, Charles Monroe, James Murray, Young Lamar, John Wright, and J. Cahoon.

There were at least forty families within a five-mile radius of the Lincoln home in 1820, which would mean, on the average, three families to each section of land. By 1822 the number of families would probably have reached fifty. Most of them had come from Kentucky, and some of them including the Carters and Gordons had been neighbors of the Lincolns in Hardin County. These families formed a nucleus of friends through which the Lincolns broadened their acquaintance.

While Abraham probably met many neighbor children on his expeditions to mill, when he went with his father on his carpentry jobs, and when the Lincoln family "went visiting" or had callers, he made most of his friends during the brief school terms that he attended. His second school in Indiana was kept by James Swaney, ward of Azel W. Dorsey, who became Abraham's third teacher. The Dorsey and Swaney families had lived near the Mill Creek farm Thomas Lincoln had acquired in Hardin County, Kentucky, in 1803. "Azel Dorsey cleared land and planted corn in 1776," and "Swaney built a cabin on Bullitt's Lick." [9] Undoubtedly the Swaneys and Dorseys knew each other there. Anyway the son of this pioneer Dorsey, also Azel, was appointed guardian of the orphaned son and daughter of Michael Swaney by the Warrick County, Indiana, court on October 26, 1817, at the town of Darlington, first county seat of Warrick County. The court document read: [10]

"Azel W. Dorsey appeared in court with James Swaney and Charlott Swaney, orphan children of Michael Swaney, Dec. and being appointed guardian of said children and on application to the court that the said James of the age of 17 and ½ years [be] bound to him for and during the term of four years and six months upon the following conditions: The said boy is to have at the expiration of the said service a horse, saddle and

• HOME SITES

1. Thomas Lincoln
2. Dennis Hanks
3. Thomas Barrett
4. Thomas Turnham
5. William Whitman
6. Thomas Carter
7. John Carter
8. Luther Greathouse
9. David Casebier
10. John Jones
11. William Wood
12. William Whittinghill
13. James Gentry
14. John Romine
15. Samuel Howell
16. Noah Gordon
17. Joseph Wright
18. William Wright
19. Moses Randall
20. Peter Brooner
21. Amos Richardson
22. David Edwards
23. Reuben Grigsby
24. Aaron Grigsby
25. Josiah Crawford
26. William Barker
27. Henry Gunterman
28. Benoni Hardin

x POINTS OF INTEREST

AB. Lincoln's original one-quarter section.
B. One half of above quarter section relinquished
C. Twenty-acre tract purchased from David Casebier
AC. One hundred-acre tract owned by Lincoln
D. Grave of Nancy Hanks Lincoln
E. Swimming Hole
F. Deer Licks
G. James Gentry's Store near his home
H. Gentry-Romine Store at the crossroads.
I. Little Pigeon Church, cemetery where Sarah Lincoln Grigsby lies buried, and site of early schoolhouses
J. Noah Gordon's horse mill.
K. Site of Swaney's school short distance to west of this point.

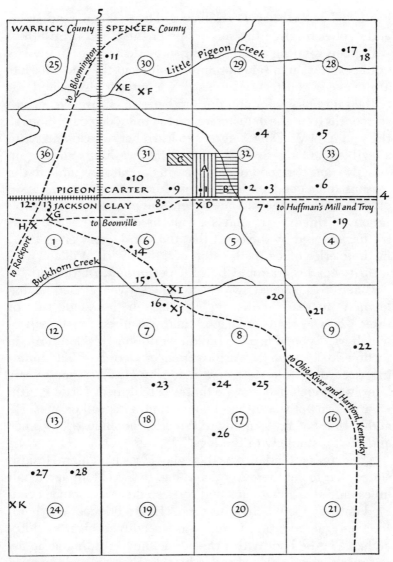

WARRICK County SPENCER County
to Bloomington
Little Pigeon Creek

(25) •11 (30) (29) (28) •17 •18

×E ×F

•4 •5

(36) (31) ░G░ ▊A▊ (32) (33)

•10 •9 •1 8 •2 •3 •6

PIGEON CARTER

12• /13 JACKSON CLAY 8• ×D 7• to Huffman's Mill and Troy

H•× ×G to Boonville •19

to Rockport (1) (6) (5) (4)

•14

Buckhorn Creek 15•

16• ×I •20

×J •21

(12) (7) (8) (9)

•22

to Ohio River and Hartford Kentucky

•23 •24 •25

(13) (18) (17) (16)

•26

•27 •28

×K (24) (19) (20) (21)

Little Pigeon Community

(1) Section Numbers
------ Roads
———— Section Lines
╫╫╫╫╫ County Boundary
———— Township Lines

SCALE: 1 INCH = 1 MILE

bridle to be worth seventy dollars and learn him to read, write and cypher through the single rule of three and furnish him with good wearing apparel and a good decent suit of clothes at the expiration of said apprenticeship; and the said Charlott at the age of fourteen years and six months is also bound out to the said Dorsey for and during the term of three years and six months from the date hereon on the following conditions as the said Azel W. Dorsey agrees to learn her to read and write a legible hand and find her meat, drink, washing and lodging and also find her good decent wearing apparel suitable to the seasons and a good feather bed and furniture at the expiration of her said servitude and one decent suit of clothes at the expiration of three years and six months aforesaid [11] and it is further ordered by the court that the said Dorsey enter bond in the clerk's office in the sum of $1000 with William Ross security for his true and faithful performance aforesaid."

When this James Swaney reached twenty-one, having learned "to read, write, cypher through the single rule of three," he was ready to teach,[12] and was hired for the school which was opened in a log building on John Hoskins' farm, in section 23, Jackson Township, Spencer County.[13] The building, according to a statement made by Hoskins many years later, was much like the one that was built near Little Pigeon Church "except that it had two chimneys instead of one." He added that he had torn down "the old schoolhouse long since and built a stable with the logs." [14]

Abraham's attendance at this school was irregular. Hoskins stated that to get there Abraham "had to travel four and a half miles; and this going back and forth so great a distance occupied entirely too much of his time. His attendance was therefore only at odd times, and was speedily broken off altogether." [15] Abe had by this time done much reading at home, and was probably well ahead of his schoolmates, perhaps even of his master. There was probably little that Swaney could have taught him. As he entered his teens reading was becom-

102

ing more important than ever before to him. He was more reflective and meditative, and giving more attention to thinking things through for himself. He had read enough so that he was beginning to develop a critical sense, an attitude of discrimination.

About the time that he was attending Swaney's school he came into possession of Murray's *English Reader,* which he considered to be the finest of all the school texts he had studied.[16] It was an excellent supplement to what he was learning at school, especially in the field of English literature.

The book is just what its title implies, a series of selections of prose and poetry suitable for reading aloud.[17] Its purpose was threefold: "To improve youth in the art of reading; to meliorate their language and sentiments; and to inculcate some of the important principles of piety and virtue." The author continues, "The language of the pieces chosen for this collection, has been carefully regarded. Purity, propriety, perspicuity, and in many instances, elegance in diction, distinguish them. They are extracted from the works of the most correct and elegant writers."[18]

One of the interesting features of the book is the introduction of twenty pages which is concerned with the "principles of Good Reading"; "Proper Loudness of Voice"; "Distinctness"; "Due Degree of Slowness"; "Propriety of Pronunciation"; "Emphasis"; "Tones"; "Pauses"; and "Manner of Reading Verse." The selections of prose and verse that follow, covering 269 pages, are arranged with these principles in mind, and give opportunity for exercising a great variety of emotions and their correspondent tones and variations of voice. The prose selections comprising Part I are arranged under these headings: "Select Sentences and Paragraphs," "Narrative Pieces," "Didactic Pieces," "Argumentative Pieces," "Descriptive Pieces," "Pathetic Pieces," "Dialogues," "Public Speeches," and "Promiscuous Pieces." The poetry selections comprising Part II are grouped under "Select Sentences and

Paragraphs," "Narrative Pieces," "Didactic Pieces," "Descriptive Pieces," "Pathetic Pieces," and "Promiscuous Pieces."

The following, taken from the "Select Sentences and Paragraphs" of Part I, demonstrate the author's moral intent.[19]

"No station is so high, no power so great, no character so unblemished, as to exempt men from the attacks of rashness, malice, or envy."

"When we observe any tendency to treat religion or morals with disrespect and levity, let us hold it to be a sure indication of a perverted understanding or a depraved heart."

"The happiness of every man depends more upon the state of his own mind, than upon any one external circumstance; nay, more than upon all external things put together."

"Amusement often becomes the business, instead of the relaxation, of young persons; it is then highly pernicious."

"Nothing is so inconsistent with self-possession as violent anger. It overpowers reason; confounds our ideas; distorts the appearance, and blackens the colour of every object."

"In judging others, let us always think the best, and employ the spirit of charity and candour. But in judging of ourselves, we ought to be exact and severe."

Also included here is Addison's essay, "The Planetary and Terrestrial Worlds Comparatively Considered," which includes the following: "The sun, which seems to perform its daily stages through the sky, is in this respect fixed and immovable: it is the great axle of heaven, about which the globe we inhabit, and other more spacious orbs wheel their stated courses."[20]

A preachment by Blair on "The Proper State of Our Temper with Respect to One Another," concludes with this observation, "The forms of the world disguise men when abroad. But within his own family, every man is known to be what he truly is."[21]

Among the "Pathetic Pieces" is one by Dr. Young entitled "Altamont," in which an "account of an affecting, mournful

exit, is related. . . ." The following are some of the exclama-
tions of a young man on the eve of his death: "I have plucked
down ruin. . . . That is the rock on which I split: I denied his
[the Redeemer's] name! Remorse for the past, throws my
thoughts on the future . . . my soul, as my body, lies in ruins;
in scattered fragments of broken thoughts. . . . My principles have poisoned my friend; my extravagance has beggared
my boy, my unkindness has murdered my wife!—And is there
another hell?" [22]

A new fund of information was opened to Abraham in the
"Descriptive Pieces" which included "The Cataract of
Niagara," "The Grotto of Antiparos," "Earthquake at Catenea."
"The Public Speeches" which Abe no doubt declaimed before
his family or any other available audience, included "Cicero
Against Verres," "Adherbal to the Roman Senate," "The
Apostle Paul's Noble Defence before Festus and Agrippa,"
"Lord Mansfield's Speech in the House of Peers, 1770."

In Part II, among the "Pieces in Poetry" Abe found a great
variety. Some of the lines which he read follow:
From Cowper's "Cruelty to Brutes Censured," [23]

> I would not enter on my list of friends,
> (Though grac'd with polish'd manners and fine sense,
> Yet wanting sensibility,) the man
> Who needlessly sets foot upon a worm.

From Whitehead's "The Youth and the Philosopher," the
following lamentation, attributed to Plato on viewing the
triumphs of a young charioteer: [24]

> With indigation I survey
> Such skill and judgment thrown away:
> The time profusely squander'd there
> If well employ'd, at less expense,
> Had taught thee honor, virtue, sense;
> And rais'd thee from a coachman's fate
> To govern men, and guide the state.

And also from Cowper, this time "Indignant Sentiments on National Prejudices and Hatred, and on Slavery." [25]

> I would not have a slave to till my ground,
>   To carry me, to fan me while I sleep,
> To tremble when I wake, for all the wealth
> That sinews bought and sold have ever earn'd
> No: dear as freedom is, and in my heart's
>   Just estimation, priz'd above all price;
> I had much rather be myself the slave,
>   And wear the bonds, than fasten them on him.

Abraham had now "been through" Dilworth's and Webster's Spellers, Scott's *Lessons in Elocution* and Murray's *English Reader*. In them he had found lessons and exercises in such basic subjects as reading, spelling, grammar, and mathematics, and some instruction in the natural and physical sciences, dialectics, and rhetoric. One outstanding feature of these and schoolbooks generally of that day was the religious and moral treatment of all subject matter. This has been mentioned before, but perhaps it cannot be stressed too much. The Preface to Murray's *Reader* states: "That this collection may also serve the purpose of promoting piety and virtue, the compiler has introduced many extracts which place religion in the most amiable light and which recommend a great variety of moral duties . . . The compiler has been careful to avoid every expression and sentiment, that might gratify a corrupt mind, or, in the least degree, offend the eye of innocence. This he conceives to be peculiarly incumbent on every person who writes for the benefit of youth."

Furthermore, all the schoolbooks mentioned above included pages of what might be called variously aphorisms, axioms, epigrams, maxims, mottoes, precepts, or proverbs. Read over and over, these sentences, tersely expounding some fundamental truth or wise philosophy, not only constituted lessons in good living and right thinking, but served as examples of clear, concise writing. Many of them were selected from

106

works of the world's great literary artists, philosophers, historians, and statesmen. Their influence and effect on Abraham cannot be measured, but their content and style should be considered as a fundamental of his education.

Some of these sentences follow:

"Revenge dwells in little minds."

"Sincerity and truth form the basis of every virtue."

"The young are slaves to novelty, the old to custom."

"Examine well the counsel that favours your desires."

"Never adventure too near an approach to what is evil."

"Gentleness corrects whatever is offensive in our manners."

"Nothing blunts the edge of ridicule so effectually as good humor."

"Narrow minds think nothing right that is above their own capacity."

"If we have sense, modesty best sets it off; if not, best hides the want."

"Let your conduct be the result of deliberation, never of impatience."

"To say little and perform much, is the characteristic of a great mind."

"The gratification of desire is sometimes the worst thing that can befall us."

"Genuine virtue has a language that speaks to every heart throughout the world."

"Our good or bad fortune depends greatly on the choice we make of our friends."

"Diligence, industry, and proper improvement of time, are material duties of the young."

"What avails the show of external liberty, to one who has lost the government of himself."

"Self-partiality hides from us those very faults in ourselves which we see and blame in others."

"Man's chief good is an upright mind, which no earthly power can bestow, nor take from him."

"To have your enemy in your power and yet to do him good is the greatest heroism."

"The desire of improvement discovers a liberal mind and is connected with many virtues."

"Guard your weak side from being known. If it be attacked, the best way is to join in the attack."

"Every man has some darling passion which generally affords the first introduction to vice."

"The first ingredient in conversation is truth; the next, good sense; the third, good humor; the last, wit."

"Intemperance engenders disease, sloth produces poverty, pride creates disappointments, dishonesty exposes shame."

"To measure all reasons by our own is a plain act of injustice; it is an encroachment on the common rights of mankind."

"No man is so foolish that he may not give good counsel at a time; no man so wise but he may err, if he takes no counsel but his own."

"When even in the heat of dispute, I yield to my antagonist, my victory over myself is more illustrious than over him, had he yielded to me."

"To deal with a man, you must know his temper, by which you can lead him; or his ends, by which you can persuade him; or his friends, by whom you can govern him."

"When upon rational and sober inquiry, we have established our principles, let us not suffer them to be shaken by the scoffs of the licentious, or the cavils of the sceptical."

"It is idle as well as absurd, to impose our opinions upon others. The same ground of conviction operates differently on the same man in different circumstances, and on different men in the same circumstances."

"Solicitude in hiding failings make them appear the greater. It is a safer and easier course, frankly to acknowledge them. A man owns that he is ignorant; we admire his modesty. He says he is old; we scarce think him so. He declares himself poor; we do not believe it." [26]

108

In decided contrast to Murray's *Reader* was another book which Abraham read about this time, *An Authentic Narrative of the Loss of the American Brig Commerce . . . with an Account of the Sufferings of Her Surviving Officers and Crew . . .* , by James Riley.[27] While it is not known just when he obtained a copy of this, it is known that it was some time after he read Weems's *Washington*.[28] The narrative relates the story of Captain Riley's shipwreck off the coast of northwest Africa, the enslavement of himself and his crew by the Moroccan Arabs, their almost unbelievable suffering on the Sahara desert, and finally the purchase of their freedom with the aid of the British vice-consul at Mogadore. According to Captain Riley's prefatory statement he wrote out his narrative and then Anthony Bleeker, at his request, "revised the whole— and suggested some very important explanations . . . his talents, judgment, and erudition, have contributed in a considerable degree, to smooth down the asperities of my unlearned style." [29]

Riley was born in Connecticut and attended a school there not unlike the ones Abraham attended in Spencer County. It was a subscription school, the patrons hiring "a teacher to instruct their children in reading and writing, and some of them are taught the fundamental rules of arithmetic. They hire a male teacher for four months in the year, say from October to March. . . ." [30] When Riley was fifteen, he wrote that he "was tall, stout, and athletic for my age; and having become tired of hard work on the land I concluded that the best way to get rid of it was to go to sea and visit foreign countries." With the consent of his parents he started on his adventures. "Having no friends to push me forward, no dependence but on my own good conduct and exertions, and being ambitious to gain some distinction in the profession I had chosen, I continued to acquire some knowledge in the art of navigation. . . ." [31]

Riley relates how he rose to become captain of his ship. Then comes the account of the shipwreck, the enslavement of the captain and crew, their grim experiences on the "frightful African Desart," and finally how they regained their freedom. The narrative includes a description of the desert, its inhabitants and their manners, customs, and dress, and other informative material that Riley had acquired. On one occasion he witnessed the devastation of the crops of a fertile valley by a veritable cloud of locusts. "We were about two hours in passing this host of destroyers, which when on the wing made a sound, as finely described in Holy Writ, 'like the rushing of horses into battle.'" The exhibition of the deadly serpents and serpent eaters at Rhabat recalled to his mind "the story of the fiery serpent that bit the children of Israel in the deserts of Arabia, near Mount Hor, as recorded in the 21st chapter of the Book of Numbers." [32] Finally Captain Riley made his way back to America where "if it is God's will," he wished ever to remain. This personal account of true adventure caught the attention of the American reading public and the book had a wide sale. Undoubtedly there were several copies available to Abe in southern Indiana. The Arab and English vocabulary and map of northwestern Africa which were part of the volume added to its interest.

In closing his narrative Riley reflects on his sufferings: [33] "I have been taught in the school of adversity to be contented with my lot . . . and shall endeavour to cultivate the virtues of charity and universal benevolence . . . when black despair had seized on my departing soul, amid the agonies of the most cruel of all deaths, I cried to the Omnipotent for mercy, and the outstretched hand of Providence snatched me from the jaws of destruction."

Then came important passages which Abraham must have pondered: "Unerring wisdom and goodness has since restored me to the comforts of civilized life, to the bosom of my family, and to the blessings of my native land, whose political and moral institutions are in themselves the very best of any that prevail in the civilized portions of the globe, and ensure to her

110

citizens the greatest share of personal liberty, protection, and happiness; and yet," he continued, "strange as it must appear to the philanthropist, my proud-spirited and free countrymen still hold a million and a half nearly, of the human species, in the most cruel bonds of slavery. . . . Adversity has taught me some noble lessons: I have now learned to look with compassion on my enslaved and oppressed fellow-creatures; I will exert all my remaining faculties in endeavours to redeem the enslaved, and to shiver in pieces the rod of oppression; and I trust I shall be aided in that holy work by every good and every pious, free, and high-minded citizen in the community, and by the friends of mankind throughout the civilized world . . . it is my earnest desire that such a plan should be devised, founded on the firm basis and the eternal principles of justice and humanity, and developed and enforced by the general government, as will gradually . . . wither and extirpate the accursed tree of slavery that has been suffered to take such deep root in our otherwise highly-favoured soil. . . ."

This book must have impressed Abraham with the reality that enslavement was not confined necessarily to those with dark skins, and that people of his own color might be enslaved by those powerful enough and disposed to carry out that purpose.

CHAPTER IX

14

Reverence

1823

THE LINCOLN FAMILY discovered upon their arrival at their Indiana home that a church had been established in the community the preceding June. The first minute book of the organization called "The Church of Christ Constituted by the Regular Baptists at Pigeon Creek," which records the business sessions of the church, fortunately has been preserved. On the second page there appears this notation: "Saterday June the 8 1816 the Baptist Church of Jesus Christ known by the name of Pigeon church Warrick County Indeanne Teritory was Constituted By Brother John Weldon & Thos. Downs a presbaty caled for that purpose whos names numbers & articles of faith and Government are as follows. . . ."[1]

The minutes reveal the progress of the meeting which followed: "First the church chose B[ro.] Samuel Bristow, moderrater and Thomas Downs clak for the meeting. 2 invited Brethren of sister churches to a seat with us. Names of Brethren that come in the bounds of this constitution. First the articles of faith read & received by the committy. Letters handed in by brethren and sisters, Mathew Rogers, 1; John Harrison, 2; Samuel Bristow; 3. John Tenneson, 4; Enuch Garison, 5; Wm. Lamare, 6; Nelley Rogers, 7; Diner Allen, 8; Jemimy Harrison, 9; Lavina Bristow, 10; Sarah Powel, 11; Patcy Garrison, 12; Lucy Lamare, 13."

112

The articles of faith and government which have already been mentioned as approved are then set down and are presented here just as they appear in the minute book.

1. we believe in one god the Father the word & the holley gost who haith created all things that are created by the word of his power for his pleasure.
2. we believe the old & new testaments are the words of god thare are everry thing contained thare in nessarssary for mans Salvation & rule of faith and pracktice.
3. we belive in the fall of man in his public head & that he is incapable of recoverry unless restorred by Christ.
4. we believe in Election by grace given in Christ Jesus Before the world began & that God Cawls regenerates & Sanctifies all who are made meat for Glory by his special grace.
5. we believe the righteous will persevere throw grace to glory & none of them finely fawl away.
6. we belive in a general resurrection of the Just and unjust and the Joys of the righteous and the punishment of the wicked Eturnal.
7. we belive that Good works are the fruits of Grace and follow after Justification.
8. we belive that babtism and the lord's supper are ordenances of Jesus Christ and that true belivers are the onely proper subjects and the onely proper mode of babtism is immertion.
9. we belive the washing of feet is a command to be complide with when opportunity serves.
10. we belive it is our duty severally to seport the lord's table and that we orght to administer the lords supper at lest twise a year.
11. we belive that no minister ought to preach the gospel that is not calld and sent of god and they are to be proven by hiering them & we allow of none to preach Amongst us but such as are well recomended And that we aurght to Contribute to him who Faithfully Labers Amongst us in word and Docttrin According to our severrel abilities of our temporal [MS torn]. . . .

John Weldon and Thomas Downs, who appear to have been largely responsible for establishing the church, had been ministers at Yelvington, in Daviess County, Kentucky, just across the Ohio River from Spencer County. William Downs, a brother of Thomas, preached for awhile at the Little Mount

Church with which the Lincolns were affiliated in Kentucky.[2]
Samuel Bristow was leading the newly organized Little
Pigeon Church group when the Lincolns arrived. He lived
about five miles from them, in Jackson Township, where he
entered land in 1818.[3]

The influx of Baptists from Kentucky caused the number of
churches in Spencer County and the surrounding country to
increase rapidly. On October 19, 1821, an association of
Baptist churches was organized, at the home of the Rev.
Young Lamar. A meeting of messengers was called to convene
at the Little Pigeon meetinghouse on the first day of the
following September. Representatives were present from
churches at Little Pigeon, Polk Patch, Cyprus, Bethel,
Hurricane Fork, Bear Creek, Gilead, Olive Union, and Shilo.
The preacher for this occasion was Alexander Devin of the
Wabash Association.[4] This was the first large assembly of
sister churches held in the new Little Pigeon meetinghouse,
and, undoubtedly, the attendance was increased by the desire
to see the new building. The association was called the Little
Pigeon Association of United Baptists. Most of the churches
were in the area drained by Little Pigeon Creek.

It may seem strange that Thomas and Nancy Lincoln, who
had been faithful members of a Baptist church in Kentucky,
did not affiliate with the Little Pigeon organization upon
reaching Indiana. They may have hesitated because it was
connected with the Regular Baptist branch, and had adopted
a written statement of "faith and government." The Kentucky
congregation, to which the Lincolns belonged, was of the
Separate Baptist branch. The latter refused to have any written creed and used the Bible alone as its only rule of faith and
practice. Whether or not Thomas refused to subscribe to the
articles of faith and government of the Little Pigeon Church
is not known. It is possible that he was not invited to unite
with the Regular Baptists because of his affiliation with the
Separates.[5]

A movement in Kentucky to bring together the two

branches of the church spread to Indiana, and when the Little Pigeon Association was formed, it was called "United Baptist Association." Apparently this appeal for unity opened the way for Thomas Lincoln to join the Little Pigeon Church. It was nearly seven years after he arrived in Indiana that he took this step, and became a member of the congregation whose building he had helped construct in 1821. On June 7, 1823, Thomas united with the church "by letter" from the Little Mount Separate Baptist Church in Kentucky. While this indicates that he was received into the body in good standing, it does not imply that by joining this church he repudiated the simple faith of the Separate Baptists. On the same day that Thomas Lincoln united with the church "by letter," his wife Sally Lincoln joined "by experience." Apparently she had never been affiliated with a church before this time.[6]

Many people today are not aware of the strict discipline maintained by the churches on the frontier. As long as a member's name remained on the active list of a church, he was expected to live according to the strict pattern of behavior demanded of him as a member of that church. Those who knew Thomas Lincoln personally have testified to his good character and moral status. "Abe got his honesty, and his clean notions of living and kind heart from his father," is typical of the statements that were made about him.[7]

It has already been mentioned that Nancy Hanks Lincoln followed the practice of reading daily from the Bible to the family. This regular religious custom was supplemented by Thomas' habit of asking grace at table. Fortunately the short supplication he invariably made has been preserved: "Fit and prepare us for humble service for Christ's sake, Amen."[8] On one occasion, when the meal consisted mostly of potatoes, Abe's strong sense of humor got the best of him, and after the blessing had been asked, he commented that these were "mighty poor blessings."[9]

There was a copy of Starke Dupuy's hymnbook, *Hymns and*

Spiritual Songs, in the Lincoln home. While Abe had no voice for singing, he was familiar with the words of many of the numbers. David Turnham, when questioned many years later, stated that he had forgotten all the songs which were sung in the community except the "pious ones." He recalled that "they were from Dr. Watts and Dupuy's hymns." The first lines of some he mentioned were "Am I a soldier of the cross. . . . How tedious and tasteless the hour. . . . There is a fountain filled with blood. . . ." [10] Starke Dupuy was of French Huguenot descent, and the son of a Baptist preacher of Woodford County, Kentucky. Despite his ill health, he compiled a hymnbook "that attained great popularity in the Southern States and especially in Kentucky and Tennessee." Of course, wherever hymns were sung, the books of Watts were familiar. The Lincolns may have been partial to Dupuy's hymns since he was a Kentucky Baptist. [11]

The religious influences in the early life of Abraham Lincoln should not be overemphasized, but they deserve careful attention, since they have so often been ignored or misrepresented. The sermons preached by the pioneer ministers were bound to be important to him. Beside their religious message, they constituted almost the only public speaking that he heard. The importance of religion to the Little Pigeon community has been well expressed as follows: [12]

"Among the backwoodsmen of Indiana, at that period sectarianism did not run as high as it probably does in the same section now [1860]. The people were glad of an opportunity to hear a sermon. . . . Thus it was at least with the father and mother of young Lincoln, who never failed to attend, within reasonable distance. They gladly received the word, caring less for the doctrinal tenets of the preacher than for the earnestness and zeal with which he enforced practical godliness. . . .

"Many of these early pioneer preachers were gifted with a rare eloquence. Inspired always with the grandeur of their

116

theme, communing daily with nature while on their long and solitary journeys from settlement to settlement, they seemed to be favored, far beyond human wont, with a very near approach to the source of all inspiration; and coming with this preparation before an audience of simple-minded settlers, preacher and people freed from conventional restraint, these men almost always moved the hearts and wrought upon the imagination of their hearers as only those gifted with the truest eloquence can."

This author then turns from the parents to Abraham himself: "Listening occasionally to the early backwoods preachers, was another means which, more than schools, and, perhaps quite as much as books, aided in developing and forming the character of young Lincoln." After dwelling at some length on the type of preaching Abraham heard, he concludes: ". . . as to the great value of the preaching here spoken of . . . there can be but one opinion. That it exerted a marked influence on the character of young Lincoln, that it thoroughly awakened the religious elements in him . . . are facts which the writer desires to place upon record. . . ."[13]

Abraham's familiarity with the Bible was not entirely due to his reading of the sacred volume. Striking Biblical texts used by the preachers whom he heard influenced his thinking as did the axioms in his schoolbooks.[14] Two of the most eloquent preachers in Kentucky, William Downs and David Elkin, served the antislavery church which Abraham's parents joined. Both preachers were strong advocates of emancipation, and even before Abraham could read or write, he learned of the wrongs of slavery by listening to these men of God.[15] One historian describes Elkin as "a man of extraordinary natural intellect, but was uncultivated, being barely able to read." One who heard him often states: "Parson Elkin was a good—true—man and the best preacher & finest orator I ever heard. I have heard his words distinctly & clearly one fourth of a mile."[16]

117

A student of Kentucky Baptist history, writing about William Downs, said: "He received a fair English education for that time. . . . His exceeding familiarity with the Sacred Scriptures, his ready wit, keen sarcasm, and brilliant oratory attracted and won the admiration of the most intelligent and refined people within the limits of his acquaintance. Hon. Benjamin Helm, one of the leading lawyers and statesmen of Kentucky, greatly admired his oratory, and embraced every opportunity to hear him." [17]

Thomas Downs who helped to establish the Little Pigeon Church was a brother of William Downs. "He was uneducated in the scholastic sense of the term; but he was a close prayerful reader of the Bible, and few men of his time were better acquainted with the sacred oracles. . . . he had an easy flow of common English words, his heart was thoroughly educated and deeply imbued with the grace of God, and he was an indefatigable laborer in the gospel of Christ." [18]

At least three different Indiana ministers were in the Spencer County home of the Lincolns to perform marriage ceremonies: Samuel Bristow, Charles Harper, and Young Lamar. The last was the local minister who presided at the burial of Abraham's mother. The first regular preacher in the Little Pigeon Church was Samuel Bristow. He and his wife Lavina were among the thirteen charter members of the church. He served as a justice of the peace and could therefore perform marriages either as a clergyman or a justice. It is not likely that he had any ministerial training but took up preaching as an elder in the church. In the spring of 1821 he performed several marriage ceremonies in Spencer County. Little is known of Charles Harper. In 1821 he signed a certificate as "minister of the gospel," and during the last four years of the Lincolns' residence in the county he became a powerful leader in the Little Pigeon Association. Often he was the messenger selected by the church to attend association meetings. [19]

118

The best-known preacher who was associated with the Little Pigeon Church was Young Lamar. His name appears on the minute book of the church in 1819, and it was at his home in October, 1821, that the Association of the Baptist Church was formed. During the entire period of the Lincolns' residence in Indiana he was living a few miles south of them on land he had entered on February 17, 1817. According to the census records, he was at least forty-five years old in 1820 and he had a family of five children. He was the outstanding minister in that section for many years, and was most often chosen to preach the sermon at meetings of the Association.

Many of the early ministers of Indiana were interested in politics. Two of the Baptist ministers whom Abraham must have heard frequently, Alexander Devin and Charles Polke, were members of the Constitutional Convention of 1816. On one occasion when the Rev. Mr. Devin was delivering a sermon during a very warm season, he removed his coat, waistcoat, and cravat, unbuttoned his shirt collar, and preached with great vigor for two hours.[20] There was also the Kentucky minister who perspired quite freely and remarked as he wiped his brow, "The trees of the Lord are full of sap." The Rev. Mr. Polke settled in Perry County in 1807. He was responsible for organizing several churches and he served congregations near Rome and Tobin's Bottom for many years.[21] He was a regular attendant at meetings of the Little Pigeon Association.

Two preachers whom Thomas Lincoln must have known in Kentucky came to Indiana, Jeremiah Cash and Matthew Rogers. The former was a son of Warren Cash, a Revolutionary soldier, and Susannah Cash. Warren and Susannah were "the first fruits to God in the wilderness of Kentucky," having been converted on Clear Creek in Woodford County early in 1785. Jeremiah Cash was a regular attendant at the meetings of the Little Pigeon Association and on one occasion became greatly offended and withdrew from the session because of theological differences. He was an Antimissionary Baptist, and ministered to a church in Gibson County.[22]

Matthew Rogers was born in Ireland and migrated to Kentucky in 1780 where he erected a fort on Beech Fork, the same stream on which Thomas Lincoln lived as a youth. He was undoubtedly well acquainted with the Lincoln family. On December 23, 1797, a certificate was issued in Nelson County which stated that Matthew Rogers had been "ordained agreeably to the order of the Church of Christ of the Separate Order and was qualified to perform marriage services." In the 1820 census of Indiana he is listed as over forty-five years of age. He had three sons who were preachers. He was still performing marriages in Spencer County in 1829.[23]

Three other Little Pigeon ministers who may have influenced Abraham were John Richardson, Adam Shoemaker, and Isaac Veatch. On November 13, 1819, John Richardson was appointed as one of a committee of ten to choose a site for the church building, and in March, 1821, according to the church minutes, he was still serving on this committee. By the 1820 census, his family consisted of a wife and six children. He was selected as an alternate to preach the sermon at the Association meeting in July, 1822. He died of the flux in August of that same year.[24]

Isaac Veatch was born in Tennessee, moved to Indiana from Meade County, Kentucky, about 1826, and settled in Luce Township. He had been a preacher at Otter Creek Church in Kentucky, but followers of Alexander Campbell took over the church shortly after Veatch came to Indiana. "He was a preacher of fair ability." [25] Adam Shoemaker was solemnizing marriages in Perry County as early as October 17, 1816, but very little has been recorded about him except that he was an ardent believer in emancipation.[26] He is said to have been the third minister at the Little Pigeon Church and was officiating at weddings in Spencer County as late as 1825.

Some other ministers whose names appear in the Spencer County records as having performed marriages and who preached at Little Pigeon Church before 1830 were Uriah Cummings, Henry Hart, Samuel Anderson, John Seaton, Thomas Summers, and Stanley Walker. The last-named was well acquainted with the Lincolns. Apparently there were preachers who visited Little Pigeon, however, who were not very welcome, as the church passed a resolution on July 12, 1823, that "this church hear after invite no strange furener to preach in the public meting house without they think he come well recommended as a preacher of the Gospel." [27]

When the Johnston children came to the Lincoln home, they provided an added incentive for Abraham's displays of oratory. His stepmother said, "He would hear a sermon [by the] preacher, come home take the children out, get on a stump or log, and almost repeat it word for word." [28] According to another member of the household, "He would come from church put a box in the middle of the cabin floor and repeat the 'sermit' from text to doxology." [29] He would not only recall the sermons word for word, but also would give some emphasis to the preacher's eccentricities both of mannerism and voice.

After the Little Pigeon Church was built Abraham was given a job which required his attendance whenever the church was open. On June 12, 1823, Thomas Lincoln became one of the trustees of the church, along with Reuben Grigsby and William Barker. This put Thomas in a position to recommend someone to take care of the meetinghouse, keep it clean and provide firewood and candles. Abraham who was fourteen years old at that time was employed as sexton. The church had a loft approached through a trap door by a ladder located in a corner of the building. Many years after the church was abandoned there was discovered in this loft "in a crevice between two of the upper logs an old faded memorandum book" which contained, among other entries, this:

"Dr. To 1 broom
   " To ½ doz tallow candles."

and signed "ABE LINCOLN, Sexton." [30]

How long Abraham served as sexton we do not know. His father continued as trustee for several years.

Fifty miles away from Abraham's immediate environment there was a religious colony that must have exerted an indirect influence, at least, on the pioneer population of the area. The most-used trail from their settlement to the state capital at Corydon passed through the Little Pigeon community. The Lincoln family must have known of their peculiar faith, and possibly met some of them as they traveled about the country selling the goods they manufactured.

About the year 1785 in Württemberg, Germany, a group called Harmonists separated from the Lutheran Church. The principal emphasis in their thinking was directed to the teaching of the Acts of the Apostles which stated that the adherents to the new Christian movement had "all things in common." In the year 1804, under the leadership of George Rapp, their pastor, one hundred and fifty families of this brotherhood migrated to America. They first settled in Butler County, Pennsylvania, where they inaugurated a system of co-operative industry under the motto "Each for all and all for each in sickness and health." By the fall of 1814 the colony moved to a new location on the Wabash fifty miles south of Vincennes which they called Harmonie.

While the religious ideals of the community were emphasized and rules enforced, the Rappites, as they were called, will be remembered primarily for their economic achievements. There can be no better illustration of their progress than their listing in the 1820 census of the machinery in their possession: 1 merchant mill by water with 3 pair stones, 1 merchant mill by steam with 2 pair stones, 2 saw mills by water, 1 oil and 1 hemp mill, 3 stocks for fulling, 4 wool carding machines, 2 cotton carding machines, 400 spindles for

122

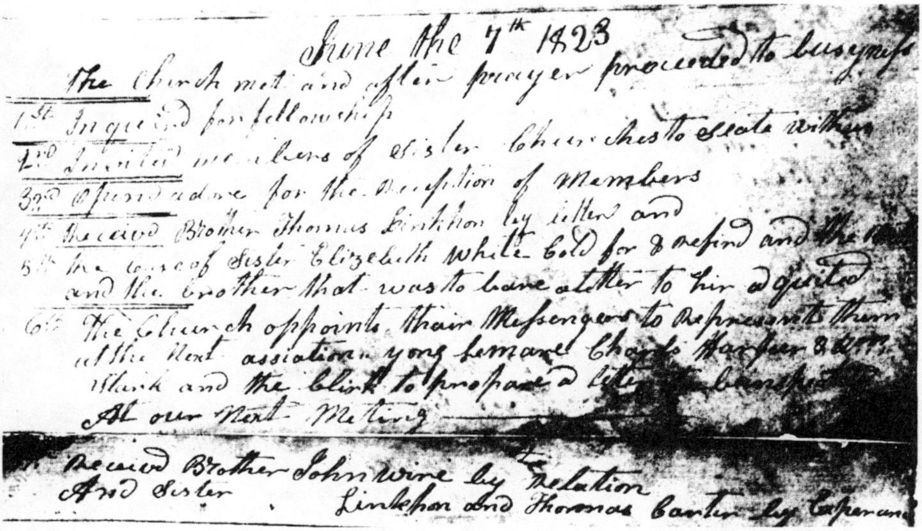
June the 7th 1823
The Church met and after prayer proceeded to busyness
1st Inquired for fellowship
2nd Invited members of Sister Churches to seate with us
3rd Opened a dore for the reception of members
4th Received Brother Thomas Linkhon by letter and
5th the case of Sister Elizabeth White [illegible] for & refered and the [illegible]
and the brother that was to bare a letter to hir appointed
6th The Church appoints thair Messengers to represent them
at the next assiation [illegible] Charls Harper & [illegible]
[illegible] and the clirk to prepare a letter [illegible]
At our next Meting
Received Brother John Wire by relation
And Sister Linkhon and Thomas Carter by Experance

Page from Minute Book of Little Pigeon Church recording the admission of Thomas Lincoln into the church

Little Pigeon Church

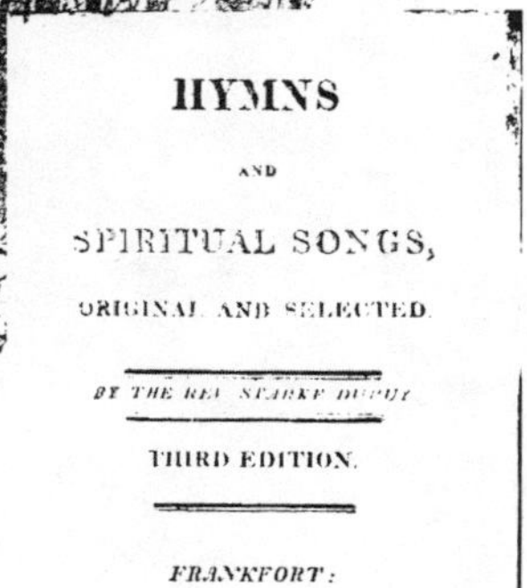
HYMNS
AND
SPIRITUAL SONGS,
ORIGINAL AND SELECTED.
BY THE REV. STARKE DUPUY
THIRD EDITION.
FRANKFORT:
PRINTED FOR BUTLER AND WOOD,
BY KENDALL AND RUSSELLS,
PRINTERS TO THE STATE
1818.

Dupuy's Hymnbook

spinning wool, 120 spindles for spinning cotton, 4 machines for shearing cloth, 11 weaving looms for wool and cotton, 4 weaving looms for stockings, 1 steam engine. The report on their manufacturing operations showed an annual consumption of 10,000 lbs. of wool, 5,000 lbs. of cotton, 5 tons of hemp, 1 ton of logwood, 1,000 beef hides, 1,000 deerskins. The number of persons employed included 75 men, 12 women, 30 boys and girls. Articles manufactured were: superfine, fine, and woolen cloths, cassimere, cassinette, flannel, linsey blankets, swansdown; plaid, chambray stripe and white cotton; blue and white cotton yarn; upper, sole, and saddle leather; various kinds of blacksmith work; tinware; spinning wheels; ropes and cordage; leather gloves, shoes and boots; saddles, bridles and harness; wool and fur hats; stockings, socks, mittens and caps; flax; rope hemp; pumgan (?) seed oil; earthenware; strong beer, peach brandy, rye and corn whiskey; wagons, carts, and plows; flour, beef, pork, butter, and wine.

But there is a discouraging note with respect to the sale of their merchandise. This was due partly, they observed, to the customers' "embarrassing circumstances of pecuniary matters." Also they complained about the difficulty in selling the products of the wool factory, "owing to the prejudice prevailing against domestic woolen goods." [31]

According to Frederick Rapp, son of George Rapp, the entire western country was financially embarrassed. "Little money was in circulation; almost none that passed at par." [32]

A flatboat sent out from Harmonie to New Orleans in 1823 carried a cargo consisting of "39 kegs of lard, 100 kegs of butter, 680 bushels of oats, 88 barrels of flour, 103 barrels of pork, 32 oxen, 16 hogs, and 40 barrels of whisky," valued at $1,369.[33] These phenomenal accomplishments effected during a period of six years within the confines of a great wilderness were a remarkable achievement. The value of the development at Harmonie by the fall of 1824 was placed by the owners at $1,000,000. This appraisal must have been inflated, because the following year it was reported that the whole Rapp establishment, including 28,000 acres of land, was sold to Robert Owen for $190,000.[34]

A visitor to one of their Sunday religious gatherings stated: "Mr. Frederick Rapp sat at an elevated desk and gave out the psalms and preached. His sermon was about friendship, working for one another, having common property, and the approaching millenium. . . . The service lasted about an hour & a half. [There were about 500 persons present.] . . . Between 12 & 1 oclock. The village band consisting of 8 or 10 wind instruments, assembled in front of Mr. Rapp's house, played one or two slow movements and then preceded us into the church. . . . They are in the habit of assembling together for the purpose of practising singing." [35]

There is no evidence that any members of the Lincoln family ever visited Harmonie but they must have heard of its steepled church and the brick church building that followed it. The presence of this communal society must have given a religious tone to all of southwestern Indiana. At Harmonie as well as in each isolated little settlement, the dominant interest of the people was the carrying out of God's will.

CHAPTER X

15

Attainment

1824

FOUR YEARS after Abraham attended Andrew Crawford's school and two years after his brief session with James Swaney, he was sent to a new school conducted by Azel W. Dorsey, who had acted as Swaney's guardian. While Swaney had been young, obscure, and ill-prepared, Dorsey was well known in Spencer County and the best trained of Abraham's teachers.[1]

It has already been noted that the Dorsey family settled in Kentucky as early as 1776, and lived not far from the property which Thomas Lincoln acquired in Hardin County.[2] Azel W. Dorsey was born in 1784.[3] The Lincolns and Dorseys were not unknown to each other. Greenberry Dorsey, brother of Azel, served on a jury with Thomas Lincoln in Hardin County in 1803. The plaintiff in the trial was Christopher Bush, father of Sally Bush Lincoln.[4] Another interesting coincidence was that on the very day on which Thomas Lincoln married Nancy Hanks (June 12, 1806), Azel W. Dorsey was in Elizabethtown buying from the Bleakley and Montgomery store "super fine cloth" for a suit, gloves, stockings, a silk handkerchief, etc., all costing £ 10/4/4½.[5] It was in this store that Thomas Lincoln had purchased his wedding outfit. Dorsey's new clothes may have been acquired not for his wedding but for courting, for he married Eleanor Spriggs in Nelson County on January 4, 1807.[6]

In the year that Abraham was born, Azel and Greenberry Dorsey, along with a George Burkheart, were farming a piece of ground located on Clear Creek close to Thomas Lincoln's Mill Creek farm. The land belonged to Michael Reuch. The fate of their venture is best told in an answer to the suit which Reuch brought to recover damages: "They [Dorsey, Burkheart, and Dorsey] did cultivate the ground in a farmer-like-manner under the term(s) leased. . . . they did pay the plaintiff ⅓ part of the corn raised on the said farm, stacked the hay in three or six stacks and gave the plaintiff one third thereof. . . . on that day there was a great tremendous flood and freshet in Clear Creek, running through the leased premises, which swept and carried off from the said premises, all the rails and fencing thereon, by means of which irresistible act of nature or God the defendants were disabled from leaving the farm in the repair required by the covenant."[7]

The last records of Azel W. Dorsey in Kentucky are found in 1813, when he listed for taxes two horses and one hundred acres of land.[8] On February 8 of that year he was appointed commissioner of revenue tax for Hardin County, a position that kept him busy for several weeks at a fair remuneration.[9] Some time between 1813 and 1816 Dorsey moved to Indiana. On May 13, 1816, he served as clerk of the election which was held in the home of William Berry in Ohio Township, Warrick County, to choose delegates to the Constitutional Convention.[10] On October 20, 1817, as has been noted, he was appointed guardian for James and Charlott Swaney. On June 10, 1818, he served as crier at the sale of lots in the new town of Rockport, which brought about five thousand dollars.[11] Rockport was platted for the county seat of Spencer County which had been established by the preceding legislature, and until a courthouse was built Dorsey's house served as headquarters for the county officers.[12] He was the first treasurer of the county, and on January 13, 1818, was elected coroner.[13]

126

Dorsey turned merchant for awhile. On March 10, 1819, he entered into a partnership with M. B. Snyder in the operation of the firm of Dorsey & Snyder.[14] Apparently they were not very successful, for the lot on which their business was conducted, No. 32 in Rockport, was sold by Dorsey on October 22, 1822.[15] Meanwhile, he had moved to Dubois County where he is listed as a resident in the 1820 census. He was also residing there as late as March of 1821. He was soon back in Spencer County, however, as he disposed of property at Rockport on June 19, 1824.[16] This county seat town was his home during most of his residence in Indiana. He is said to have taught the first school there. The patrons of the Little Pigeon school must have felt themselves fortunate to secure this well-known citizen as a teacher for their children. Dorsey had a good cultural background, and although he may not have been a college-trained professor, he was capable of instructing the children of Spencer County, Indiana, during the first decade of the state's history. As far as is known he had no eccentricities for which he would be remembered. Reading, writing, and arithmetic were the three essentials which he emphasized. The schoolhouse in which Dorsey taught was near the Little Pigeon Church. Before it was built classes may have been held in the church. The school building conformed to the general rule for pioneer schools: "a rude pole cabin with huge fire-place, rude floor of puncheons and seats of the same, and a window made by leaving out a log on the side to admit light [through the opening], often covered with greased paper to keep out the wind. . . ."[17] Dorsey's school has been more particularly described: "He presided in a small house near Little Pigeon Creek meeting-house, a mile and a half from the Lincoln cabin. . . . It was built of unhewn logs, and had 'holes for windows,' in which 'greased paper' served for glass. The roof was just high enough for a man to stand erect. Here he taught reading, writing, and ciphering. They spelled in classes and 'trapped' up and down."[18]

Dorsey, in recalling Abraham as his student, said that he "was marked for the diligence and eagerness with which he pursued his studies, came to the log-cabin school-house arrayed in buck skin clothes, a raccoon-skin cap, and provided with an old arithmetic which had somewhere been found for him to begin his investigation into the 'higher branches.'" [19]

The outstanding contribution which the Indiana schools made to Abraham in his quest for an education was the excellent foundation he acquired in arithmetic. This is one branch of learning in which we can follow him through the stages of his advancement with some degree of success. In his earlier schooling he had probably learned simple arithmetic, and now in Dorsey he had a teacher who would be able to take him through what was known as "The Rule of Three" or proportion, or at least set him on the way to this goal. Abe's father encouraged him because he was "determined that some how or other Abraham should cipher through the book." [20] The text was probably Pike's *Arithmetick,* a copy of which was in the Lincoln family. [21]

Nicholas Pike was a native of New Hampshire. After graduating from Harvard with an M.A. degree, he engaged in teaching and engineering. In 1786 he completed his manuscript on mathematics, and it was published two years later. In the five hundred pages comprising the text the student was taken through plane geometry, trigonometry, solid geometry, and given an introduction to algebra. [22] The fifth edition of the book, published in 1804, was "abridged for the use of schools" and contained 352 pages. Abraham probably used the abridged edition, as it concluded with the rule of three and related subjects. [23]

On the back of the title page of the 1804 edition there appears an "Explanation of characters *used* in this *Treatise,*" with illustrations of how each may be correctly used: sign of equality; addition; subtraction; multiplication; division (by

128

two different signs), and also "fractionwise"; proportion, illustrated with the line called the "Vinculum"; the second power or "square"; and the third power or "cube."

The "Contents" of the volume gives some idea of the subject matter covered: numerations, simple and compound addition, subtraction; vulgar fractions; double rule of three; conjoined proportion; fellowship by decimals; square, cube, biquadrate and sursolid roots; geometric progression; interest; discount; barter; insurance; pensions; simple and double proportion; and the use of logarithms.

In a footnote one finds that familiar chant of the seasons:

Thirty days hath September, April, June, and November;
February twenty-eight alone, and all the rest have thirty-one.

This is followed by the statement: "When you can divide the year of our Lord by 4, without any remainder, it is then Bissextile, or Leap Year, in which February has 29 days."

On the end sheet of the copy of the book examined by the author[24] the following lines have been penned under the date of June 16, 1822, by an unknown student:

If wisdom's ways you'd wisely seek
Five things observe with care
To whom you speak, of whom you speak,
And how, and when, and where.

Possibly some of the children's games at school were suggested by the problems submitted in the arithmetic book. This one by Pike recalls a familiar procedure: "Suppose a number of stones were laid a yard distance from each other for the space of a mile, and the first a yard from the basket; what length of ground will that man have to travel over, who gathers them up singly, returning with them one by one to the basket?" While the space of a mile covered with stones would be prohibitive, the same process for a distance of ten or fifteen yards would make the problem an interesting one to demonstrate.[25]

Abe also studied the arithmetic compiled by Nathan Daboll, a popular text of the day.[26] A copybook which Abe made was based apparently on Pike, Daboll, and Dilworth's arithmetics. This "sum book" was made of ledger paper measuring 9 by 12 inches sewed together. Only ten of the pages seem to have survived.[27] They are extremely valuable because they carry the only extant specimens of Abe's early penmanship and ciphering. The following is a description of these ten sheets arranged as nearly as can be determined in their original order.[28]

1. A badly mutilated sheet with no captions but presenting the first signature of Abraham Lincoln thus far discovered. The obverse side contains, besides remnants of ciphering, these lines: "Abraham Lincoln his hand and pen he will be good but god knows When." This doggerel was penned by schoolboys before the beginning of the nineteenth century. It appeared in an old copybook belonging to one James Wilson dated 1793 at one time in the possession of a family in Elizabethtown, Kentucky. On the same page Abraham then wrote: "Time What an emty vaper tis and days how swift they are swift as an indian arr[ow] fly or like a shooting star the present moment Just [is here] then slides away in [haste] that we [can] never say they ['re ours] but [only say they're] past."

The edges of this sheet are badly torn which makes an exact transcription impossible. However, it can be seen that Abe fell down on the spelling of the words "empty" and "vapor." On the reverse side there are exercises in subtraction. It may be noted that Abe apparently had difficulty making the figure eight.[29]

2. At the top of the obverse side of this sheet the words "Long Measure &C &C" are written in bold script. Below is a table of "long measures" followed by exercises in miles, furlongs, poles, yards, feet, and inches. On the reverse are the headings "Subtractions of long Meas[ure]," "of Land Meas-

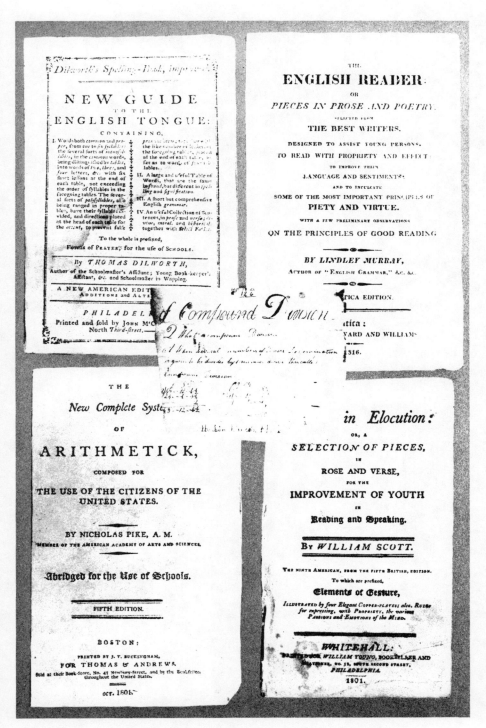

Some of Abraham's schoolbooks, with portion of a page from his copybook

ure," and "of Dry Measure," with examples of each. In the lower left-hand corner these lines again:

> Abraham Lincoln
> his hand and pen
> he will be good but
> god knows When [30]

3. "Multiplication 1824" heads the obverse of this sheet. Below are several multiplication problems and their solutions. On the reverse is the heading "Multiplication Continued" and more problems. In large script in the lower right-hand corner are the words "Abraham Lincolns Book." [31]

4. This sheet also is badly torn. Apparently the heading on the obverse side was originally "Long Division 1824," but the word "Long" has been torn away. At the bottom, on the left, are again the words "Abraham Lincolns Book." On the reverse is the heading "Long Division C[ontinued]," followed by problems, and in the lower right-hand corner this verse:

> Abraham Lincoln is my name
> And with my pen I wrote the same
> I wrote in both haste and speed
> And left it here for fools to read.

This is followed by a date which is partially obliterated but is probably 1826. If these lines were written by Lincoln, he took greater pains with his penmanship than elsewhere.[32]

5. The obverse side of this sheet is labeled "[Co]mpound Multiplication." Below is the question "What is Compound Multiplication," followed by the answer, "When several numbers of divers Denomination are given to be multiplied by one Common Multiplier this is called Compound multiplication." Below is ciphering and a "story" problem. On the reverse side, the heading "To Exercise Multiplication" is followed by another story problem. In the middle of the page in large script are the words "Of Compound Division" followed by the definition: "When several numbers of Divers Denomination are given to be divided by a common divisor

131

this called Compound Division," and more ciphering. At the bottom of this page Abe printed his name and the words "His Book." This is the earliest example of his printing extant.[33]

6. The heading of this page is "Simple Interest." Both sides of this sheet are full of problems and their answers. One of the problems under the subheading Case 1, reads: "A testator left his son, besides providing for his education &c $1500 to receive the amount thereof at 6 percent per an[num] when he should arrive at the age of 21 years which his guardian then found to be $2332-50 Cents how old was the Boy at his fathers decease." Abe's solution is worked out beneath.[34]

7. Both sides of this sheet are devoted to "Simple Interest." Cases 2 and 3 are explained and examples given.[35]

8. Both sides of this sheet are concerned with "Compound Interest." The edges are torn and the rules and ciphering are difficult to read.[36]

9. The obverse side of this reads: "Discount March 1st, 1826." Below are a definition of discounting, rules for figuring, and examples. On the reverse is the heading "Discount 1826," and a series of examples. This sheet is of interest because it indicates that Abe continued studying arithmetic after he left Dorsey's school in 1824.[37]

10. The final sheet is devoted to "The Single Rule of Three," the goal that Thomas Lincoln set for his son. Two neat lines are ruled under the heading and the rest of the page divided into two columns. Three problems are copied here, followed by Abe's solutions. On the reverse side are five questions concerning proportion and answers to them. The final one is "How many sorts of proportion are there," and the answer follows: "two direct and indirect." [38]

How far Abe progressed in his arithmetic under Dorsey's tutelage and how much he did on his own after he left school cannot be determined. As observed above, apparently he was still working at it in 1826. As a student Abraham made an impression on his schoolmates. One recalled that he stood out in spelling matches, "always ahead of all the classes he ever was in." He "was always at school early. He easily stood at the head of his class and passed the rest of us rapidly in his studies."[39] Another declared, "Lincoln had a strong mind. I was older than he was by 6 years and further advanced but he soon outstripped me. . . ."[40]

One of the basic factors in Abraham's successful pursuit of an education was the helpful and sympathetic attitude of his parents and his stepmother as well. Nancy Hanks Lincoln, who has been described "as a woman known for the extraordinary strength of her mind . . . a brilliant woman,"[41] was largely responsible for Abraham's intellectual curiosity. His stepmother, although unable to contribute much in the course of intellectual guidance, did in every way possible create about him an atmosphere congenial to study and also greatly encouraged him. His father had great respect for learning, and made it possible for his children to attend whatever schools were available to them. Sally Lincoln herself said, "As a usual thing Mr. Lincoln never made Abe quit reading to do anything if he could avoid it. He would do it himself first." She insisted that his father was anxious that he advance in all his studies. "Mr. Lincoln could read a little & could scarcely write his name; hence he wanted, as he himself felt the uses and necessities of education, his boy Abraham to learn & encouraged him to do it in all ways he could."[42]

Sally was impressed with young Abe's unusual eagerness to know, and his persistence and concentration. She said, ". . . when old folks were at our house, [Abe] was a silent & attentive observer—never speaking or asking questions till they were gone and then he must understand every thing—even to the smallest thing—minutely and exactly—he would then repeat it over to himself again and again—sometimes in one form and then in another & when it was fixed in his mind to suit him he became easy and he never lost that fact or his understanding of it."[43]

The only time young Abraham is supposed to have exhibited a display of temper was when he himself was unable to express clearly an idea or when those with whom he was talking could not "explain plainly what he wanted to know." It always irritated him when he heard someone talking who was not specific and hence difficult to understand.[44]

Before leaving Abe's school days, mention should be made of a tragedy that befell one of his schoolmates, Matthew Gentry, in 1824, which made a deep and lasting impression on him. The Gentrys were the "rich" family of the Little Pigeon community. James Gentry, the father, had been born in North Carolina in 1788, and migrated to Ohio County, Kentucky, where he married Elizabeth Hornbeck in 1803.[45] They moved to Spencer County, Indiana, where he entered a thousand acres of land in 1818. There were eight children in the Gentry family, Matthew, Agnes, Allen, Hannah, Sarah, Joseph, Elizabeth, and James. Abe knew them all and went to school with the older children.[46] Matthew, who was three years older than Abe, was known as "a rather bright lad," and since he was the eldest son of *the* rich man" of a "very poor neighborhood," he was held in a particular regard by his teachers and fellow pupils. Then one day, without warning, Matthew became "unaccountably furiously mad." Apparently Abe was present when his friend was stricken, and saw him attempt to maim himself, fight his father, and attack his mother. Seeing this "fortune-favored child" so horribly struck down shocked and bewildered Abe. It was a grim experience for a young sensitive boy to have undergone. The awful scene seemed to haunt him, and its lasting effect on him cannot be measured. We know that he brooded over it, wondering the meaning behind such a cruel fate.[47]

There was time for recreation in the form of sports before and after the school sessions and at lunchtime. We have observed already how Abraham read in Weems's book about the athletic ability of George Washington. We find Abraham at fifteen approaching that season in his life when he enjoyed displaying his great physical strength. Also, he was reaching towards his maximum height of six feet four inches. He was "stout, withy, and wiry." ". . . he . . . greatly excelled in all those homely feats of strength, agility, and endurance as practiced by frontier people. . . . In wrestling, jumping, running, throwing the maul and pitching the crow-bar, he always stood first among those of his own age . . . and even when pitted against those of maturer years, he was almost always victorious." [48]

Abe's long arms and legs gave him tremendous advantage in such contests as throwing the maul and the crowbar, feats similar to hurling the hammer and the javelin. The maul was a heavy mallet of walnut or some other hard wood, with a hickory handle. The contestant would swing this maul around his head two or three times and then let go to see how far he could throw it. In place of the classical javelin the pioneers threw a crowbar. These crude devices meant that superior strength rather than skill was required to win. Weight-lifting contests of various sorts were engaged in by both boys and men. There was also wrestling where usually some generally accepted rules were observed, and Abraham particularly excelled in this. Occasionally matches degenerated into "no holds barred" contests. Abe's long legs carried him to the fore in running and jumping competition. He was supposed to have been able to cover forty-one feet in what was called the "three hops."

There are many tales told of Abe's sheer strength. A neighbor said that he once saw young Abe "pick up and walk away with a chicken house made of poles, pinned together and covered, that weighed at least six hundred pounds, if not more." Another story went that one day he observed three or four men preparing sticks on which to move some posts, and brushing the men aside, he shouldered the posts singlehanded and deposited them at the place at which they were to be

135

used. In fact, one person insisted that with straps and ropes properly adjusted Abraham could lift a thousand pounds easily.[49] It is impossible to untangle the legends and truths of Abe's great physical prowess, but certainly by his sixteenth year he was commanding the attention, respect, and even wonder of the Little Pigeon Creek community.

Now that Abraham's school days were over at fifteen years of age it is of interest to summarize his progress in formal instruction. He had been sent to two consecutive terms of school in Kentucky by the time he was seven years of age. After an interval of four years, when eleven, he attended his first school in Indiana. Another term at thirteen was provided and his final course of instruction as we have just observed was conducted in 1824. At each of these periods he had a different teacher which probably was to his advantage.

The subscription schools on the frontier usually were in session for two or three months after the late harvests had been gathered and before the early spring plowing season. During December, January, and February in both Kentucky and southern Indiana the youth could be spared most conveniently from the duties common to pioneer life. Five terms of school for Abraham, or the aggregate of a year's formal training would be considered in that day a common-school education. The courts insisted that a child bound out to a guardian should have "one year's schooling in the English language."[50]

Abe advanced just as far as the primitive school system permitted. His formal education in the "three R's" was comparable to the instruction acquired by the average youth growing up in southern Indiana at that time. He should not be considered an underprivileged child with respect to education for the period in which he lived.

There were many factors besides books and schools which contributed to Abe's general education. He was often at Rockport, county seat of Spencer, and also at the seats of government of the adjacent counties of Warrick, Dubois, and Perry. On one occasion, at least, in company with his friend Henry Brooner he went to Vincennes, the old territorial capital, and en route they must have passed through Petersburg in Pike County. One of his most interesting early journeys was to Princeton, the county seat of Gibson. The best date for this trip seems to be in the year 1824, when he was fifteen years old. He rode "across the country on a flea-bitten gray mare, with a bunch of wool which his mother had sent along to be carded." [51]

Abe's business interests in the town have been recalled by the youth employed at the mill where the carding was done: "In the afternoon of a particularly warm day in August, 1827 [probably 1824], a tall, beardless, long-legged boy about my own age dressed in a suit of well-worn brown jeans, the trousers of which he had long before outgrown, and wearing a woolen hat and coarse, heavy, plain-cut leather shoes of the style then in vogue among the backwoods people, came riding up to the mill. Behind him, tied over the horse's back, was a bunch of wool, which, after dismounting, he carried across the road and dropped at my feet, asking if it could be carded." John M. Lockwood, the attendant, told him that he would have to wait his turn, but when he learned that the boy had ridden forty miles from Spencer County, he promised he would try and work his lot in ahead of some of the others. Lockwood continued, ". . . he gave me his name, but, being new to me and one I had never before heard, he looked over my shoulder and carefully spelled it for me. . . ." Cash or toll was used in payment at the mill. Abe said, "I have no money . . . so you will have to keep out enough toll for your pay." Lockwood remembered that there were eighteen pounds and he tolled "one sixth of it or three pounds." Abe is said to have lingered about the mill for some time watching the machinery at work and then walked up into the town.[52]

Abraham was greatly impressed upon entering the town

"with a quaint sign on the corner of the public square. It stood out in bold relief, Robert Stockwell merchant." [53] There were a half dozen other stores, at least three taverns, a few brick dwellings, several frame houses, and about eighty log cabins in the community. "The inhabitants were principally *Kentuckians*." [54] The village was halfway between Vincennes and Evansville. Abe was a keen observer, and wherever he went nothing escaped him, which added tremendously to his store of knowledge.

CHAPTER XI

16

Action

1825

SCHOOL DAYS were over for Abe by the time he reached the age
of sixteen. The one objective before him now was the securing
of steady employment that would pay a favorable wage. Usually a boy on the frontier followed the vocation of his father
and Thomas was interested primarily in carpentry. One of his
Kentucky acquaintances said that he had "the best set of
carpenter's tools in Hardin County." [1] J. L. Nall, a nephew,
observed that Thomas was "a cabinetmaker and thrifty when
he lived in Kentucky." [2]

Several products of his handiwork have been identified.
Samuel Haycraft, Elizabethtown historian, called attention to
"a house rather better than usual for that day, the carpenter's
work of which was executed by Thomas Lincoln. . . . most
of that work is to be seen to this day [1865] sound as a trout
although done upwards to sixty years ago." [3] Referring to this
same structure Haycraft pointed out that "the joiners work"
also was done by him. [4] Some of the decorative mantels made
for the early homes in the town are identified as his work.
Several pieces of furniture that Thomas made in Kentucky
have been preserved, including a cherry bed and corner cupboards which seemed to be his specialty.

Upon reaching Indiana Thomas Lincoln continued in his
vocation and one of his new neighbors observed that he "was a

139

carpenter by trade, relied upon it for a living, not on farming."[5] Dennis Hanks stated that his carpenter's tools were "a wonder to the hull deestrict."[6] William Wood, a prominent resident of the community, recalled that: "Thomas Lincoln, often and at various times worked for me, made cupboards, etc., other household furniture; built my house, made floors, ran up the stairs, did all the inside work for my house."[7]

David Turnham also reported, "I have a cupboard in my house which Thomas Lincoln made for me about 1821 or 1822. It is about 2½ feet high, 1½ ft. wide, has six drawers and is made of walnut and poplar, the boards used are whipsawed."[8] While the pioneers could construct their crude bedsteads, tables, and benches, a good corner cupboard, almost indispensable in a cabin home, required the skill of a cabinetmaker. In Kentucky as well as Indiana this was Thomas Lincoln's distinctive creation. Eight of these pieces of furniture which he is known to have made are extant.[9]

These corner cupboards vary but little in construction, most of them made apparently from the same pattern. They are of walnut or cherry, about seven feet tall, and weigh about three hundred pounds. For the cornice Thomas cut out an ornamental piece in what was known as the "hole and tooth" design. Ida M. Tarbell, in describing one of these cupboards, stated that it had "an inlaid decoration in white ash running down the door jambs on each side. . . . The design is crude, to be sure, but it shows a sense of decoration and patriotism combined, for the curving streamer falls from a star and at each bend there arises a tiny flag. The inlaying is so well done that in spite of full ninety years of scrubbing and scouring it remains intact."[10] Undoubtedly Abraham assisted his father by whipsawing the lumber and doing other rough work necessary. In his cabinetmaking Thomas Lincoln apparently drifted into a practice of puttering around with his inlay work. As one neighbor stated, he "was not a lazy man but a piddler, always doing but doing nothing great."[11] This artistic urge

140

Corner cupboard made by Thomas Lincoln,
now owned by R. Gerald McMurtry

Detail showing scroll

which his father displayed did not interest one of Abraham's temperament or mentality. Also, there was no demand for another cabinetmaker in the community.

Thomas Lincoln also farmed, and although Abe was "raised to farm work" [12] he did not like it any better than carpentry. Father and son with the aid of John Johnston by hard labor had cleared close to twenty acres of land for cultivation. "About half of it [was put] in corn, the rest of it in wheat and oats, and an acre in grass. They were also able to keep sheep, hogs, and several head of cattle by this time." [13] The abundance of several kinds of nuts, hazelnuts especially, on the Lincoln tract, made it possible for the hogs to live on the mast through the winter without any other means of sustenance.

All implements and gear on the farm were very primitive. The plowshare and bar were usually of iron, but the moldboard was of wood. Harrows were made entirely of wood and all the connecting rings for both plow and harrow were of rawhide. A pitchfork was usually formed from a young forked dogwood sapling, the bark taken off and the two points sharpened for tines. Rakes were made from deer horns, and hickory, properly seasoned and shaped in the form of a large scoop, served as a shovel. Corn shucks plaited in ropelike cords and sewed together served as horse collars. [14]

While Abe and John Johnston were plowing one day, an enormous "chin fly" attacked their horse. This made him move around the field at a very lively gait. Abraham noticed how severely the horse was being bitten and presently killed the fly. Johnston asked, "Why did you do that, Abe?" Upon the reply that he did not want the poor horse tortured, Johnston observed: "Well it made him step and we would get the plowing done so much sooner." [15]

There is more or less support for the tradition that Abraham told one of his employers that "his father taught him to work but never learned him to love it." [16] This was especially true of most kinds of menial labor which he was compelled to do at

141

home and employed to perform by the neighbors. The same informant noted above states, "Abe was awful lazy; he worked for me, was always reading and thinking; used to get mad at him. . . . he would laugh and talk and crack jokes and tell stories all the time, didn't ever work but dearly loved his pay. He worked for me frequently, a few days only at a time." [17]

However, another neighbor states, "Abe worked for us at various times at 25¢ per day, worked hard and faithful and when he missed time would not charge for it." [18] Still another employer comments, "He was mighty conscientious about getting in a full day. There were always results from his labors and he spoke very little when at work. Now and then after an hour or so, we would sit on a log to catch our wind and Lincoln would tell some yarn he had heard, mostly something funny, always interesting." [19]

Apparently it depended much on what Abraham was employed to do, as to whether or not he displayed much energy in his work. Possibly the average pioneer looked upon a boy's interest in books as a symptom of laziness. It is difficult, however, to associate the term "lazy" with one who had particular pleasure in utilizing his great strength in the constructive work of the pioneer. No man who was lazy would find a congenial place among those who were clearing the forests.

There was one type of manual labor in which father and son had been engaged that gave Abraham much satisfaction; that was using an ax. As soon as the family reached the new homesite when Abraham was but seven years old, he had "an ax put into his hands at once. . . . and he was almost constantly handling that most useful instrument—less of course in plowing and harvesting seasons." [20]

Abraham loved the feel of an ax and he was physically equipped to use it. His hands had a vicelike grip and his long arms gave tremendous power to his blows. One of his companions stated, "My how he could chop. His ax would flash and bite into a sugar tree or sycamore, down it would come. If

142

you heard him felling trees in a clearing, you would say there were three men at work, the way the trees fell." [21] One who worked with him states, "He was a master woodsman and could size up a tree that would work up well into rails at almost a glance." [22]

As the open places were enlarged for cultivation, there was an urgent demand for rail fences. The work of a lifetime on the frontier might be confined to the use of rail-splitting implements which included an ax, a maul, and a set of wedges. The maul with its heavy cheese-shaped head and long hickory handle was a powerful instrument in the hands of a rail splitter. With it iron wedges were driven into logs to start cleavage, then followed those made of dogwood or ironwood, which completed the task of quartering the log. Finally the triangular-shaped rails would be produced. Ash, hickory, oak, poplar, or walnut trees were most often worked up into rails. Usually they were made about ten feet long and four inches across. An expert woodsman could make as many as four hundred rails from sunrise to sunset. Usually a flat rate of twenty-five cents a day was paid but occasionally the laborer did piecework for a certain amount per hundred. The rail splitter was often retained to put up a fence and usually the contract called for getting out rails and fencing in a lot. The *Revised Laws of Indiana* defines a lawful fence as one "at least five feet and a half in height, the uppermost rail in each panel thereof supported by strong stakes, strongly set and fastened in the earth, so as to compose what is commonly called staking and ridering, otherwise the uppermost rail in each panel, shall be braced with two strong rails, poles, or stakes, locking each corner or angle thereof; and in all the foregoing materials, the apertures between the rails, pailings and [or] palisadoes within two feet of the surface of the earth, shall not be more than four inches, and from the distance of two feet from the surface, the apertures between such rails, pailings or pali-sadoes, shall not be more than six inches; and that in all worm

143

fences staked and ridered, and the worm shall be at least four feet six inches; and if locked as aforesaid, the worm shall be at least five feet. . . ." [23]

The pioneer boiled down all this legal vernacular by this simple rule that a rail fence should be horse high, bull strong, and pig tight: high enough so a horse could not jump over it, strong enough so a bull could not push it over, and tight enough so a pig could not squeeze through it. Abraham could have found employment at rail splitting at twenty-five cents a day as long as he desired that kind of labor. [24]

One job in which Abraham was engaged brought him out of the woods for a season, at least, and established him on the banks of the Ohio River. In August, 1826, Dennis Hanks, Squire Hall, and Abraham got a notion that they could make a lot of money by cutting cordwood for passing steamboats. These craft used wood for fuel and acquired their supply as needed from the great piles of cordwood that were stacked up close to the river bank. [25] The place the trio had chosen to operate was not far from the mouth of the Anderson River. They were told they might have to take their pay in merchandise. The price usually received was twenty-five cents per cord. It is said Abe received for his share of the proceeds "nine yards of white domestic." Out of this Abe had a shirt made and "it was positively the first white shirt which, up to that time, he had ever owned or wore." [26]

While helping to load the fuel Abraham had a chance to talk with the captain and members of the crew and on occasion with some of the passengers. This river experience opened up an entirely new outlook on life for the boy who had lived in the midst of the wilderness for nearly a decade.

Not far from the place where Abe had been cutting cordwood a packinghouse and ferry were operated by James Taylor where Anderson River flows into the Ohio. Taylor may have observed Abe at work and offered him a job or possibly Lincoln solicited the place then open. However, we find him

144

now living at Taylor's, securing his meals there and sharing a room with the proprietor's son Green. His wage was six dollars a month.

One of Abraham's regular tasks was the running of a ferry across Anderson River about three hundred yards from its mouth. At this point it was about one hundred feet wide and fifteen feet deep. Taylor owned the tract adjacent to the Spencer County landing which was one of the oldest ferry sites in the state of Indiana. As early as 1802 small settlements had sprung up on both sides of the Anderson River which made the ferry of local importance.[27] An elderly woman stated that when she was a little girl Abe worked on the ferry. She remembered "his gentle manner to the children," while the other hand employed there was very "brusque." For the convenience of foot passengers Lincoln used a row boat much lighter than the regular ferry. For this service he received a picayune, 6¼ cents, for the round trip. This early patron of the ferry said, "I can see now, how with one sweep of the oars, he could send his boat from shore to shore at low water."[28]

Not only did little girls remember the tall ferryman, but big boys soon learned that Abraham had a wealth of stories which would make the ferry landing an interesting loafing place. Here Abraham attracted new audiences and more mature listeners to hear his stories and recitations.[29]

Green B. Taylor recalled many years later an incident which occurred when Abe was living in his home and working for his father. "It was during the season that Abe was operating the ferry across Anderson River for my father that we were told to go into the crib and husk corn, while we were husking the corn, Abe taunted me about a certain girl in Troy that I did not like and kept it up until I tore the husk off a big ear of corn and threw it at him. It struck him just above the eye." In relating the story at another time Taylor said that "this blow left a scar that Lincoln carried to his grave," and added that he [Green] "went crying to his mother who gave him what

145

Lincoln would not give him, a sound cuffing." On the other hand, there is a tradition that the whole affair occurred at a husking bee, and Taylor's indignation was aroused when Abe found a red ear and kissed Green's girl. Also, according to another story, Green was supposed to have been "disposed to ill-use the poor hired boy." That would have been something to see: the twelve-year-old Green abusing the sixteen-year-old, six-foot-four Lincoln.[30]

During his spare time Abe had built a small row boat at the Ohio River landing. One day, two men came up and singling out him and his boat, asked him to row them with their luggage to a packet that was coming down river. He agreed, and carried them out to the waiting steamer and saw them and their gear safely aboard. Before they steamed away they each tossed a silver half dollar into his little boat. He could scarcely believe his eyes—"a poor . . . boy [earning] a dollar in less than a day." The "world seemed wider and fairer"and he was "a more hopeful and confident being from that time."[31]

Apparently after that he offered such service to other steamer passengers and his private little business finally got him into the clutches of the law. Two brothers who lived on the Kentucky side of the river, John T. and Len Dill, had the ferry rights across the Ohio from a point opposite Anderson River. They regarded Abraham's ferrying of steamer passengers as an encroachment upon their jurisdiction, and had him brought before Samuel Pate, a justice of the peace near Lewisport, Kentucky. The pertinent clause of Kentucky law was read: ". . . if any person whatsoever shall, for reward, set any person over any river or creek, whereupon public ferries are appointed, he or she so offending shall forfeit and pay five pounds current money, for every such offence, one moiety to the ferry-keeper nearest the place where such offence shall be committed, the other moiety to the informer; and if such ferry-keeper informs, he shall have the whole penalty, to be recovered with costs."

146

Ohio River steamboat General Pike

A clearing with a woodman's hut

Wooding station for steamboats

craft were added. From 1811 through 1826 there were 160 ships built and launched in the West. However, the fatalities were heavy. Of this number ninety were no longer running, having been lost or destroyed by accident or disaster. In 1825 there were 143 steamboats on the western waters. Of these 109 had been built in western shipyards.[37]

One of the most famous river disasters had occurred above Troy in the spring before Abraham began working on the river, and no doubt he heard the story repeated many times. In May, 1825, the Marquis de Lafayette, on his triumphal tour through the United States, left Nashville, Tennessee, on board the steamboat *Mechanic*. It came up the Mississippi and entered the Ohio, bound for Louisville. At a point on the river at the site of Cannelton the boat hit a snag and sank. No lives were lost. The Marquis' party spent the night on the Kentucky shore. The next morning they were picked up by the steamboat *Paragon* and taken on to Louisville. There is a pleasant little story that Lafayette sought refuge in a cabin on the Indiana shore belonging to a Mr. Cavender, and held a kind of reception for the neighbors the following morning. Unfortunately, there is no evidence to support this.[38]

Steamboat traffic brought a cosmopolitan touch to the river towns. Arrivals and departures provided never-ending excitement. On board were prospective settlers and immigrants with their families and curious travelers from the East and Europe, as well as merchants and boatmen. Visions that Troy might become a flourishing river town and trading center never materialized. But in 1825, when young Abe was working along the river, he was living on the main street of western transportation and travel. The months he spent there afforded him an education as important as any he had received in the schoolroom. His eyes were opened to the world that lay outside the Pigeon Creek wilderness. His imagination was aroused and his ambition whetted. After this sojourn he could never have been content to live quietly in the backwoods.

149

CHAPTER XII

17

Romance

1826

WITH THE COMING OF SPRING Abraham was needed at home to assist in putting in the crops, and he returned to Little Pigeon Creek from his several months of labor at Anderson River. While as far as is known his fancy had not turned to love at this season, his sister's had. Sarah had wonderful news for him. She was engaged.

Little has been said of Sarah[1] since she was twelve years old and a stepmother had come to relieve her of the burdensome household tasks she had been performing since her own mother's death. But she had not relinquished her interest in and watchful care over her younger brother. When Abe would start out with the boys for an evening's fun, Sarah "admonished him as to his conduct." [2] While he may have resented her "motherly" anxiety, he had a deep affection for her.

On February 10, 1826, Sarah became nineteen years old.[3] She was described by her stepmother as being "short of stature and somewhat plump in build, her hair was dark brown and her eyes were gray." [4] John Hanks, a cousin, stated that "she was kind, tender and good natured and is said to have been a smart woman. That is my opinion." [5] Her facial expression resembled Abraham's, somewhat: "in repose it had the gravity which they both, perhaps, inherited from their mother; but it was capable of being lighted almost into beauty by one of her brother's ridiculous stories or rapturous sallies of humor. She was a modest, plain industrious girl. . . ." [6]

On April 8, 1826, probably in anticipation of her marriage, the Little Pigeon Church "received Sister Sally [Sarah] Lincoln by experience of grace." [7] This was a step taken by pioneer young people who came from good Christian families before establishing their own homes. There were few young people accepted into membership of the pioneer churches. Parents who were church members assumed the responsibility for keeping their families "under the same order and discipline as they themselves . . . [were] bound to observe, both in their walk and conversation." [8] Marriage and church affiliation seemed to go hand in hand in those days.

A year before the Lincolns arrived in Spencer County a family by the name of Grigsby settled about three miles south of the site of the Lincoln cabin. This family had moved from North Carolina to Kentucky, and were living in Ohio County in that state in 1810. The United States census for that year lists the family as consisting of Reuben, under forty-five years of age, his wife under twenty-six, and a boy and a girl under ten. The boy's name was Aaron and he was born in 1801. In 1826 he became engaged to Sarah Lincoln.

Very little is known of Aaron Grigsby's youth. His parents were ardent members of the Little Pigeon Church and were well regarded in the community. Probably intellectually and economically their status was comparable with the Lincolns'. There is nothing factual to support a tradition that Aaron Grigsby had received a superior education and had studied law. In fact, the only document that has been found signed by him shows that he did so by making his mark. [9]

Aaron and Sarah had lived in the same community for ten years. Their parents were members of the same church and they would have seen each other often. Only one piece of folklore associated with Aaron's courtship has come down to us. Sarah was visiting some neighbors of the Grigsbys one day

151

and Aaron happened by. The little boy of the family, seeing them together, ran into the house exclaiming, "Mother! mother! Aaron Grigsby is sparking Sally Lincoln; I saw him kiss her." The boy's mother told him to stop watching Sarah or he would not get an invitation to the wedding. The trouble with this story is that the little boy who had been so observing was only seven months old when the Grigsby-Lincoln rites were solemnized.[10]

The marriage was performed on August 2, 1826, by Charles Harper,[11] minister of the Little Pigeon Church, probably in the Lincoln cabin.[12] Church weddings were not customary in that day. We may be sure there was no dancing at this wedding because of the strict discipline of the church to which the families belonged. There is a story to the effect that Abraham wrote a poem which was read on this occasion, entitled "Adam's and Eve's Wedding Song." While the verses may have been read, Abraham most certainly was not the author. The first stanza reads:

> When Adam was created
> He dwelt in Eden's shade,
> As Moses has recorded,
> And soon a bride was made.[13]

Aaron and Sarah must have looked into the future with much hope. They had a new cabin on a tract of land but a half mile from Aaron's people, and only two miles from Sarah's. It is reasonable to assume that Thomas Lincoln presented Sarah, upon her marriage, with the dowry usually allotted a daughter at that time. By law even an orphan girl who was bound out was given the following property upon fulfilling her time of service: "a new feather bed, with all necessary clothing, with pillow and bolster, all of decent home manufacture."[14] Certainly Sarah would have all this, plus suitable clothing for herself and undoubtedly a cow and calf. Often a father would also give a horse and saddle as a wedding present.

Sarah was popular with her in-laws. Her brother-in-law,

152

Nathaniel Grigsby, portrayed her as a "woman of an extraordinary mind." "Her good-humored laugh I can hear now, is as fresh in my mind as if it were yesterday." "She could, like her brother Abe, meet and greet a person with the kindest greeting in the world, make you easy at the touch and word." Grigsby concluded by saying that Sarah was "an intellectual and intelligent woman. However, not so much as her mother." [15]

The Grigsby-Lincoln nuptials were scarcely over when Thomas and Sally Lincoln began preparing for another wedding in their home. This time the prospective bride was Matilda Johnston, Sally Lincoln's younger daughter by Daniel Johnston. Matilda was born in Elizabethtown in 1811 and was five years old when her father died. There has been little occasion to mention her but there is one girlhood incident of interest told by Matilda herself. Unfortunately, the scribe who recorded it added so many of his own theories that the simple tale related by Matilda has been obscured. [16] The time must have been a year or two before 1826. She opened her story by stating that she and Abraham "grew up together loving one another as brother and sister." One morning Abe shouldered his ax and started down the well-worn path for a day's work in the woods. Tilda had been forbidden to follow him. She slipped away, however, and trailed a short distance behind Abe without his being aware of her. Suddenly she slipped up behind him, "bounced on his back like a panther, putting her knees in the small of Abraham's back and locking her hands around his neck . . . threw Abraham down on his back. . . . In pulling Abraham backward, 'Tilda fell on the sharp keen edge of the ax and cut herself badly and quite severely." Abe saw that she had received a deep wound, and tearing off part of his shirt, did his best to staunch the flow of blood. Then came the following dialogue:

Abraham—"Now what are you going to tell your good mother, 'Tilda?"

Tilda—"Why Abe, I'll tell my mother that I cut myself badly on the ax and that will be the truth about it."

Abraham—"Yes, that will be the truth but it won't be the whole truth, 'Tilda. 'Tilda, the very very best thing you can possibly do is to tell your mother the whole truth and nothing but the truth and risk your mother. This I advise you to do." [17]

Matilda had now reached the age of fifteen, one year older than was her sister Elizabeth when she married Dennis Hanks. How long Squire, son of Levi and Elizabeth Hall, had been keeping company with Matilda we do not know. He was born in Kentucky, presumably in 1805, but we are unable to learn when he came to Indiana.[18] The wedding of Squire and Matilda took place in the Lincoln cabin on September 14, 1826, and Young Lamar was the minister officiating.[19] After the wedding it is likely that they went to live temporarily with Dennis and Elizabeth Hanks. Squire was a half brother of Dennis.[20]

In the romantic atmosphere created by these two weddings in 1826 one might expect to find Abraham's interest turning to girls. Psychologically the age of seventeen is about the time a youth begins to think of romance and the Lincoln home was full of it. The acquisition of his first white shirt the year before shows that Abe was beginning to think of his personal appearance. His stepmother encouraged him to dress up on Sundays and when he went visiting of an evening. Dennis Hanks said that "Abe had more pride 'n the rest of us. He always had an extry pair of butternut-dyed jeans pants, an' a white shirt." [21] It cannot be said that Abe's personal appearance was magnetic at this time. He was exceedingly tall with very long arms and legs, and of a leathery complexion. In fact, one of the young ladies of the neighborhood said, "All the young girls of my age made fun of Abe." She added that she did not think that it disturbed him, and since he was such a good fellow his gawky appearance was somewhat discounted.[22]

Abe's stepbrother, John D. Johnston, who was about his

154

own age, commented that "Abe didn't take much truck with girls. . . . he was too busy studying at the time."[23] John Hanks who observed him in his Indiana years, stated that he could never get Abe in the company of girls, although he was not timid "in this particular, but did not seek such company."[24] David Turnham, a schoolmate, said, "Abe did not much like the girls . . . didn't appear to."[25]

According to the testimonies of several young ladies of southern Indiana who felt that they could have become Mrs. Abraham Lincoln, had they so desired, it appears that Abraham might not have been bashful at all. But many of the claims do not stand up under close scrutiny. A roll call of these "brides that might have been" could start with a story which Abraham told about his first romance.

"The Covered Wagon Girl"—One day a pioneer's wagon broke down near the home of the Lincolns, and while it was being repaired the family to whom the wagon belonged cooked their meals in the cabin. There were two girls in the family and Abraham took a great fancy to one of them. After they were gone he began day dreaming about her. "I thought I took my father's horse and followed the wagon, and finally I found it, and they were surprised to see me. I talked with the girl and persuaded her to elope with me; and that night I put her on my horse, and we started off across the prairie. After several hours we came to a camp; and when we rode up we found it was the one we had left a few hours before, and we went in. The next night we tried again, and the same thing happened—the horse came back to the same place; and then we concluded that we ought not to elope. I stayed until I had persuaded her father to give her to me." Abraham added that he considered writing out this story, but then decided it did not amount to much. He finished by saying, "I think that was the beginning of love with me."[26]

Polly Richardson—Polly, daughter of John and Nancy Richardson, claimed, "I was Abe's first sweetheart." There is a story that Abraham protected Polly and her mother against a pack of wolves the first night they spent in Indiana. Polly further recalled that later he took her to church, spelling bees, and other neighborhood affairs, and concluded, "Abe wanted me to marry him, but I refused." Actually, Abraham was but eight years old when the Richardsons arrived in 1817, and but twelve years old when Polly married Robert Agnew on March 15, 1821.[27]

Elizabeth Tully—Born in Kentucky, Elizabeth came to Spencer County in 1824. She said that she met Abe at the Little Pigeon Church and claimed that she was his "first regular company." "Abe asked to see her home and she agreed," she later recalled. "A hundred yards from the church they sat down and took off their shoes to save leather and Abe carried both pair." She claimed that they kept company for several months, and when asked if Abraham ever proposed to her, she replied, "No, but I could tell from his chat he wanted to marry me." She later married a Mr. Hession.[28]

Elizabeth Ray—A grandson of Elizabeth has preserved "one of a pair of earrings which he said Lincoln gave to his grandmother when he wanted her to marry him." The mate to this earring has been lost. The grandson also had a copy of a biography of George Washington which Lincoln was supposed to have given to Elizabeth when they were courting. Elizabeth Ray married Reuben Grigsby, Jr., on April 16, 1829.[29]

Caroline Meeker—When Abraham Lincoln was working as a ferryman for James Taylor on the Ohio, at the mouth of Anderson River in 1826, he is said to have crossed over to the Kentucky side quite often to call on Caroline Meeker, niece of Squire Pate whom Abe knew. Once at a husking bee Caroline discovered a red ear which she shyly slipped to Abraham. Caroline later married Eli Thrasher.[30]

Matilda Johnston—It cannot be said that Matilda Johnston ever claimed that Abe had anything but a brotherly feeling for her. One of her interviewers, however, has tried to make it appear as if there was a love affair brewing between them. Neither Abraham nor his sister ever entertained any prospects of matrimonial affiliations with the Hankses, Halls, or Johnstons.[31]

Elizabeth Wood—This girl was a daughter of one of Abraham's best friends whom he called Uncle Wood. That Abraham was often in their home is a fact. David Turnham, a neighbor of the Wood family, was asked once if there was not a love affair between Abraham and Elizabeth Wood, to which Turnham replied, "No such thing as courting or proposing was ever thought of." Elizabeth once said that she was sure that Abraham wanted to become better acquainted with her, but she declined his company because of "his awkwardness and large feet." Elizabeth married Samuel Hammond on January 10, 1833.[32]

Hannah Gentry—This alleged romance was probably confined to the schoolroom. Hannah was one of the girls whom Abraham was supposed to have helped out in a spelling match. She was described as "a beauty noted for her amiable disposition, and her father was the richest man in the community." According to neighbors in Spencer County, she would have been Mrs. Lincoln, if Abraham had not been "too fond of onions, as she could not endure them." Hannah Gentry married John Romine on April 2, 1829.[33]

Sarah Lukins—What Sarah's maiden name was is not known. She told a friend, "I could a' been Abe Lincoln's wife, if I'd wanted to, yes sirree." On being pressed for particulars, she said, "Well, Abe tuk me home from church oncet." [34]

Julia Evans—According to this story, Abraham went to Princeton, Indiana, to have some wool carded and related: "I passed on the street a very beautiful girl, the most bewildering creature it seems to me I had ever seen. My heart was in a flutter. The truth is I was so thoroughly captivated by the vision of maidenly beauty that I wanted to stop in Princeton forever." The young lady who bowed to him on the street of

157

Princeton was Julia Evans, "admittedly the village belle." One of Abe's friends claims that Abe said that *this* "was the scene of my first love." [35]

Ann Roby—The most widely circulated story of a romance during Lincoln's youth features Miss Roby. She attended school with him but later moved to Rockport where Abe was engaged in building a flatboat in the late fall of 1828. Ann "described with self-evident pleasure the delightful experience of an evening's stroll down to the river with him, where they were wont to sit on the bank and watch the moon as it rose slowly over the neighboring hills. Dangling their youthful feet in the water, they gazed on the pale orb of night. . . ." Ann was married to Allen Gentry on March 20, 1828, and in December their first child was born. Any romance at this time between Abraham and Ann would be preposterous. [36]

These traditions imply that Abe was a youth whose affections were constantly shifting; it is doubtful that he seriously considered matrimony while living in Indiana. [37]

The problem of housing usually follows marriage and while Abraham did not have to worry about finding a home for a wife, the Hankses, the Grigsbys, and the Halls all were now established in their own cabins. It might be well to see how Thomas Lincoln had fared in financing his home and farm on which he had made the first payment ten years before.

It will be recalled that on October 15, 1817, Thomas Lincoln went to the Vincennes Land Office and entered the southwest quarter of section 32, T 4 S, R 5 W. This tract contained one hundred and sixty acres and the government price for the land was $320.00. The initial payment necessary to secure the land was $16.00 which Thomas paid at the time the land was entered. Two months later he paid $64.00, making a total of $80.00 which was the required one-quarter payment due on the land. [38]

An act approved March 2, 1821, provided that any freeholder could relinquish certain tracts of land to the government and receive credit to be applied as payment on the remainder of his holdings. On April 28, 1827, the three Thomases who lived side by side in Carter Township, Thomas Lincoln, Thomas Barrett, and Thomas Carter, arrived at Vincennes and each relinquished one half of his respective quarter section. Thomas Lincoln applied the credit on the total amount due on his remaining eighty acres. Nearly all of Thomas Lincoln's neighbors took advantage of this relinquishment act, because it allowed them to surrender the poorer and undeveloped part of their land for the same price per acre that the better part cost them. It was a good business deal and alert landholders took advantage of it.[39] Thomas was able to complete the payment for the one-half quarter section amounting to $160.00 by applying to it another relinquishment to which he had title amounting to $80.00. On June 6, 1827, he received a patent signed by John Quincy Adams, President of the United States, for the west half of the quarter section.[40]

During the ten years in which Thomas Lincoln had completed payment for the eighty acres he had elected to keep, he also made a purchase from David Casebier of twenty acres in Section 31, adjoining the northwest corner of his land.[41] This gave him one hundred acres free from debt. This is a somewhat different picture than is usually drawn of Thomas Lincoln's landholdings in Indiana. Apparently he had accomplished what he had set out to do on leaving Kentucky: he had realized economic security in his land transactions which hitherto he had not been able to achieve.[42]

Apparently the twenty acres Thomas Lincoln purchased from Casebier was partly if not all under cultivation, as he is said to have had about forty acres of ground available for farming. When Herndon visited the homesite in 1865, he observed, "It has an orchard on it, part of which Abraham Lincoln planted with his own hands." He further states, "saw five or six old, old apple trees."[43]

159

CHAPTER XIII

18

Idealism

1827

WHEN Aaron and Sarah Lincoln Grigsby moved into their new home shortly after their wedding, their closest neighbors were Josiah and Elizabeth Crawford who lived but one-half mile to the east. They were also from Kentucky and many of their relatives had settled in the Little Pigeon community. Aaron was just a year older than Josiah and Sarah was the same age as Elizabeth. Naturally a friendship sprang up between these two young couples. The young women especially had much in common and Sarah must have been delighted to learn that Elizabeth was interested in garden flowers such as Nancy Hanks Lincoln had grown.

Some of the plants which the pioneer women in Indiana used to cultivate were "the sweet pink, the poppy, the marigold, the larkspur, the touch-me-not, the pretty-by-night, the lady-in-the-green, the sword lily, the flower bean, the hollyhock, the bachelor's button. . . . the roses, the sweet or damask rose, the pinny, the old maid's eyes, the velvet pink, the mullen pink, the garden sweet williams, the carolina pink." There were also an abundance of wildflowers such as: "the wild sweet william, wild pink, lady slipper, wild roses, butterfly weed, wild honeysuckle, blue flag, yellow flag." [1] Of course, there were the many kinds of violets, and also the chalk white blossom of the poison snakeroot.

The Crawfords upon arrival had employed Thomas Lincoln
to assist in the construction of their home. With the aid of
Abraham he had whipsawed planks for the floor and also made
the mantel, doors, and sashes.[2] Among the pieces of furniture
which he fashioned for the Crawfords was a corner cupboard
and a wardrobe made of black walnut and inlaid with white
oak.[3] There is no evidence that Thomas worked for Crawford
or anyone else as a day laborer to "clear and fence the land
and assist in planting and cultivating the crops" as has been
alleged. It is true his son Abraham often assisted Crawford in
this capacity.[4]

Just as groundless is the assertion that Sarah Lincoln
worked as a domestic in the Crawford home.[5] During the short
period of time that the Crawfords lived in Spencer County
before her wedding Sarah may have helped Elizabeth with
her two children, but after she married into the Grigsby family
she would not be hiring out to any one. Neither the Crawfords,
the Grigsbys, nor any of the other Little Pigeon families out-
ranked the Lincolns socially, and only the Gentrys excelled
them economically.

Not only has the relationship of Thomas and his daughter
with the Crawford family been misrepresented, but even
Abraham's contacts with them have been misinterpreted.
Crawford has been portrayed as an overbearing employer
much older than Abe, when less than seven years separated
them.[6] Mrs. Crawford has been described as a woman of
uncertain age who took a "mother's interest" in Abe.[7] Since
she was born September 23, 1807, she was but a year and a
half older than the tall youth who often worked for her
husband.

Abraham learned that "Mr. Crawford had in his house
Ramsay's Life of Washington—a book which he was told gave
a fuller and better account of Washington and the Revolution
than the volume (Weems) he had read with so much
pleasure. He at once borrowed the book, and devoured its

contents. By some accident the volume was exposed to a shower and badly damaged. Young Lincoln had no money, but he knew how to work. He went to Crawford, told him what had happened, and expressed his readiness to work out the full value of the book. Crawford had a field of corn, which had been stripped of the blades as high as the ear, preparatory to cutting off the tops for winter fodder for his cattle. He expressed his willingness to square accounts if Lincoln would cut the tops from that field of corn. The offer was promptly accepted, and after three days of hard labor the book was paid for, and young Lincoln returned home the proud possessor of another volume." [8]

Abe, himself, in relating the story, said, "You see I am tall and long-armed, and I went to work in earnest. At the end of the two days there was not a corn-blade left on a stalk in the field. I wanted to pay full damage for the wetting the book got, so I made a clean sweep." [9] Elizabeth Crawford said that when Abe told her husband that the book had gotten water-soaked, Josiah simply said, "Abe, as long as it is you, you may finish the book and keep it." "Abe pulled fodder for a day or two for it," she added. [10]

While the story of how Abraham acquired the book has been widely circulated and is of much human interest, the contents of the volume are of more importance. Even the frontispiece, although a simple drawing of a large stone with the waves beating upon it, greatly impressed Abe. Inscribed on the boulder was the single name "WASHINGTON" and underneath the picture the tribute: "Firm as the surge-repelling rock." [11]

Ramsay's dedicatory statement in his *Life of George Washington* [12] reads: "To the Youth of the United States, in the hope that from the Example of their common father, they will learn to do and suffer whatever Their Country's Good may require at their hands, the following life of George Washington, is most affectionately inscribed by the author."

162

Books Abraham read in his late teens

Ramsay served as a field surgeon during the Revolution, having graduated from the medical department of the University of Pennsylvania, and as a member of the Continental Congress from 1782–86. He authored other volumes including a history of the Revolution.

The Contents of this *Life of George Washington* show that Abe found here a more detailed account of the Revolution than he had in Weems's volume, and more information about the beginnings of the Federal government.

Chapter 1. "Of George Washington's birth, family, and education. Of his mission to the French commandant on the Ohio, in 1753. His military operations as an officer of Virginia from 1754–1758. . . ."

Chapter 2. "Retrospect of the origin of the American revolutionary war. Of George Washington as member of Congress, in 1774 and 1775. As Commander in Chief of the armies of the United Colonies in 1775 and 1776, and his operations near Boston in these years."

Chapter 3. "Campaign of 1776." This includes the battles of Long Island, Trenton, and Princeton.

Chapter 4. "Campaign of 1777." This includes the battles of Brandywine and Germantown, the distresses of the American Army, and its winter quarters in Valley Forge.

Chapter 5. "Campaign of 1778." Herein Washington surprises the British and defeats them at Monmouth.

Chapter 6. "Campaign of 1779." This covers the distresses of the American Army and the expedition against the Six Nations of Indians.

Chapter 7. "Campaign of 1780." Herein the Marquis de la Fayette arrives and gives assurance that a French army might soon be expected.

Chapter 8. "Campaign of 1781." Herein Washington extinguishes the incipient flames of civil war, and makes Cornwallis and his army prisoners of war.

Chapter 9. "1782 and 1783." Herein Washington recommends measures for the preservation of independence, peace, liberty, and happiness; dismisses his army and retires to Mt. Vernon.

Chapter 10. "General Washington . . . devotes himself to agricultural pursuits. Favours Inland Navigation. . . . Regrets the defects of the federal system, and recommends a revisal of it. . . . Is solicited to accept the presidency. . . ."

Chapter 11. "Washington Elected President. . . . Fills up public offices wholly with a view to the public good. . . ."

Chapter 12. "General Washington attends to the foreign relations of the United States. . . . The free navigation of the Mississippi is granted. . . . Negotiations with Britian. . . . Declines a re-election, and addresses the people. . . . Recommends a navy, a military academy, and other public institutions."

Chapter 13. "Washington rejoices at prospect of retiring. . . . Pays respect to his successor, Mr. John Adams. . . . Resumes agricultural pursuits. General Washington dies. Is honoured by Congress, and by the citizens. His character."

In the appendix Abe found an address and petition to Congress from the Officers of the Army of the United States, Washington's Farewell Address, and Washington's will.

The story of the damaged book and its contents invites an enumeration of other volumes which came into Abraham's hands about this time. One of the oft-repeated fallacies about Abraham Lincoln during his Indiana years is that he "got hold of and read every book he ever heard of within a circuit of 50 miles." [13] Within this region were the Indiana towns of Boonville, Corydon, Evansville, New Harmony, Princeton, Rockport, Troy, and Vincennes, and across the Ohio in Kentucky, still within fifty miles, were Brandenburg, Calhoun, Cloverport, Hardinsburg, Hartford, Hawesville, Henderson, and Owensboro. While Abe was an avid reader, and no doubt went to great pains to secure books, it is unreasonable to assume that he read every book within this area.

164

As exaggerated as this fifty-mile radius story, have been the reports of the size of the private libraries to which he is supposed to have had access. One person has declared that at least 750 volumes were available to him, and estimated that three of the prominent men of the region, John Pitcher, Daniel Grass, and Reuben Grigsby, Sr., each had a hundred books in their libraries.[14] No authentic clue as to the actual size of either Pitcher's or Grigsby's library has been found. Pitcher was a resident of Rockport, and Grigsby was a neighbor of the Lincolns. An inventory of Grass's estate listed "1 book case" valued at $1.00, and "books" valued at $10.00. Gideon Romine is credited with having a sizable library, but in the settlement of his estate, the appraisers found only one book, a dictionary, which sold for twelve and a half cents. Another Spencer County citizen, William Ray, said to have had an impressive library, left in his estate but "one parcel of books" valued at $2.00. The legendary library of Josiah Crawford actually contained but seven books at his death which brought at sale $2.45.[15]

A claim appears in the *History of Warrick, Spencer and Perry Counties* to the effect that "After 1820 Spencer County at Rockport boasted of a public library of several hundred volumes." The author also makes this observation: "The name of Lincoln does not appear once on the record as a borrower," and comments that undoubtedly Abraham was in Rockport several times a year with his father and that they "could easily have obtained the books if they had desired." However, the same history clearly reveals that no books were purchased for the said library by the county until April, 1831, when two hundred and fifty dollars was appropriated for the first acquisition. "So far as known this was the founding of the county library." The Lincolns by this time were in Illinois.[16]

While David Turnham admitted, "We had but few books at that time," and another of Abe's friends stated that "It was almost impossible to get books," Abe "read everything that he could lay his hands on and the[se] books he read and reread and studied thoroughly. [He] . . . was always reading, studying, thinking," "whenever Abe had a chance in the field while at work, or at the house, he would stop and read." "When he went out to work anywhere, he would carry his books with him and would always read while resting," "always sitting on his shoulder blades." [17]

Having enjoyed Weems's *Washington* so much, he must have been delighted when two more biographies by this author came his way, one of Benjamin Franklin and one of Francis Marion, the Revolutionary hero of the South. The style of these had the same grandiloquence as the Washington biography, as witness the following conversation between Marion and a British officer. Weems has Marion say, "I am in love and my sweetheart is Liberty. Be that heavenly nymph my companion, and these wilds and woods shall have charms beyond London and Paris in slavery. To have no proud monarch driving over me with his gilt coaches; nor his host of excisemen and tax-gatherers insulting and robbing me; but to be my own master, my own prince and sovereign, gloriously preserving my national dignity—and pursuing my true happiness; planting my vineyards, and eating their luscious fruits; and sowing my fields, and reaping the golden grain, and seeing millions of brothers equally free and happy as myself." After listening to Marion, the British officer reported to his superior, "I have seen an American general and his officers, without pay, and almost without clothes, living on roots and drinking water; and all for Liberty. What chance have we against such men?" [18]

Abe also studied two recitation books, *The Columbian Class Book* and *The Kentucky Preceptor*. The former, compiled by A. T. Lowe, and published in Worcester, Massachusetts, in 1824, consisted of "Geographical, historical and bibliographical extracts compiled from authentic sources." "Whoso readeth, let him understand."

166

The Kentucky Preceptor, containing a Number of Useful Lessons for Reading and Speaking, was a loan from Josiah Crawford.[19] Like Scott's *Lessons in Elocution,* it contained "a number of useful lessons for reading and speaking." Compiled "by a teacher," it was, primarily, a new edition of Caleb Bingham's *The American Preceptor,* published in Boston. The Crawford copy was the third Kentucky edition, published in Lexington, Kentucky, in 1812. The following well-known lines appear on the title page:

> Delightful task! to rear the tender thought,
> To teach the young idea how to shoot,
> To pour the fresh instruction o'er the mind,
> To breathe the enlivening spirit, and to fix
> The generous purpose in the glowing breast.

A statement in the Preface reveals the moralizing tone of the selections: "Tales of love, or romantic fiction, or anything which might tend to instil false notions into the minds of the children have not gained admission."

Next on Abe's list of books came Nathan Bailey's *A Universal Etymological English Dictionary,* the extended title of which gives a good idea of the wealth of information it contained: "Comprehending the derivations of the generality of words in the English tongue. . . . And also a brief and clear explication of all different words. . . . Together with a large collection and explication of words and phrases used in our ancient statutes, charters, writs. . . . Also a collection of our most common proverbs, with their explication. . . ."[20] It would be difficult to overemphasize the importance of such a volume to an ambitious boy who had so few sources of information open to him.

Words interested Abe, and from Bailey he could learn their origin and history. The Introduction points up the tremendous importance of words to mankind: "The Faculty of Speech, which makes so considerable a Difference between a Man and a Brute, is of excellent Use, as it renders Mankind conversable one with another, and as the various natural Endowments, Observations, Experiences, and Attainments of every individual Man, are hereby, with a wonderful Facility, mutually communicated. And we may add to this the Invention of Letters, by means of which we are not confined within the narrow Limits of our Acquaintance and Cotemporaries, but one Man may be acquainted with the Attainments of Multitudes of the wisest Men in Present and Ancient Times, either in his own or remote Countries. Words are those Channels, by which the Knowledge of Things is convey'd to our Understandings and therefore, upon a right Apprehension of them depends the Rectitude of our Notions." Abe also had at hand a copy of Barclay's *Dictionary*. It was said that he would sit "in the twilight and read a dictionary as long as he could see." [21]

It may have been while Abe was in Troy that he was introduced to a new field of reading. Since that town was an official post office newspapers were delivered there by the post rider and were available to anyone who could read them. Gentry's Store, located only one mile and a half from the Lincoln cabin, became a post office on June 15, 1825, with Gideon W. Romine as post master, and no doubt newspapers were received there. Sixteen papers were published in Indiana in the mid twenties.[22] How many of these reached Gentry's Store, of course we do not know. But certainly at least occasional copies of the Vincennes *Western Sun,* Corydon *Gazette,* New-Harmony *Gazette,* and the Terre Haute *Western Register,* the Indianapolis *Gazette* and *Journal,* came through, as well as papers from Louisville, Cincinnati, Lexington, and eastern cities. They might be days, weeks, or a month or more old, when they arrived, but their news would still be news to the people of Little Pigeon Creek.

Abe's stepmother thought that "newspapers were had in Indiana as early as 1824. . . . Abe," she said, "was a constant reader of them. I am sure of this for 1827–28–29–30." [23] John Romine, son of Gideon Romine, remembered lending a paper to Abe containing an editorial on Thomas Jefferson. When the boy returned it, Romine said, "it seemed he could repeat every word in that editorial and not only that but could recount all the news items as well as all about the advertisements."[24] This paper may have been published in July, 1826, during which time the papers were filled with articles and editorials occasioned by the celebration of the fiftieth anniversary of the signing of the Declaration of Independence and the almost simultaneous deaths of two of its Signers— Thomas Jefferson and John Adams—[25] on the Fourth of July, 1826.

Reading such items it was natural that it would not be long before Abe tried his own hand at such writing. The Lincoln neighbor, William Wood, related that "A. wrote a piece on national politics, saying that the American government was the best form of government in the world for an intelligent people; that it ought to be kept sacred and preserved forever. . . . that the Constitution should be sacred, the Union perpetuated, and the laws revered, and enforced. . . . This was in 1827 or '28." Wood showed the article to John Pitcher, a lawyer practicing in Posey County at the time. "I told him one of my neighbors' boys wrote it; he couldn't believe it till I told him Abe did write it . . . said to me this: 'The world can't beat it.' He begged for it. I gave it to him and it was published, can't say what paper it got into."[26]

The reading of newspapers which encouraged Abraham to try his hand at writing copy also contributed to the scrapbook he made. Since these papers were usually borrowed and had to be returned, "when he came across a passage that struck him he would write it down on boards if he had no paper and keep it there till he did get paper."[27] He had been writing short essays since his school days, when, as Nathaniel Grigsby stated, one day at school Abraham "came forward with an awkward bow and a deprecative smile to read an essay on the wickedness of being cruel to helpless animals."[28]

169

A scrapbook kept by John H. Huffman, son of the miller who lived several miles north of the Lincoln home, has been discovered. It is dated 1830. The book contains three sentences each written twenty times over, either as a practice in penmanship or as a punishment for the infringement of the school rules. Whatever the reason for writing, the morals of the sentences must have made a deep impression on the student:

"If you would be wise be studious; if rich be industrious."

"Goodness usually leads to universal esteem. Modest deportment ever commands admiration."

"Let prudence and moderation govern your actions." [29]

Joseph Gentry had a copybook, and inasmuch as "it was considered at that time that Abe was the best penman in the neighborhood. . . . I asked him to write some copies for me." Gentry continued that Abraham wrote several and recalled this one:

> Good boys who to their books apply
> Will all be great men by and by.[30]

William Wood also related that among the newspapers to which he subscribed, was a temperance paper. "Abe used to borrow it, take it home and read it, and talk it over with me. . . . One day Abe wrote a piece on temperance and brought it to my house. . . . I gave the article to one Aaron Farmer, a Baptist preacher; he read it, it struck him; he said he would like to send it to a temperance paper in Ohio, for publication; it was sent and published. I saw the printed piece, read it with pleasure over and over again." [31] A temperance wave was sweeping the country and frequent articles on the subject appeared in the press. In 1829 the *Western Sun* published nine sermons on the subject by Henry Ward Beecher. While Abe's article was in tune with the times, it was also a sincere expression of his own convictions. Wood said that "Abe once drank, as all people did here," but his stepmother declared that on no occasion did he use intoxicants, and three of the boys with whom he grew up said that he "never at any time so much as tasted intoxicating liquor of any sort, nor did he use tobacco, either chewing or smoking." [32]

According to David Turnham's story, Abe had at least one brush with the evil effects of intemperance in Indiana. "One night Abe and I were returning from Gentryville," so Turnham said, "we were passing along the road in the night, we saw something lying near us in a mud hole, and saw that it was a man. He was dead drunk. The night was cold—he was nearly frozen, we took him up—rather Abe did—carried him to Dennis Hanks', built up a fire and got him warm. I left, Abe staid all night." [33]

Henry Brooner related an interesting episode to J. T. Hobson. He recalled that when he was about twenty-five years old, which would be about 1829, "Abraham Lincoln came to my house, where I now live and left an article of agreement for me to keep. At that time one mile north of here, there was a distillery owned by John Dutton. He employed John Johnston, Lincoln's stepbrother, to run it that winter, and Lincoln left the article of agreement between the parties for me to keep." Apparently, on occasion, Abraham helped Johnston fulfill his contract with Dutton.[34]

While a temperance movement was waxing on the frontier, another type of social reform had been inaugurated at New Harmony, on the Wabash, fifty miles to the southwest of the Little Pigeon community. Robert Owen, the founder of the New Harmony experiment, was born in Wales in 1771. He acquired a large fortune as a British industrialist and gained public attention as a philanthropist and social theorist. Desiring to continue his utopian experiments on a larger scale he came to America in 1824 and purchased the Rappite settlement on the Wabash and called it New Harmony. In his introductory address in 1825 Owen stated: "I am come to this country to introduce an entire new state of society; to change it from the ignorant, selfish system to an enlightened social system, which shall unite all interests into one, and remove all cause for contest between individuals." [35]

There is no reliable evidence that Abe was well-informed about or in any degree influenced by the ideas of the social reformers in the new utopia. Insofar as Owen's beliefs were known in the Little Pigeon community it may be assumed logically that they would have been rejected. A communal society, religious infidelity, and radical theories of marriage and education would have found scant favor with the individualistic, devout, and conservative pioneers who predominated in southern Indiana at the time. Nor would the British origins of the New Harmony leader have commended the experiment to the settlers of Indiana who treasured memories of two wars with England.[36]

CHAPTER XIV

19

Adventure

1828

ON January 20, 1828, Sarah Lincoln Grigsby, in her twenty-first year, died in childbirth. She and Aaron had been married but a year and a half. They had built a new cabin on their own tract of land and had, as a niece of Aaron's observed, "a very bright future before them for the people of that day, and Sallie Grigsby was much thought of and loved by all her husband's people." [1]

"I remember the night she died," a neighbor recalled years later. "My mother was there at the time. She had a strong voice, and I heard her calling father. . . . He went after a doctor, but it was too late. They let her lay too long." [2] On the night Sarah passed away Abe was at the Reuben Grigsby, Sr.'s house. He "was out in our little smoke house at our house doing a little carpenter work," one of the family said, "when Aaron, Sarah's husband, came running up from his house a quarter of a mile away and said that Sarah had just died. We went out and told Abe. I never will forget that scene. He sat down in the door of the smoke house and buried his face in his hands. The tears slowly trickled from between his bony fingers and his gaunt frame shook with sobs. We turned away." [3] "This was a hard blow to Abe, who always thought her death was due to neglect," one of his friends said. "From then on he was alone in the world, you might say." [4]

Unfortunately Dr. Edmund Moore who had practiced medicine at Rockport for several years and had been "frequently called upon to attend the Lincoln family" had moved to Illinois in 1827.[5] There was a Dr. John Allen practicing at Troy at this time, who may have been the doctor summoned for Sarah, but too late to save her.[6]

On December 10, 1825, the Little Pigeon Creek Baptist Church had ordered three of its members, Reuben Grigsby, William Barker, and Noah Gordon, "to Lay of[f] the burying ground."[7] It was located on land next to the meetinghouse belonging to Gordon. Sarah had joined the church in April, 1826,[8] four months before her marriage, and she, with her stillborn baby in her arms, was one of the first to be buried in the new cemetery.[9] A slab of sandstone inscribed with her initials marked her grave.[10] Abe and his father no doubt would have liked to have had Sarah's grave next to her mother's, but it was probably her husband's wish that she be buried in the churchyard.[11]

Sarah's death had a profound effect on Abraham. He was given to periods of depression and despondency, "was witty and sad and thoughtful by turns."[12] He had a strong tendency toward pensiveness and introspection, probably inherited from his mother.[13] Something happened to him when he was eight years old when he shot the handsome wild turkey and watched it drop to the ground. He never killed for sport thereafter. When he was nine years old his mother whom he loved more than anyone else in the world died, and her grave on the little hill near the cabin kept the painful incidents of her death constantly on his mind. When he was fifteen, he had witnessed the awful mental collapse of his schoolmate, Matthew Gentry, a demonstration of the "human form with reason fled," "the burning eyeballs . . . maniac laughter," the victim of the "pangs that killed the mind," who "begged, and swore, and wept and prayed." During the months that followed, after Matthew had become less distracted, Abraham would

174

approach the Gentry home to listen to his mournful song and seemed to derive some comfort from the plaintive sound. Even in the early morning, before the other members of his household were awake, Abe would steal out to "drink its strains," when even the "trees with the spell seemed sorrowing angles."[14]

Then four years later came the tragedy of the death of Sarah, his only sister who had played with him, studied with him, and looked after him following their mother's death. These harsh experiences left lasting marks deep within his mind and spirit, and he endured long periods of melancholic brooding and depression. At the same time these tragedies made him deeply sympathetic with others in grief.[15]

Toward the end of the year Abe had an opportunity to get away from these scenes of sadness and he seized it with enthusiasm. James Gentry, owner of Gentry's Store, was sending a flatboat down river to New Orleans and he asked Abe to help man it. Gentry's son Allen was in charge of the boat. Abe was to receive eight dollars a month plus his passage back by steamboat.[16] Allen Gentry was a year or two older than Abraham, and had been to New Orleans once before with his father, who had made the trip several times.[17] Allen had moved to Rockport in 1826, apparently to facilitate the family's flatboating operations, occupying a cabin on land he acquired from his father that year.[18]

It was the most exciting and important experience of Abe's Indiana years. When he started, he was nineteen years old, but he probably did not get back until after his twentieth birthday. His father had made at least one trip to the strange and exotic city at the mouth of the Mississippi, and the tales he had told of his journey made Abe eager to see for himself. While working on the Ohio he had observed steamboats going down and coming back from New Orleans and talked with their passengers and crews, as well as with the men who manned the hundreds of flatboats that passed on their way

175

down river. Now he was going himself. He plied his father with questions about the problems and pitfalls of operating a flatboat, about the courses of the Ohio and the Mississippi, and about the great city he would see. Thomas reviewed the high points of his own experience, not forgetting to remind his son that in 1806 there had been no steamboats to bring the flatboat crews upstream. They had had to walk or ride horseback to get back to their homes.[19]

Much of the business in the local stores in the pioneer days was by barter. This left the storekeeper with a considerable amount of goods on hand—generally farm produce—which he was able to dispose of advantageously in New Orleans and at stops on the way down. Flatboats were the means used to convey these goods to market. Apparently James Gentry was a successful trader. On one occasion being asked what per cent he was making on the sale of his goods, he replied, "God bless your soul. I don't know anything about your per cent., but I know when I buy an article in Louisville for a dollar, and sell it in Gentryville for two dollars, I double my money every time."[20]

While Abe was preparing for the trip, he lived at the home of Alfred Grass, son of Daniel Grass, Rockport's first citizen during its early history. Even during these busy days Abe would use every free moment for reading. One of the family recalled that he "would sit in the evening near the table with the rest of the family until the tallow dip had burned out; then he would lie down on his back with his head toward the open fire place, so as to get the light upon the pages of the book, and there he would often read until after midnight." ". . . he would bake the top of his head or wear himself out for want of rest, but he was always up in the morning ready for work."[21]

Rockport, the county seat of Spencer County, occupied a picturesque location on top of some impressive limestone cliffs. It was first called Hanging Rock, then Mt. Duvall, and

176

finally Rock Port or Rockport. A post office was established there on May 9, 1825, which would mean that newspapers and magazines would be available. In 1828 its population was about one hundred.

Very fortunately there is a document in the Spencer County courthouse which describes a boat which must have been very much like the one that Allen and Abraham took down river.[22] The written contract was entered into on August 21, 1833, by William Jones, with John E. Cotton and James Wakefield for the construction of a flatboat for the sum of $97.50. The boat was to be delivered not later than December 1 of that year. A penalty for failure to comply with the agreement would cause a forfeit of "double the amount of the cost of the said boat," to be assessed against the builders. Jones was a former clerk employed by Gentry who apparently purchased the Gentry store and needed a boat similar to the 1828 craft.

The specifications of the contract called for a flatboat "65 feet long the gunwales to be of good poplar 2 feet in width and nine inches thick . . . the said boat to be 18 ft. wide the bow of said boat to be very strong with a good solid piece of timber to strengthen the bow. . . . the bottom plank to be of gum or poplar 2 inches thick substantially put on . . . the cabin to be of gum or oak 1½ inches thick 7 inches wide the studding to be three feet apart . . . the roof to be first-rate and not to leak . . . the boat is to be on each side 4½ feet high in the middle . . . a first-rate streamer [extended rudder] and two first-rate sweeps."[23]

In the construction of a flatboat the hull was built bottom-side up near the water's edge. For launching, rollers were placed under the gunwales. Midway on one of the gunwales a rope was attached, then thrown over a stout limb of a tree extending over the water. Oxen were hitched to the end of the rope and driven forward so that the boat was turned over in the water right side up ready for further construction. If windlasses and levers were available, they may have been used instead of oxen. The above-water structure was then completed and a coil of rope was obtained for the check post.[24]

After the crops had been harvested and produce was ready for shipping, Allen and Abraham began to build their boat. In order to be done by December they would have had to start in October. If they chose a name for their craft, there is no record of it,[25] nor do we know exactly what cargo they carried, nor its weight. The Vincennes *Western Sun* of June 17, 1826, noted that during that spring twenty-four flatboats, two from Vigo County and twenty-two from Knox County, bound for New Orleans, carried the following total amount of produce: 57,250 bushels of corn; 20,550 lbs. bulk pork; 2,273 bacon hams; 1,501 barrels pork; 280 barrels corn meal; 41 live cattle; 780 chickens; 160 bushels oats; 5,013 lbs. bees wax; 3 barrels beans; and 410 venison hams. Abe and Allen probably loaded their boat with similar produce. There is a tradition that Abe and his father built a wagon for James Gentry.[26] If so, it may have been used in moving goods to the flatboat. John Romine recalled hauling bacon to the landing at Rockport to be loaded.[27]

After the boat was ready, its departure was delayed because Allen refused to leave until after the birth of his son which occurred on December 18. About the time that Allen Gentry settled in Rockport, the Roby family—Abraham Roby, his wife Polly, and their two daughters, Ann and Elizabeth, moved to the county seat from the Little Pigeon Creek community. Allen and Ann were married on March 19, 1828.[28] One evening before the eagerly awaited baby was born, Abe was sitting with Ann and Allen on the flatboat, talking. Ann remembered, "I said to Abe that the sun was going down. He said to me, 'that's not so; it don't really go down; it seems so. The earth turns from west to east and the revolution of the earth carries us under; we do the sinking, as you call it. The sun, as to us, is comparatively still; the sun's sinking is only an appearance.' I replied, 'Abe, what a fool you are!' I know now

178

Ohio and Mississippi River steamboats

that I was the fool, not Lincoln. I am now thoroughly satisfied that he knew the general laws of astronomy and the movements of the heavenly bodies. He was better read then than the world knows or is likely to know exactly. No man could have talked to me as he did that night unless he had known something of geography as well as astronomy. . . ." [29] It will be recalled that in Murray's *English Reader* Abe had read Addison's essay on "The Planetary and Terrestrial World Comparatively Considered," and newspapers of that day frequently carried scientific articles.

Two weeks after the baby, called James after his paternal grandfather, was born, the flatboat embarked. This would have been around the end of the month.[30] The boys prepared their meals and took turns sleeping in the cabin. During the day Abe was assigned to the bow and took care of the sweeps or extended oars, while Allen attended the streamer. They had to man their posts almost constantly when the boat was in progress.[31]

There are available many diaries written by early travelers going up and down the Ohio and Mississippi. Among them is one kept by Colonel John Baillie, an Englishman and member of Parliament, who made the downriver journey just before Abraham and Allen. Colonel Baillie started his river trip at Wheeling, and upon reaching Louisville noted, "The number of steamboats here is almost incredible. I understood there were upwards of 500 on the Mississippi and Ohio alone." He continued, "Went on board several that were lying below us. The largest called the *Washington* is built like a three storied house, and with every accommodation that could be found in a good hotel." But about the flatboat he was not so enthusiastic, saying that it was "built something like an immense coffin. . . ." [32]

Colonel Baillie saw much that Allen and Abraham were to see as he continued down river from the cliffs at Rockport, though the change in season made the landscape that the boys saw less attractive. Baillie commented that the forests were "still clothed in all the luxuriance of their foliage, or rather in all the beauty of their autumnal tints. . . ."[33]

The Colonel noted passing the Tennessee River. Here he observed, "We saw several flocks of wild turkeys on the shore; one of our party killed a bird from the boat with his rifle. Most of the Americans in this part of the country are excellent shots." On November 19 his boat reached the Mississippi. "You soon discover the difference in the character of the 2 rivers," he said, "the Ohio moving slow and placid, whilst the Mississippi sweeps along with a fierce and tempestuous current. . . ."[34]

The loneliness of the landscape impressed him: ". . . during the whole day we had no view save the interminable forest, and dull ragged banks on both sides. Subject as this part of the country is to yearly inundation, very few settlements have yet been attempted and these generally on high bluffs. . . . We passed only one today, where I observed something like the appearance of a village. . . ."[35]

On the 22d he wrote that during the past week the passengers had "lived almost entirely on the wild Turkeys which are excessively cheap in this country. I am quite decided that they are the finest flavored birds I ever tasted." River water was all that was available for drinking. "They say it possesses medicinal qualities being impregnated with salt. I cannot however say I discovered this merit. . . ."[36]

At one point when the boat stopped to take on wood he went ashore where he was impressed by the great cottonwood and sugar trees: "the largest trees I ever beheld in England were nothing to them."[37]

On the 24th the boat stopped briefly at Natchez, "a place of some trade, with a population of 5,000. . . ." On the 25th, below Natchez, Baillie observed that "the forests are now covered everywhere with Spanish moss, which attached itself to the trees, but particularly to the Cypress . . . you see it hanging

180

from all parts of the trees in dark and somber festoons, adding a funereal aspect to the dark and dreary view: quite in character however with the deadly malignity of the climate." [38]

In the afternoon Baton Rouge, 150 miles above New Orleans, was reached. Here the sugar plantations commenced and the levees to hold back the river. Then came the exotic city itself. New Orleans "is built very like an old French provincial town: the same narrow streets, old fashioned houses, and lamps suspended by a chain across the road. Many of the houses are however picturesque, with their large projecting roofs and painted sides and windows, quite a contrast to the brick and mortar towns we have lately seen. . . . The population including blacks is upwards of 40,000, the greater part of which are still French, or speak only that language. The whole place has quite the air of a French town. I cannot conceive of a more unhealthy, deadly situation than New Orleans during the last of summer. Bogs, swamps, morasses, in every direction, which they do not attempt to drain. Mosquitoes are of course abundant, even now they swarm in mirriads as bad as in the worst places in the West Indies." [39]

"There are 2 Catholic churches and one small Presbyterian church for the whole population. . . . I should suppose that New Orleans like the small town of Natchez . . . is not famous for its morality or religious feeling. Those who come here on account of trade, think only of making money as fast as they can, and trouble themselves very little about other matters." [40]

"There is a public ball here 2 or 3 times a week, which includes all the colored ladies of the place known by the name of quadroons. Many I have seen are really very beautiful girls; their blood is a mixture of Indian, African, and French. . . . I see many of the Indians in town every day." [41]

"I observed in walking through the streets several large rooms fitted out as slave markets, and generally filled with un-

181

happy blacks, dressed up for the occasion. The men and women are ranged on opposite sides of the apartment, where they may traffic for human beings with the same indifference as purchasing a horse. New Orleans I conclude is a good market for this kind of human stock. . . ."[42]

The New Orleans newspapers of that day reveal the active trading in the slave markets. The New Orleans *Argus* for December 27, 1828, advertised "Virginia and North Carolina slaves for sale. 29 young Virginia slaves of both sexes to be sold cheap for cash. 43 Virginia slaves, women, men, girls, and boys, may be bartered for sugar or to be sold on a liberal credit say for one or two years on undoubted paper. 24 North Carolina slaves of both sexes to be sold cheap for cash or on a short credit. North Carolina slaves being 5 large robust men and four women and girls in which a bargain will be offered. John Clay, 44 Gravier St."

Earlier in the month these announcements appeared in the *Argus:* "Just arrived in the ship Lafayette from Baltimore 180 negroes, about 100 likely young men; a cooper, a carpenter, a blacksmith and a butcher. May be seen at 113 Charles St.," and "37 slaves both sexes for sale; 2 coopers, one shoemaker, one tanner, 2 hands at whipsaw. On board schooner Transport at the Levee."[43]

On December 20, 1831, Simon Cameron, writing from New Orleans to Dr. Sheldon Potter of Philadelphia, gave his reaction to the city:[44]

"I like the city exceedingly, the people are kind and hospitable and the place itself will some day be one of the greatest in the Union. The shipping now along the wharves far exceeds that of Philadelphia. Vessels are now waiting in port for cotton and sugar, the latter is scarce and of course rising in price in consequence of the early rains and frost injury to the cane.

"Everybody makes money here. Raw materials are all cheap and labor of every kind dear. The whole western world must come here and they do come and leave their money which is generally picked up by Yankees but they are clever Yankees.

"Next Saturday I shall go to a masquerade if I have time. On Sunday perhaps to the French Theatre. All matter of pleasure are attended to on Sunday and many of the stores are open on that day."

In contrast to Colonel Baillie, Cameron was favorably inclined toward the climate and location of New Orleans: "I think this as healthy as any place along the Susquehanna. In the winter, it is healthy as any place in the world. I never was more healthy in my life."

The American and Orleans theaters were both open. At the auction store of Messrs. George W. Boyd & Company an Egyptian mummy with its sarcophagus upwards of three thousand years old was on exhibition, and it was announced that the patrons would be waited on by the American Dwarf.

Such were the beautiful, strange, and stimulating sights, sounds, and even smells that met Abe and Allen, two boys from the Indiana wilderness, as they followed Colonel Baillie down river only a few weeks later. The distance from Rockport to New Orleans by water was 1,222 miles. Unfortunately, neither of them kept a diary showing what they saw and how they reacted to it. But they had their eyes and ears open. They were used to the interminable forests and lonely stretches showing no sign of human habitation that had so impressed the Colonel. On the other hand Natchez was probably the biggest town Abe had seen up to that day. Allen having been down the year before served as guide as they explored its streets. They continued down past the moss-festooned forests of the Lower Mississippi. The funereal atmosphere noted by Baillie had its effect on Abe who still suffered periods of the sadness and loneliness that had almost overpowered him when his sister died. But the constant demands of his navigation job kept him from giving way to depression.

183

As soon as the boys entered the Mississippi, they began trading their cargo for cotton, tobacco, and sugar. All went peacefully for them until just below Baton Rouge. Here were the prosperous sugar plantations noted by Colonel Baillie, extending down to the river. The story is that "a part of the cargo had been selected with special reference to the wants of the sugar plantations and the young adventurers were instructed to linger upon the sugar coast for the purpose of disposing of it. On one occasion they tied up their boat for the night near a plantation at which they had been trading during the afternoon. The negroes observing that the boat was in charge of but two persons, seven of them formed a plan to rob it during the night. Their intention evidently was to murder the young men, rob the boat of whatever money there might be on it, carry off such articles as they could secret in their cabins then by sinking the boat destroy all traces of their guilt. . . . They had not, however, properly estimated the courage and prowess of the two young men in charge. The latter, being on their guard gave the would-be robbers and assassins a warm reception and not withstanding the disparity in numbers, after a severe struggle, in which both Lincoln and his companion were considerably hurt, the former were driven from the boat. At the close of the fight, the young navigators lost no time in getting their boat under way." [45]

This near tragedy is supposed to have taken place at the plantation of Madame Duchesne. Abraham carried a scar as a souvenir of this battle, one story claiming it was over his right eye and another that it was over his right ear.[46]

When the boys reached New Orleans, they disposed of the remainder of their cargo, and then sold their boat since it was of no more use to them. Their job done, they had a few days to see the sights. Perhaps the docks interested them as much as anything, with the great variety of vessels from the East Coast cities and European ports. The *New Orleans Price*

Current and Commercial Intelligencer[47] noted that on one day in 1828 there were docked in the harbor 66 ships, 85 brigs, 30 schooners, 6 sloops, and 20 steamboats, destined for such far away ports as Hamburg, Gibralter, Aberdeen, Bremen, Nantz, Havana, Cowes, Compeche, Vera Cruz, and Rio Grande, and American ports of Philadelphia, New York, Bristol, Baltimore, Providence, Portland, and Pensacola.

Leaving the docks the boys walked the streets, gazing at the handsome buildings and the people who were so different from their Indiana neighbors. Who did they talk to? Did they venture into a theater? Did they sample some of the strange and unusual foods? Allen recalled that, "We stood and watched the slaves sold in New Orleans and Abraham was very angry. . . ."[48]

Possibly Abe noted the sign printed over the large store of Lincoln and Green, at 11 Camp Street, seeing for the first time how his name would look in big letters. Did the boys indulge in a little shopping? Since Allen had so recently become a father, he may have sought out some of the toys left over from Christmas that had been advertised early in December in the papers: "250 dozen of assorted animals, hobby horses, musical friars, carriages, wagons, and 90 dozen jumping frogs."[49]

But they could not linger too long. Allen had to return to his family responsibilities and they both had to get back to Rockport to settle with their employer. All that remained for them to do was to select a boat to take them back up river. It was probably Abe's first trip on board a steamer, certainly his first journey of any distance.

A logbook of a steamer coming down the Ohio and Mississippi noted that on December 1, 1828, it had passed the following boats also going down: the *DeWitt Clinton, Car of Commerce, Isabella, Natchez,* and the *Attakapas* with flatboats in tow. It had met the following going up river: the *Ontario, Patriot, Maryland, Oregon, Essex, Lady Washing-*

ton, Montezuma, Helen McGregor, Bolivar, and the *Opelousas.*[50] The boys had probably seen these and many more on their trip down. The *Amazon, Atlanta, Belle Creole, Belvidere, Calidonia, Cincinnati, Crusader, Cumberland, Daniel Boone, Diana, Feliciana, General Marion, General Wayne, Huntress, Lady of the Lake, New York, Paul Jones, Stranger, Triton,* and the *William Tell* were among the many others that regularly were plying up and down the rivers at this period.[51]

On May 24, 1828 the Vincennes *Western Sun* carried this notice which gives some idea of the speed and service offered by the steamboats: "The steam boat Amazon, capt. Paul, arrived at Louisville on the 25th ult. from New Orleans, in nine days from port to port, with a cargo of three hundred and eighty four tons, eighty three cabin and four hundred and thirty one deck passengers. The Amazon made the trip from Louisville to New Orleans and back, in less than three weeks— Let the eastern steam boats beat this, in speed, quantity of cargo, or in number of passengers." The *Amazon,* three hundred tons, had been launched at Cincinnati in 1826. She was to be lost by sinking in 1831.[52]

Abe and Allen came back on board one of these craft and no doubt enjoyed every aspect of the experience. If their boat engaged in any one of the frequent races that the river steamers participated in, they may have helped feed wood for the boilers. Just how long they were gone from home we do not know. They lost some time trading on the way down, but their experience at Madame Duchesne's may have curtailed their stops at other sugar plantations. They were probably gone two months—eight weeks that were full of new experiences and new sights that added up to a very important part of Abe's education.[53]

CHAPTER XV

20

Awareness

1829

ABRAHAM MAY HAVE CELEBRATED his twentieth birthday in New Orleans, but he was back home by the first of March and assisted in putting in the crops. It must have been a trivial task to turn the soil slowly, patiently drop the seed, and tediously cultivate the slow-growing vegetation. His mind was on the fascinating river but a few miles away over which people of all types and circumstances were moving on rafts and floating palaces; also, where wages were paid for exciting occupations. Abraham had already been making inquiries about the possibility of getting a job on the river and William Wood, a neighbor, stated that on behalf of Abe he had seen "merchants in Rockport and mentioned the subject to them. In 1829 this was."

Apparently Abe had performed his tasks on the flatboat competently and after his return he may have been employed in the store at intervals by Gentry. Goods had been sold originally by James Gentry at his home, but about 1826 some business arrangement was made with Gideon W. Romine. A storehouse was used at the crossroads about one-half mile west of the Gentry home. This same year, on June 15, a post office called Gentry's Store was established at the new location, and Romine was appointed post master.[1] On October 20, 1828, Gentry sold Romine "a tract of land ten rods in length and eight rods in width situated where the state road leading from Rockport to Bloomington, intersects the state road from Corydon to Boonville." The beginning point of the tract survey is cited as "the northwest corner of the said G. W. Romine's storehouse."[2] The Gentry and Romine businesses probably became a family enterprise, because James Gentry's daughter Agnes married Benjamin Romine on January 12, 1825, and another daughter, Hannah, married John Romine on April 5, 1829.[3]

Just how William Jones fits into the Gentry-Romine trading picture is not very clear, although he is said to have clerked for them. The post office at Gentry's Store was discontinued October 29, 1829, and it was not until March 31, 1831, that it was re-established with Jones as postmaster.[4] By this time the Lincolns had been gone a full year. Late in that same year, 1831, Jones purchased from William Whittinghill for the sum of $7.50 "a parcel of land 210 feet in front running back 225 feet," at this same crossroads where the Gentry-Romine store was located.[5] It has already been mentioned that Jones contracted for the construction of a flatboat in 1833 at Rockport.

A grandson of Jones has stated that his grandfather was born "at or near Charlesville, North Carolina, prior to 1800. He came to Terre Haute, Indiana, and later went to Louisville, Kentucky, where he married. He then came to Spencer county and settled on Section 2, Township 5, Range 6. . . ." The grandson added that he had been told his grandfather "gave Lincoln his first job and later hired him as clerk in the store for about two years."[6] Certainly Jones was not Abe's first employer, and if Abe worked for him at all, it could not have been for as long a period as two years. Jones apparently did not go into business for himself until after the Lincolns left Indiana.

Of more interest and importance than a possible business relationship between Jones and Abraham is the influence

188

Jones is alleged to have asserted over the youth politically. Nathaniel Grigsby told Herndon that "Jones was Lincoln's guide and teacher in politics." [7] Jones may have supplemented Abe's knowledge about the Whigs and their leader Henry Clay, but to conclude from this statement that Abe received his earliest political impressions from Jones is misleading. Perhaps his chief contribution was to supply Abe with newspapers to read.

In attempting to recreate Abraham's political background, we have one solid and indisputable fact with which to start: "he was always a Whig." [8] This statement is supplemented by John Hanks who went one step further when he affirmed: "I can say that Abe was never a Democrat, he was always a Whig; so was his father before him." [9]

As noted earlier, the great majority of the early immigrants to Indiana were from Kentucky, and they fall into two categories. There were those who had originated in the slave states farther south and had taken up a temporary residence on the Kentucky side of the Ohio. These formed a political element distinct from the Virginia Revolutionary soldiers who had settled in Kentucky before the turn of the century. Those from the Carolinas and Tennessee were usually followers of Jackson, while the fact that Clay had come from Virginia and settled in Kentucky gave him what might be called a "provincial" support by the earlier settlers in that state.

More important than any secondary influence on Abe's politics, such as may have been exerted by Jones, was the primary contribution to his thinking that he derived from the atmosphere of the Lincoln home. To this little attention thus far has been paid. Politically men tend to follow in the footsteps of their fathers. It has been noted that Thomas Lincoln was a Whig.

Conversation in the Lincoln family of an evening was about politics.[10] The father had been an ardent member of an antislavery church in Kentucky, which would have definite influence on his political viewpoint. Furthermore, he belonged to that class of pioneers, of whom his father was one, whose forebears had settled in Kentucky following the Revolution. Their outstanding political spokesman was Henry Clay, the advocate of internal improvements, high protective tariffs, and a national bank. An uncle of Thomas Lincoln, for whom he was named, lived in Lexington, Clay's home. In Indiana, Thomas Lincoln was surrounded by neighbors who had likewise migrated from Kentucky and were followers of Clay as were the majority of the voters of Carter Township.[11]

Abraham's stepmother also came from a home where politics was evidently a frequent subject of conversation. Her father, Christopher Bush, was a sheriff of Hardin County, Kentucky, for several years and his sons likewise filled public office. One of his sons-in-law, Ichabod Radley, served as a deputy sheriff, and Thomas Lincoln was appointed to a patrol of which Christopher Bush, Jr., was captain. It will be recalled that Sally Bush Lincoln's first husband had been jailor in Hardin County. Therefore, it is not strange that the Lincoln family talked politics. Abraham's stepmother once told him that he "ought to go into politics, because when he got to argyin' the other feller'd purty soon say he had enough."[12]

The first Presidential campaign and election which Abraham could have observed with any intelligent interest was that of 1824. He was fifteen years old at the time. This was a struggle between great leaders rather than a contest of political parties. There were four candidates, John Quincy Adams, Henry Clay, William H. Crawford, and Andrew Jackson. There were no definable parties; there were Jacksonians, anti-Jacksonians, Clay men, Adams men, etc. As early as February 22, 1823, the Vincennes *Western Sun* reported: "On Friday last upwards of one hundred citizens of this borough and vicinity met [at Vincennes] . . . for purpose of ascertaining public sentiment in this part of the state, in the choice of a president of the United States, to succeed the illustrious patriot, and distinguished statesman, James Monroe—The votes taken, were 58 for Clay, and 56 for John Quincy Adams— no other candidate was voted for."

During the campaign the Vincennes *Western Sun* was full of political items. Of special interest to the Lincoln family would have been a series of articles reprinted from the Cincinnati *Gazette,* signed "Seventy-Six," showing why Clay should be elected over the other candidates.[13] Particular attention was paid to his opposition to slavery and advocacy of gradual emancipation. Abe must have seen some if not all the issues of this paper, and, at the impressionable age of fifteen began to form certain opinions in respect to the conduct of public affairs which were to become basic elements in his theory of government.

Four years later, at nineteen, Abe naturally was more interested in the Presidential contest. By this time the Jackson-Calhoun faction and the Adams-Clay faction were developing into the Democratic party and the Whig party. The newspapers were full of political articles, addresses, and reports of conventions and rallies. The weekly *Western Sun,* having devoted a good portion of two of its four January issues to printing the President's message to Congress, devoted several columns of two February issues to an address of Henry Clay to the Public, dated December, 1827. In his concluding statement he said, ". . . my anxious hopes will continue for the success of the great cause of human liberty."[14] The *Western Sun,* however, was a pro-Jackson paper and during June, July, August, and September, published a series of letters in support of Jackson signed by the pseudonym "Jefferson." Indiana gave her five electoral votes to Jackson rather than Adams, which must have been a disappointment to Abe.

One local politician who probably had a real influence on Abe in the matter of speechmaking was Ratliff Boon, a Democrat. He had been born in Franklin County, North Carolina (his birthplace is sometimes given as Georgia) on January 18,

1781. Boon came to Warrick County, Indiana, in 1809, settling about twelve miles from the site of the Lincoln cabin. He was a member of the Indiana House of Representatives when the Lincolns arrived, two years later he was elected to the state Senate, and in 1820 elected lieutenant governor on the ticket with Jonathan Jennings. He succeeded to the Governorship in 1822, when Jennings resigned to enter Congress. He was re-elected lieutenant governor, then in 1824 elected to Congress. He was defeated in his bid for re-election in 1826, but was successful in 1828.[15] Such a political record must have made an impression on Abe. Boon was an intensive personal campaigner. The story goes that while his opponent was trying to talk a voter—say a blacksmith—into supporting him, Boon would be at the forge finishing some job which the smith had under way. Abe must have heard Boon speak often. A letter to the citizens of Indiana written during his campaign for lieutenant governor closed with these words:

"In presenting myself to you, Gentlemen, as a candidate for the office in question, I have nothing to claim through my ancestors, nor from former services; but alone depend on what may be thought I justly merit, and the disposition of those who have the right to determine, who shall be jointly charged with the administration of the state government. . . . Should my wishes meet the approbation of the majority of my countrymen, they will confer on me a lasting obligation, for which, I here pledge myself to use every exertion in my power to promote the interest of the state, and the happiness of its citizens."[16]

Gentry's store served four townships that cornered there. One of these was named Jackson, after "Old Hickory," another Clay. Interestingly, the former was Democratic, and Clay was Whig. These township names alone suggest that the crossroads store was a political forum. Here Abe probably heard his first political discussions and first expounded his own opinions, illustrating his points from his growing fund of stories.

Perhaps even more popular as a gathering place for settling the political issues of the day was the blacksmith shop. Just who was the blacksmith in the community has not been determined. According to one source, the first smith in Carter Township was John Morris.[17] William Davis was the one identified as "Abe's particular friend" by the editor of a Spencer County newspaper, although at a later date he was uncertain about this.[18] Dennis Hanks's statement that John Baldwin was the name of the famous story-telling blacksmith has been generally accepted.[19] It has even been suggested that from him more than anyone else Lincoln got his early supply of stories.[20] No biographical information on him has been found.

No matter how proficient a raconteur the legendary blacksmith may have been, it was not from him but from his own father that Abe got his sense of humor and his story-telling proclivities. One who lived in the Lincoln home declared, "From his father Lincoln inherited his conversational habit and love of anecdote. Thomas Lincoln was brilliant as a storebox whittler and leader of grocery-story dialogue. His chief earthly pleasure was to crack jokes and tell stories in a group of chums who paid homage to his wit by giving him the closest attention and the loudest applause."[21]

Dennis Hanks stated, "Thomas Lincoln . . . could beat his son telling a story, cracking a joke."[22] Another said, "From his father came that knack of story telling."[23] Possibly, years later, when the old people of Spencer County were recalling some of the humorous stories Abraham had told, they should have credited them jointly to Thomas Lincoln and son.[24]

As Abe grew older the contest of wits that developed between him and his father must have been lively. The following story and pun is typical of the kind that delighted both Thomas and Abe. A calf owned by Thomas Lincoln was mired in a swamp and drowned. Abe was told by his father to take the skin down to Hammond's tannery near Grandview and

193

have it properly treated. Abe told the keeper that "his father wanted his hide tanned." [25]

Here is a story which illustrates how Thomas was always ready with a piquant retort: One day Sally Lincoln said to her husband: "You have never yet told me whom you like best, your first wife or me." Thomas replied, "Oh, now, Sally, that reminds me of old John Hardin down in Kentucky who had a fine-looking pair of horses, and a neighbor coming in one day and looking at them said, 'John, which horse do you like the best?' John said, 'I can't tell; one of them kicks and the other bites and I don't know which is wust.' " [26]

It must have been about this time, when some of Sally Lincoln's grandchildren were beginning to walk, that Abe played a practical joke on his stepmother. She had just had the interior of the cabin newly whitewashed. Abe saw one of the youngsters playing in the mud in the yard, and picking it up and holding it with its feet free, "walked it" up one side of the cabin, across the ceiling and down the opposite side, leaving little footprints on the fresh white surface. Sally observing this phenomenon had to laugh with the others. Abe good-humoredly repaired the damage with new whitewash, feeling the reaction to the joke was well worth the effort.[27]

There is a book of humor which Abe is said to have read during his Indiana's days, and it is submitted here on the be-lated testimony of one of his boyhood associates. If read, it does not seem to have become a source for his own stories. Nathaniel Grigsby when interviewed by Herndon on September 12, 1865, stated, "I cannot remember of his [Abraham's] reading any book or books except Æsop's Fables, The Bible, Robinson Crusoe." But when Grigsby was questioned by William Fortune in 1881, fifteen years later and fifty-one years after the Lincolns left Indiana, Grigsby recalled that there was a book called "The King's Jester" and "Lincoln would read it to us out in the woods on Sundays."

Mr. Fortune put forth considerable effort to identify the

194

HON: HENRY CLAY

Engraved for the Analectic Magazine

book, and finally concluded that it was actually entitled *Quin's Jests,*[28] not "The King's Jester" as reported by Grigsby. The book, published in London by S. Bladon in 1776, is a compilation of jests running to 104 pages. In the preface Bladon wrote: "Many of his [Quin's] jokes and impromptus were indelicate and indecent. These the editor thought the duty he owed the public, compelled him to suppress, though they might have swelled his work to a much greater size and, of course increased his profit. The following sheets then contain nothing but what may be called the quintessence and refinement of Mr. Quin's wit and humors divested of every gross and indecent idea that might offend the chastest and most delicate ear and in this point of light, the editor thinks this performance may be no invaluable acquisition to the polite and even the learned."

After reading through the text it appears to the author that the editor put down his blue pencil too soon. The continued use of "G—," as the editor printed it, and the recurrence of certain vulgarisms still remain to offend "the most delicate ear." It does not seem that the stories couched in the language of the stage and referring to the English playwrights, actors, and other celebrities, would be of interest to pioneer youths who knew nothing of the English theater or society.

Abraham's humor on one occasion was said to have been directed to a facetious satire entitled "The Chronicles of Reuben." The Biblical account in the fifth chapter of I Chronicles which begins: "Now the sons of Reuben the first born of Israel . . . ," may have suggested this composition which is patterned after the literary style of these two Old Testament books. The original copy is not extant and the only version that we have was written from memory thirty-five years after the incident which it concerned. The traditional first line states: "Now there was a man whose name was Reuben, and the same was very great in substance; in horses and cattle and swine, and a very great household. . . ."[29]

Two brothers, sons of Reuben Grigsby, were married on the same day, April 16, 1829. Reuben, Jr., and Elizabeth Ray were married in Spencer County and Charles and Matilda Hawkins in Dubois County.[30] The reception for both couples was held at the home of Reuben Grigsby, Sr. This is the subject of "The Chronicles," and its climax is the confusion in assigning the bridegrooms to their proper rooms. One of the brides, Mrs. Betsy Grigsby, left this version of the affair:

"We formed a procession, my husband and me, Charles and his wife in front. The messenger [Josiah Crawford] led the way down the long lane blowing all the time on his tin horn. Old man Reuben Grigsby met and welcomed us. The home was two stories high and made of hewed logs. Mr. Lincoln and Abe made the stairs and shutters and finished it. . . . There was a big crowd and we did not finish eating until after dark. We played all that evening 'Old Sister Phoeby' and other kissing games. . . . Yes they have a joke on us. They said my man got into the wrong room and Charles got into my room, but it wasn't so. Lincoln just wrote that for mischief. Natty Grigsby told us it was all written down, all put on record. Abe and my man often laughed about that." [31]

A result of the writing of "The Chronicles" is said to have been a fight between William Grigsby and John D. Johnston. The accounts of the cause, time, place, and result of this contest are so confusing and contradictory that there is no possibility of learning just what took place. Most versions agree that the grievance was between Lincoln and Grigsby, but Johnston was substituted because he was nearer the size of Grigsby than the much larger Abe.[32] The fight is attributed to Johnston's making up "The Chronicles" story, Abe's writing it out, and a dispute between Grigsby and Abe over the owner-ship of a spotted pup.[33] The time of the fight varies with the cause, from the heated argument over the pup in 1826 to the period after the writing of "The Chronicles" in 1829. There are at least half a dozen places where the fight is said to have taken place and one eyewitness stated "every township in the county was represented" among those who saw it. Another claimed that he climbed a tree that he might see over the heads of the people who gathered around.[34] The results given of the contest are just as confusing, one being that Johnston was soundly thrashed, another that Grigsby was the first to cry "enough," and still another that because of foul play Lincoln stepped in and broke up the battle. Apparently, we have several community squabbles all rolled into one grand championship exhibition.

Since considerable attention has been given by many authors to the influences that directed Abraham Lincoln to the law as a profession, some consideration should be given to these here. By the time he was twenty years of age, he had become interested in the proceedings of the near-by courts, which while meting out justice served also as a source of entertainment. The people expressed great disappointment and disapproval if a case was dropped or dismissed, because they had come to hear the lawyers plead their cases and they did not want to miss this exhibition of oratory. Abraham lived about equally far—say fifteen miles—from the courthouses of Warrick, Spencer, and Perry counties. While this distance would prevent frequent attendance at the courts, on special occasions he probably managed to be present.

John A. Brackenridge was one of the prominent local lawyers whom Abraham observed in action. He was born in 1800 and educated in the College of New Jersey which later became Princeton University. He arrived in Indiana as a youth about twenty years old, and settled in Warrick County near Darlington.[35] On April 6, 1827, the Rev. Joseph Pierson married John A. Brackenridge to Isabella Helena McCullough. Apparently soon after their wedding they moved to Rockport where they were living in 1830.[36] As early as 1824 the name Brackenridge appeared on the court records of Spencer County as a witness to a deed and thereafter quite frequently up to 1830.

197

During these years Brackenridge was undoubtedly trying cases at Rockport, Boonville, Rome, and other county seat towns in southern Indiana. A Warrick County history notes that in September, 1831, "John A. Brackenridge . . . was fined $1.00 for contempt of court." "This man," the history continued, "had already become a prominent lawyer. . . . He was perhaps the ablest local attorney that ever practiced at the Warrick County bar." [37]

Tradition sometimes goes on a rampage, completely ignoring time and place factors. This seems to be true in the attempts to show that there was close association between John A. Brackenridge and Abraham Lincoln in Indiana. For instance, there is the "murder trial" story. The informant largely responsible for this is S. T. Johnston, a local man of some prominence. In Johnston's statement to Herndon on September 14, 1865, he said, "I am aged thirty-four years, resided in the county [Spencer] twenty-five years from the year 1831 to 1856." [38] This would mean he was born the year after Lincoln left Indiana. Yet Beveridge wrote, "Johnston was present at the trial [in Boonville] and saw and heard what he relates." Beveridge also says Johnston often saw Lincoln at the Warrick County Court at Boonville.[39] A careful reading of the Johnston statement, however, will disclose that he is reporting what a man by the name of Summers, who attended the court at Boonville, had observed and who noted that Abraham "always attended court and paid strict attention to what was said and done." [40]

The murder trial of which Johnston made special mention was supposed to have occurred in 1828. According to him, Lincoln was present and complimented Brackenridge upon his argument. Other authors have claimed that the attorney was "one of the Breckinridges, from Kentucky." [41] Furthermore, a very careful search of the Warrick County court records has not revealed a murder trial on the docket for 1828 or 1829.

The generally accepted tradition that Brackenridge loaned

Abraham books and entertained him at his home does not square with documentary evidence. J. Edward Murr puts this bit of folklore into these words: ". . . the ambitious youth frequently made pilgrimages to this gentleman's home [near Boonville] to borrow his law books, sometimes remaining throughout the day and night reveling in the mysteries of the law."[42] It has already been observed that there was no Brackenridge home near Boonville until after 1830, as Brackenridge was living in Rockport at that time. A county history also places the move of the Brackenridge home to Warrick County after 1829.[43] This evidence removes the possibility of Abraham having visited Brackenridge near Boonville or borrowed books from his library at that place.[44] If Abe visited the Brackenridge home, it must have been at Rockport.

Another attorney whom Lincoln heard in the courts, especially in Rockport, was John Pitcher. It must not be assumed that either Brackenridge or Pitcher were fatherly old men looking for a chance to help some ambitious youth. Brackenridge was but nine and Pitcher but fourteen years older than Abraham. Both were still comparatively young, anxious to get ahead in their professions, neither having as yet won the honors that later were bestowed on them.

John Pitcher was born in Watertown, Connecticut, in 1795, and was tutored in law at Litchfield. He was admitted to the bar at Hartford in 1815. The following year he married Eliza Gamble and they started for the West immediately.[45] He and his wife are listed in the 1820 census as residents of Vincennes. They had no children.[46] In the October, 1820, term of court in Pike County a John Pitcher was admitted as "an attorney and counsellor-at-law."[47] Petersburg, county seat of Pike County, was but twenty miles from Vincennes. In this same county, at the September, 1823, term of court, it was ordered that "an allowance be made of $100. for his [John Pitcher's] services as prosecuting attorney for the year 1823."[48]

Perhaps the earliest record of Pitcher's presence at Rockport is his signature as witness to a deed on August 3, 1821. Thereafter his name appears constantly in the records of Spencer County as attorney, administrator, commissioner, post master, and sheriff, all before 1830. He may have been contemplating a removal from Rockport in 1829 when he sold three pieces of property. On May 2, 1829, he joined with his wife Eliza in one sale, but in August she is not named in the deed of sale, and apparently had died.[49] On October 25, 1829, John Pitcher was married to Amanda Cissna at Rockport by John Greathouse, a justice of the peace.[50]

John Pitcher's name heads the list of twenty-two families comprising 108 individuals living in the town of Rockport when the 1830 census was taken. He lists his own age as between twenty and forty, his wife's age between fifteen and twenty, and three boys, two under five years, and one between five and ten.[51]

Abraham must have heard Pitcher in court often. A sketch of him in a local history declared, "John Pitcher was a practitioner of marked ability. . . . He was a hard student, deep in law, extremely accurate in his judgment, and was therefore a safe counsellor. . . . The character of his address to court or jury was always dignified and at times brilliant and eloquent. He was extremely forcible, as quick as powder to grasp a point. . . ."[52]

Such a successful lawyer would have made an impression on Abe sitting in court and observing the proceedings. There is no substantial evidence that Pitcher had any more direct influence on the youth. The contradictory testimony gathered by those who interviewed Pitcher when he was an old man only add to the folklore about his interest in Tom Lincoln's boy. In fact, Pitcher may have been somewhat confused about Abraham's identity, as he mentioned that the father of Abraham had operated a mill. There was another Lincoln in Spencer County who was a miller.[53]

Pitcher, in an interview with Jesse Weik, is reputed to have said, "I understood he [Abraham] wanted to become a lawyer and I tried to encourage him." [54] Another time he is reported as recalling that "he advised Lincoln to study law," and added, "He was nothing but a long, lean, gawky country jake. In fact, I did not think he had it in him." [55] Herndon only added to the confusion by crediting Pitcher with the statement that on one occasion Abraham expressed a desire to study law with him. [56]

This variance in the stories as to just what Pitcher did advise Abraham to do about studying law, if he advised him at all, somewhat impairs the strength of the statement credited to Pitcher that he "did loan him [Abraham] books—moreover law books," which he took home with him to read. One of the many people who interviewed Pitcher in his home in later years was shown a two-volume set of Blackstone "in which on the fly leaf [of one] was inscribed the name A. Lincoln." [57]

There are four Spencer County citizens and one Kentuckian who claimed or are said to have loaned Abraham law books: Aaron Grigsby, John A. Brackenridge, John Pitcher, David Turnham, all of Indiana, and Samuel W. Pate, across the Ohio, in Kentucky. [58] The statements of David Turnham have been most carefully recorded and should probably be given greatest credence. He was one of Abraham's closest friends and nearest neighbors, living but a mile away. Although he was six years older, he went to school with Abe. [59]

According to Turnham, it was in his house that Abraham found the one law book he is known for sure to have read before he left Indiana. It impressed him deeply. It was a copy of *The Revised Laws of Indiana* [1824] . . . *to which are Prefixed, the Declaration of Independence, the Constitution of the U. S., the Constitution of the State of Indiana, and Sundry other Documents, connected with the Political History of the Territory and State of Indiana.* [60] The title indicates the voluminous mass of information it contained. How Abraham reveled in it we can well imagine. Over and over again he must have read the Declaration of Independence and the Constitution of the United States contained therein.[61]

There are traditions that before Abraham left Indiana he had assumed the role of a lawyer. One of them concerns the "Old Gray Goose Case." Two of the Lincoln neighbors each had a flock of geese and one of them missing a goose, professed to find it in his neighbor's flock. The ensuing dispute was taken to the local court. One version states that the lawyer for the defendant was unable to attend and "Abraham was asked to take his place and won the case." [62] Another version has it that the whole neighborhood came to hear the case, and while they waited for the justice of the peace to make his appearance, Abe rose and made such an eloquent appeal to the litigants that by the time the magistrate arrived the two neighbors involved "were shaking hands." [63]

There is no evidence that by the time Lincoln left Indiana he had made up his mind to become a lawyer. He had heard outstanding attorneys plead their cases, had tried out his own oratory on legal subjects, and read at least one law book. By his twentieth year he had come to realize something of the professional and trading opportunities that were open to an ambitious young man in the West under the American system of free enterprise. That was as far as he had gotten by that time.[64]

CHAPTER XVI

21

Independence

1830

ON THE TWELFTH DAY of February, 1830, Abraham Lincoln reached his twenty-first birthday, and, from a legal viewpoint, became independent. Every normal youth anticipates the time when he will be on his own. That Abraham had been planning for such a day is evident from his activities during the preceding fall, when he helped his father in the erection of a new home. William Wood, a neighbor, recalled that he "saw him cutting down a large tree one day; I asked him what he was going to do with it; he said he was going to saw it into planks for his father's new house. . . . Abe cut the tree down and he and one Levi Mills whipsawed it into planks."[1]

Abe was anxious to get his father and stepmother comfortably established before he left home, and the building of the new cabin was part of his plan.

Apparently there were three structures erected by Thomas Lincoln on the crown of the hill he had selected for the homesite in 1816. Upon his initial visit he had thrown up a half-face camp to show possession which had been later occupied for a short time by the Sparrows. Immediately upon the arrival of the Lincoln family, Thomas with the help of his neighbors, had put up a typical pioneer log cabin in which the family lived for fourteen years. The hewed log cabin started by Abe and his father in the fall of 1829 was never completed or occupied by the family, though it is the building usually identified as the Lincoln family home. There is dependable evidence that while they built it, the Lincolns never lived there.[2]

But even while the new house was being constructed, the family was receiving letters from John Hanks [3] then living in Macon County, Illinois. John had come to Spencer County in 1822, lived near the Lincolns for about four years, then returned to Kentucky, and in 1828 moved to Illinois. He was enthusiastic about the opportunities there and wrote fabulous tales about the fertility of the soil, with the land ready to cultivate but for the turning of the sod. Dennis Hanks decided to go out and look over the situation. He was greatly impressed with the prospects and returned home determined to move to the prairies. He had no difficulty selling the idea to his half brother Squire Hall. Dennis and Squire, it will be recalled, had married, respectively, Elizabeth and Matilda Johnston, daughters of Sally Lincoln, and it was not long before the mother came to the conclusion that she "could not think of parting with them." [4] Through Sally, Thomas Lincoln was influenced, and in a very short time "the proposition of Dennis met with the general consent of the Lincoln family. . . ." [5] It was decided to move early in the spring of 1830. It is not very likely that Thomas was ever enthusiastic about the move, and Abraham's prospects of securing work on the Ohio River would now be cut off.

It is apparent that as early as September, 1829, while Abe and his father were working on the new cabin, Sally Lincoln was aware of the western fever that had attacked her daughters and their husbands. She had retained the town lot and cabin where she had lived in Elizabethtown, Kentucky. Faced with the possibility of moving farther west, she and her husband returned to Elizabethtown, and on September 8, 1829, joined in the sale of the property for which she received $123.00. This was a good business deal, as she cleared nearly $100.00 on the $25.00 investment made a dozen years before.[6]

204

A week or ten days before the time set for removal, the families disposed of their lands and their stock. According to Dennis Hanks's own testimony, he personally had never had more than "a kind of pre-emption right on the land he had acquired, and this he sold."[7] Thomas Lincoln, however, had two tracts of land, one of eighty acres and one of twenty. For an unknown amount, on November 26, 1829, Charles Grigsby secured a bond from Thomas for the eighty-acre tract. On February 20, 1830, a warranty deed was made in which "Thomas Lincoln and his wife Sarah for and in consideration of the sum of one hundred and twenty-five dollars to them in hand paid doth . . . sell to said Charles Grigsby . . . the west half of the southwest quarter of Section thirty-two in Township four south, Range five west, containing eighty acres. . . ." To this deed Thomas signed his name and Sarah made her mark.[8]

The above property was free from encumbrance and had been for four years. Thomas owned another piece of land containing twenty acres in Section 31 which was adjacent to the home tract. While proof of his ownership appears in the records, it is not clear to whom he sold it, although it eventually came into possession of Gentry. John Romine claimed that he traded a horse for some land belonging to Thomas Lincoln. Possibly this twenty acres was the tract, as it would be worth just about the value of a good animal.[9]

After the disposal of his real estate, Thomas sold his stock and grain. David Turnham said, "I bought the hogs and corn of Thomas Lincoln when he was leaving for Illinois; bought about 100 hogs and 4 or 5 hundred bushels of corn. paid 10 cts. per bushel for the corn, hogs lumped." Turnham also stated that "Thomas Lincoln had about 40 acres of land under cultivation when he left for Illinois."[10]

These property sales give a dependable estimate of the economic condition of the Thomas Lincoln family when they finally left Indiana. Their cash in hand amounted to nearly five hundred dollars. Whether or not Thomas had saved any of the money he had received for his carpentry work and farm operations we do not know.

At the time Thomas Lincoln was persuaded to move from Indiana, he was comfortably situated, and the fact that he had a new house under construction clearly indicates that he was satisfied with his location. He had one hundred acres of land free from debt and forty of it under cultivation. It would seem likely that, having one hundred hogs to sell, he also had other stock not enumerated. The surplus of five hundred bushels of corn after the winter's feeding, indicates that his farm was productive. Certainly there was no lack of food for the family. He had established himself as a carpenter and cabinetmaker in the community and could have continued his vocation. He was fifty-four years old. Considering all this, it seems that some pressure must have been brought to bear on him to win his consent to start life over again on a new frontier.[11]

One unpleasant incident that threatened to mar the departure of the Lincolns should be mentioned. It will be remembered that both Thomas and Sally Lincoln were members of the Little Pigeon Church. Thomas had served as a moderator at its meetings, had been a member of its board of trustees, represented the church as a delegate to association meetings, and had helped erect the building in which the congregation worshiped. In 1829 difficulty within the congregation developed. In the minute book of the Little Pigeon Association for 1829, there is an entry which reads: "It is a notorious fact that the war is between the Armenian [Arminian] and the predestinarian principles; or that of works and grace. They are the two opposites."[12] The issue came before the Little Pigeon Association in 1829 when a neighboring Primitive Baptist group demanded that they discipline an individual who had denounced predestination and declared those who preached it were lost. On the other hand those who opposed the doctrine of election were styled Campbellites.[13]

206

On December 12, 1829, the minute book of the Little Pigeon Church records that "The church granted Brother Tho. Lincoln and wife a letter of Dismission," requested, no doubt, in anticipation of their departure from Indiana. At the January business meeting, as recorded in the minutes, "Sister Nancy Grigsby informed the church that she was not satisfied with Bro. and Sister Lincoln. . . . The church agreed and called back their letter until satisfaction could be attained. . . . The parties convened at Wm. Hoskins and agreed and settled the difficulty."

Doubtless the Grigsby complaint was a doctrinal one; certainly it had nothing to do with the moral character of either Thomas Lincoln or his wife. At the next business meeting of the church, on February 13, 1830, "Sister Grigsby laid in a charge against Sister Elizabeth Crawford for falsehood." Thomas Lincoln was appointed to a committee of five men to "settle the above case," and it was ordered that "the decision of the above committee shall be the decision of the church." This appointment indicates that Thomas had been restored to good standing in the church.

Several weeks of preparation were necessary after the three families had made the decision to move. "Their mode of conveyance was wagons drawn by ox-teams." [14] Probably three wagons had to be built, one for each family. [15] A description of one of the vehicles states: "There was not a nail or a piece of iron in it. The whole structure was fastened together with wooden pins and the tires were made of rawhide." [16]

While the wagons were being constructed, the animals to pull them had to be acquired. Apparently there were two yoke of oxen for each of two wagons, and two pairs of horses for the third. Oxen in Spencer County at that time brought about $25.00 a yoke, while a pair of horses would bring twice that amount. Two of the oxen were purchased from Shadrach Hall, father of Wesley Hall, and two from William Wood. The horses undoubtedly were from their own stock, and there were also two saddle horses used by the party.

A tradition which has found expression in many forms concerns the purchase by Abe of an assortment of goods that he planned to sell along the road to Illinois. One version has it that he made his purchase at Jones's store.[17] However, James Gentry, Jr., claims that the items were bought at his father's store and that "he [James, Jr.] and Lincoln spent considerable time on that last night [before departure] making selection of notions" to be sold on the journey. James further stated that they did not retire until two A.M.[18] Young Gentry was just eleven years old at this time. While there are many pieces of folklore in both Indiana and Illinois relating to the alleged business transaction, no substantial evidence supporting it has been found.[19]

The family of four Lincolns who had come to Indiana from Kentucky in 1816 had disintegrated. Nancy Lincoln and her daughter Sarah were dead. Thomas had married a widow with three children and become closely identified with her family. Abraham, now twenty-one, stood alone, and was ready to go out on his own. This 1830 migrating party is no longer a Lincoln one; it is more Johnston, Hanks, and Hall, and of a different cultural status than the Lincoln family that had come from Kentucky fourteen years earlier.[20] Before starting out on that journey Abe had gone with his mother to pay a last visit to the grave of his younger brother Thomas. Now, before leaving Indiana, he would probably make a lonely visit to the graves of his mother and of his sister.

After having lived in the community for so many years certainly some of their friends would be present to bid them farewell. James Gentry stated, "I well remember the day when the Lincolns started for Illinois. Nearly all the neighbors was there to see them leave." Redmond D. Grigsby recalled, "I helped to hitch the two yoke of oxen to the wagon, and went with them half a mile."[21] The caravan must have made an impressive sight, and a noisy departure as well. Above the final shouts of "good luck" these primitive homemade vehicles "were very musical, for the more grease one put on the wooden axle to make it run lightly the more it would squeak and squeal, making a noise that could be heard for a mile." [22]

The migrating party that bid good-by to their Little Pigeon Creek neighbors on the first day of March, 1830, consisted of thirteen people. Thomas and Sally Lincoln, Abraham, and John D. Johnston comprised one unit. The Hanks family consisted of Dennis and Elizabeth and their four children, Sarah Jane, John Talbot, Nancy, and Harriet, all between the ages of eight and four inclusive. Squire and Matilda Hall and their son John Johnston Hall, less than a year old, completed the company.

There can be little question that the route the party followed was the Troy-Vincennes trace, an old ridge road running about four miles north of their Pigeon Creek homes. Thomas knew the road well. He had come over a part of it when he came to Indiana in 1816, and he had followed it to Vincennes on at least two occasions. Abe is supposed to have visited Vincennes once with David Turnham. Upon reaching the trace they passed through Polk Patch and Petersburg on the way to Vincennes. The distance was about fifty miles. [23] Dennis Hanks who had just returned from a trip to their place of destination knew the route to follow after they crossed the Wabash.

Augustus H. Chapman, son-in-law of Elizabeth Hanks, stated that Abraham told him that "the settlers passed through Vincennes, where they remained a day." Chapman also claimed that Abraham recalled, "they saw a printing-press for the first time." [24] Nothing would be more natural than for Abraham to want to see the press on which the newspaper he had so often read was printed. He may have seen the Vincennes *Western Sun* for Saturday, March 5, come from the press.

Before the departure of Abraham from the State of Indiana, where we have observed his gradual development, it is well for us to pause and consider briefly how he has progressed through his formative years. There was once a youth, about whom Abe was well informed, of whom it was said that he "increased in wisdom and in stature, and in favor with God and man." [25]

Certainly Abraham had "increased in stature" while in Indiana. When he came, he was "large for his age" of seven years.[26] He grew rapidly until his unusual height became his most conspicuous physical feature. He was described as gawky and ungainly during his school days when he is said to have been called "long shanks." His father would say that "Abe looked as if he'd ben chopped out with an ax an' needed a jack-plane tuk to him." [27] Someone else remarked that "he looked as if he were made for wading in deep water." [28] Abe himself always seemed to be very conscious about his height.[29]

Abe's stepmother said that he was "more fleshy in Indiana," than thereafter.[30] The year after he left the state he was described as being "fine and noble-looking, weighed two hundred and ten pounds, was six feet three or four inches in height, and of florid complexion." [31]

Abraham's physical development would not indicate that he was undernourished. Neither could it be said that he was underprivileged in his educational pursuits. In fact, his "increase in wisdom" seemed to keep pace with his "increase in stature."

He had attended what subscription school classes were open to him. As a pupil, he had learned to read, write, and figure through the rule of three. To be able to write well at ten years of age was an accomplishment of distinction, and in this art Abraham excelled. His stepmother stated that he was "diligent for knowledge, wished to know, & if pains & labor would get it was sure to get it." [32] He did not advance through the accepted channels of higher education as he "was never in a college or Academy as a student." [33] He followed a program of reading and study which he set up for himself, and his self-

210

"The Meeting of the Two Emancipators," by Albert Turner Reid. This painting hangs in the Elihu Stout Print Shop Memorial, Vincennes. Here Abraham views a printing press for the first time, in the shop of Elihu Stout, editor of the Vincennes Western Sun, *in March, 1830, on his way to Illinois.*

imposed discipline was rigid. His desire to know, to understand, was unquenchable.

Abraham "majored" in declamation and in storytelling. Fortunately the books that were available to him were particularly useful in this field. *Æsop's Fables,* which he memorized at an early age, gave him a supply of strange and mythical stories to recite. The lectures against cruelty to animals which he delivered to his playmates and the recitations he made in school gave him practice in speechmaking. Scott's *Lessons in Elocution* provided instruction in the fundamentals of public speaking. Then came *The Kentucky Preceptor* and *The Columbian Class Book,* published especially to provide practice pieces in rhetoric, but at the same time affording the reader selections of good literature and a wealth of information. The simple diction of the Bible with which Abraham was so familiar had a marked influence on his selection of words and his phraseology. Franklin's *Autobiography* and Weems's *Washington* contributed to the development of a genuine patriotism. By perusing the dictionary he increased his vocabulary and learned the importance of using the right words to convey his thoughts exactly. Then came newspapers which posted him on current events.

His own sister and his stepsisters and stepbrother were his first listeners; then in the schoolroom he found an audience. Later farm boys gathered in a fence corner to hear him, and finally at the village store or blacksmith shop adults would stop to listen, marveling at his ability to expound political theory so strongly and clearly. He evolved through these practice years a mode of expression which became unique.[34] By the time he was twenty-one years old, he had developed into an able and eloquent orator.[35]

That Abraham's speeches were couched in Biblical language would imply that he had "increased in favor with God." If such measurement rested on a knowledge of the Bible and keeping of the Ten Commandments, then Abraham would certainly fulfill it. The primary factor in the religious experience of young people was parental guidance. Abraham was fortunate in having a father and mother who were devout church members. He himself said that "his mother had interested him in Bible stories before he had learned to read . . . when he read certain verses which he had in early boyhood committed to memory by hearing her repeat them as she went about her household tasks, the tones of his mother's voice would come to him and he would seem to hear her speak those words again." [36]

The religious fervor was kept alive in the Lincoln home after his mother's passing by his father who was also an ardent Christian. "He read the Bible daily and his grace at every meal was of the briefest and simplest sort, 'Fit and prepare us for humble service, for Christ's sake, Amen.'" [37] One who knew Thomas Lincoln well said, "He was truly a good man. He was the soul of honor. He was well informed. He was truthful in every word and deed. . . . He was a mindful reader and student of the Bible." [38]

The Bible was the most influential book that Abraham read in his parent's home. According to John Hanks, Abraham "kept the Bible and Æsop's Fables always within reach, and read them over and over again." [39] One author well acquainted with Abraham wrote, "Except for the instruction of his mother, the Bible more powerfully controlled the intellectual development of the son than all other causes combined." [40]

That Abraham took seriously the teachings of the Bible and the religious discipline of the home is quite evident. In fact, he appears to have set a higher standard for himself than most church members. His stepmother has summarized his behavior: "He never drank whisky or other strong drink, was temperate in all things. . . He never told me a lie. . . . He never swore or used profane language. . . . Abe was the best boy I ever saw or ever expect to see." [41] Possibly it is not out of the way to repeat that he never used tobacco in any form.

With all his religious training it might seem strange that Abraham did not affiliate with the Little Pigeon Church to which his parents and sister belonged. Actually it would have been strange if he had signified his desire to become a member. Young unmarried people seldom joined the frontier churches. Church membership was a too serious responsibility for young people to assume. It was not undertaken until they were married and settled in life. One church set it down this way: "It is the duty of all heads of families in this church to keep those of their families that are under their care, under the same order and discipline as they themselves are bound to observe in their walk and conversation." [42]

There is no evidence whatever that during these years Abraham repudiated the simple faith of his father and mother, and there is no reason to believe that he would not have affiliated with their church if he had married in Indiana and established a home as did his sister. [43]

Finally, during his Indiana years Abraham "increased in the favor of man." "To pursue virtue through the paths of literature" was one of the objectives of the education of that day. The first and most important factor in the selection of articles for textbooks and children's books was their character-building potential. Proverbs, axioms, and fables teaching morals and religious lessons supplemented essays and dissertations which stressed virtue, integrity, nobility, and ethical behavior. Instruction in moral rectitude along with the three R's was a prime requisite in the schools of the frontier. The exemplary conduct of the persons of renown whom Abe met in his reading—both fictitious heroes and historical characters—became his models. Newspapers introduced him to statesmen such as Henry Clay who were worthy of imitation. [44]

There was no outstanding personality with whom Abraham came in daily contact in the Spencer County community. None of his immediate neighbors were superior to his own father intellectually or morally. Thomas Lincoln, by example, apparently played the most important role in his son's character building. Sally Lincoln said that her husband "was kind and loving, and kept his word, and always paid his way, and never turned a dog from his door." [45] John Hanks stated that Abraham "settled all the disputes in the neighborhood and his decisions were always abided by. I never knew a man so honest under all circumstances." [46] Another associate in Indiana wrote, "Abe was notoriously good-natured, kind, and honest. Men would swear on his simple word; had a high and manly sense of honor; was tender, gentle, etc. . . ." [47] A sort of group testimonial to the esteem in which Abraham was held is the following: "All old settlers will testify to the uniform urbanity, integrity of character, industry, and good sense that characterized his boyhood." [48]

An excellent sketch, not overdrawn, which shows how well he was oriented to the community in which he lived, states ". . . Thus young Lincoln grew to manhood . . . mingling cordially with the simple-minded, honest people with whom his lot was cast, developing a kindly nature, and evincing social qualities which rendered his companionship desirable; . . . everywhere a favorite, always simple, genial, truthful, and unpretending, and always chosen umpire on occasions calling for the exercise of sound judgment and inflexible impartiality. . . . In such daily companionship, he grew up in full sympathy with the people, rejoicing in their simple joys and pleasures, sorrowing in their trials and misfortunes, and united to them all by that bond of brotherhood among all honest poor—a common heritage of labor." [49]

The spark of genius that enlightened Abraham during these impressionable years was within him. His mother had sensed this unusual gift very early in his life and nourished it. His father, also, wanted it cultivated, and his stepmother, observing that he was "diligent for knowledge," encouraged him in every way possible. Others in the home noted that he was "ambitious and determined." [50] It was persistence and determination that motivated him during these formative years.

Abraham Lincoln was born in 1809, the very year that Indiana became a separate territory. He came to Indiana in 1816, within a few days of December 11, the birthday of the state. He himself was but a small lad, and the state comprised but fifteen counties. Now in 1830, as the state's pioneer period was drawing to a close, Abraham had come of age and stood six feet four inches tall. "He grew up . . . on our own good soil of Indiana." [51] The state also had grown, and comprised sixty organized counties.

The great seal of Indiana portrays the rising sun in the background and a buffalo sporting in a clearing. The center of interest is a tall frontiersman with ax in hand engaged in felling a tree. This woodsman might well symbolize Abraham Lincoln, Indiana's finest contribution to civilization.

Notes

CHAPTER I

1. Waldo Lincoln, *History of the Lincoln Family* (Worcester, Mass., 1923). See also *The Lincoln Kinsman*, No. 15 (September, 1939).
2. Clarence W. Fearing, *Contemporary Kindred of Abraham Lincoln* (Weymouth, Mass., 1928).
3. "The Lincolns—Frontiersmen All," in *Lincoln Lore*, No. 415 (March 22, 1937).
4. Hardin County (Ky.) Tax Book, 1797. The pages in the Bible where Abraham entered the family records in 1847 or later were removed from the volume, and while in the hands of Dennis Hanks badly mutilated. A lost fragment contained the following entry, according to a contemporary copy made by John D. Johnston: "Thos. Lincoln was born Jan. the 6th A.D. 1778 and was married June 12th 1806 to Nancy Hanks who was born Feb 5 1784. Sarah, Lincoln, daughter of Thos. and. . . ." At this point the preserved part of the record begins. While we lack the above writings in Lincoln's own hand, inasmuch as it presumably was copied from the fragment before it was lost, we shall accept the dates as recorded. The tombstone of Thomas Lincoln bears this inscription: "B. 1, 6, 1778 D. 1, 15, 1851." We should keep in mind that court records indicate that Thomas was born as early as 1776. The Bible record made by Lincoln is given in The Abraham Lincoln Association, *The Collected Works of Abraham Lincoln* (8 volumes plus index. Rutgers University Press, 1952–55), II, 94–95. The original pages from the Bible as well as the contemporary copy made by John D. Johnston were formerly in the Oliver R. Barrett Collection. All writings and speeches of Abraham Lincoln used in this volume follow the version adopted in the *Collected Works*.
5. Abraham Lincoln, "Autobiography Written for John L. Scripps," in *Collected Works*, IV, 61. This sketch was prepared by Lincoln for Scripps, probably in June, 1860, to aid Scripps in writing a campaign biography. Certainly no more dependable evidence could be found about the Lincoln family.
6. Helm-Haycraft Manuscript Collection, Lincoln National Life Foundation, Fort Wayne, Indiana.

7. "Autobiography," in *Collected Works*, IV, 61. John Lincoln named his first three sons Abraham, Isaac, and Jacob. "The Tennessee Lincolns," in *The Lincoln Kinsman*, No. 14 (August, 1939).
8. Washington County (Ky.) Tax Book, 1799, 1800, 1801.
9. Mordecai Lincoln, eldest son of Abraham and Bathsheba (Herring) Lincoln was married to Mary Mudd in 1792. Nelson County (Ky.) Marriage Register. On February 3, 1801, Ann [Nancy] Lincoln married William Brumfield; on February 22, 1801, Josiah Lincoln married Caty Barlow; and on August 4, 1801, Mary Lincoln married Ralph Crume. Washington County (Ky.) Marriage Register. For biographical sketches of these Lincolns see *The Lincoln Kinsman:* "Nancy Lincoln Brumfield," No. 41 (November, 1941); "The President's Uncle Josiah," No. 39 (September, 1941); "Lincoln's Aunt Mary," No. 42 (December, 1941); and "Uncle Mordecai Lincoln," No. 12 (June, 1939).
10. Charles Melton to Thomas Lincoln, Hardin County (Ky.) Deed Book, B-1803, p. 255.
11. Hardin County (Ky.) Court of Quarter Sessions, Order Book, October 19, 1803; Court of Common Pleas, Order Book A, p. 524, and Order Book B, p. 17.
12. Robert Bleakley and William Montgomery, merchants, Day Book, February 18, 1806. This Day Book and also a Ledger of Bleakley & Montgomery, for the years from 1805 to 1807, were discovered by the author in Dallas, Texas, and are now in the Lincoln National Life Foundation, Fort Wayne. They are extremely important in establishing the economic status of Thomas Lincoln at the time of his marriage in 1806.
13. Bleakley & Montgomery Day Book, May 16, 20, and 22, 1806.
14. *Ibid.*
15. There has been a tendency to associate Thomas Lincoln with "The Poor White Trash of the South." There is no evidence that the Lincolns were ever poverty-stricken, nor were any of the family associated with that class of people the South knew as "poor whites." See "The Poverty Myth," in *The Lincoln Kinsman*, No. 34 (April, 1941).
16. Bleakley & Montgomery Day Book, May 16, 20, 22, 1806.
17. The date of Nancy Hanks's birth is said to have been entered by Abraham Lincoln on a now lost fragment of the family Bible record as February 5, 1784. Her tombstone, however, bears this inscription: "Died Oct 5 A.D. 1818 Aged 35 years." See note 4, above. No record of the marriage of James Hanks and Lucy Shipley has been discovered, but the Shipley family traditions support the fact that they were married and Nancy was the child of this union. See "Five Shipley Sisters," in *The Lincoln Kinsman*, No. 4 (October, 1938).
18. "Came John Dawson of the county of Ann Arundel, merchant, and proved right to 500 acres of land for transporting: Christopher Shaw, John Brown, Adam Shipleigh, John Risk, Thomas Mason, William Barton, Richard Prewitt, Richard Battson, Thomas Wood, John Dixon, in February 1668." Maryland Land Grants, Box 13, p. 17. Annapolis Hall of Records.
19. Louis A. Warren, "The Shipley Ancestry of Lincoln's Mother," in *Indiana Magazine of History*, XXIX (1933), [203]–212; "Five Shipley Sisters," in *The Lincoln Kinsman*, No. 4 (October, 1938).
20. Jesse W. Weik, *The Real Lincoln* (Boston and New York, 1922), p. 46.

21. For a full discussion of the story of Lucy Shipley Hanks, see Louis A. Warren, *Lincoln's Parentage and Childhood* (New York, 1926), Chapter II, and the following articles in *The Lincoln Kinsman:* "The Unknown Hanks Ancestry," No. 2 (August, 1938); "Five Shipley Sisters," No. 4 (October, 1938); "The Richard Berry Family," No. 16 (October, 1939); "The Maternal Lineage Myth," No. 33 (March, 1941); "Squire Thompson and Charlotte Vawter," No. 47 (May, 1942); and "Caroline W. and Charles S. Hanks," No. 48 (June, 1942).

22. Washington County (Ky.) Court Order Book, February 7, 1793.

23. Washington County (Ky.) Tax Book, 1792.

24. Washington County (Ky.) Will Book C, pp. 346, 349.

25. Account by Mrs. C. H. S. Vawter, granddaughter of Sarah Mitchell, in Louisville *Courier-Journal,* February 20, 1874. See also Chapter III, pp. 33–34, below. The story is substantiated by a letter from Mary Mitchell, grandmother of Sarah, to Governor Isaac Shelby, May 1, 1793, seeking information of her granddaughter "taken prisoner by the Indians in the wilderness last fall two years, her name is Sally S. Mitchell daughter of Robert Mitchell, deceased." Letter quoted in Warren, *Lincoln's Parentage and Childhood,* pp. 311–12, from original in Durrett Collection, University of Chicago.

26. Account of Mrs. C. H. S. Vawter in Louisville *Courier-Journal,* February 20, 1874, and Mitchell Thompson in *ibid.,* January 5, 1881.

27. Washington County (Ky.) Marriage Register, June 12, 1806.

28. Account by Dr. Christopher Columbus Graham, March 20, 1882, Durrett Collection, University of Chicago. This and another account are quoted in Warren, *Lincoln's Parentage and Childhood,* pp. 69, 70.

29. Having heard the story of the court's adjournment in Washington County, the author determined to search the records for any substantiating evidence. In the Circuit Court Order Book he found the court was in session on Monday, June 9, Tuesday, June 10, Wednesday, June 11, and Friday, June 13. Under the date line, Thursday, June 12, the day of the Lincoln-Hanks wedding, the only entry was "Court adjourned for the day." Richard Berry, who gave the bride away, was serving on the jury, Mordecai Lincoln, who may have been best man, had a case on the docket on the day before, and Jesse Head, the minister, was serving as a witness in a case. The court adjourned on June 12, and we may suppose the judge and attendants went to the wedding six miles away.

30. Hardin County (Ky.) Tax Book, 1806.

31. Bleakley & Montgomery Day Book, June 13, 1806.

32. Hardin County (Ky.) Will Book A, p. 291: "Thomas McIntire Sale."

33. "Autobiography," in *Collected Works,* IV, 61.

34. Hardin County (Ky.) Tax Book, 1815.

35. "Autobiography," in *Collected Works,* IV, 61.

36. In later years Lincoln said that the Bible which his mother read and "had taught him to read was the greatest comfort he and his sister had after their mother was gone." Henry B. Rankin, *Personal Recollections of Abraham Lincoln* (New York, 1916), pp. 320, 321.

37. Elizabethtown Academy, Record Book I, Town Hall, Elizabethtown.

38. Hardin County (Ky.) Court, Order Book A, p. 231.

39. "Autobiography," in *Collected Works,* IV, 61.

40. Hardin County (Ky.) Marriage Bonds, 1816: Caleb Hazel and Mary

Stevens, October, 1816. Caleb's first wife, whom he married in 1786, was the widow of James Hall.

41. John Locke Scripps, *The First Published Life of Abraham Lincoln, Written in the Year MDCCCLX...*, reprinted by the Cranbrook Press (Detroit, 1900), p. 16. This biography should not be confused with the autobiographical sketch which Lincoln prepared for Scripps, although the author used the sketch as a source for his book. Lincoln read the manuscript copy of the Scripps book and made several deletions and corrections, so that Scripps complained that Lincoln insisted on pruning out of it many of its most readable and interesting passages in regard to his early life and other matters. Joseph Medill to Grace Locke Scripps Dyche, 1895, in *ibid.*, Preface, p. 6. We may rely upon what Lincoln left standing in this biography. The Cranbrook Press edition of this book is cited because of the rarity of the two editions published in 1860, one by the Chicago Press and Tribune Company and the other by H. Greeley and Company of New York, and the edition published by M. L. Houser in 1931.

42. Robert H. Browne, *Abraham Lincoln and Men of His Times* (2 volumes. New York, 1901), I, 83.

43. Lewis Collins, *Historical Sketches of Kentucky ...* (Cincinnati, 1848), p. 23.

44. Hardin County (Ky.) Deed Book B, p. 255.

45. Hardin County (Ky.) Circuit Court, Equity Bundle No. 11: Richard Mather *vs.* David Vance, Isaac Bush, and Thomas Lincoln.

46. Hardin County (Ky.) Circuit Court, Equity Bundle No. 18: Thomas Stout and others *vs.* Thomas Lincoln.

47. Hardin County (Ky.) Deed Book E, p. 193: Thomas and Nancy Lincoln to Charles Melton.

48. "Autobiography," in *Collected Works,* IV, 62.

49. *Ibid.*, IV, p. 61.

50. Some students of the Lincoln family have denied that slavery had anything to do with their removal from Kentucky: "Not the faintest evidence has been found indicating that slavery was so much as a contributing cause for their departure...." Albert J. Beveridge, *Abraham Lincoln, 1809–1858* (2 volumes. Boston and New York, 1928), I, 33. "... that his father left Kentucky to avoid the sight of or contact with slavery, lacks confirmation. In all Hardin county ... there were not over fifty slaves." William H. Herndon and Jesse W. Weik, *Herndon's Life of Lincoln ...*, with an introduction and notes by Paul M. Angle (A. & C. Boni, New York, 1930), p. 20. However, there were 1,238 slaves listed in the Hardin County Tax Book in 1816. In 1813 one man alone listed fifty-eight negroes in his possession. Louis A. Warren, *The Slavery Atmosphere of Lincoln's Youth* (Fort Wayne, 1933).

51. South Fork Baptist Church Record Book, July 3, 1808, and July, 1810, photostats in Lincoln National Life Foundation, Fort Wayne. See also Warren, *The Slavery Atmosphere of Lincoln's Youth.*

52. The *Western Sun* at Vincennes announced on August 24, 1816, "The Constitution of the State of Indiana has just been published and is for sale at this office. Price 25 cts." In the debate with Douglas at Alton, Lincoln put the rhetorical question, "How many Democrats are there about here who have left slave states and come into the free State of

Illinois to get rid of the institution of slavery." The reporter claims that one voice interrupted and said, "A thousand," another voice added "a thousand and one," to which Lincoln replied, "I reckon there are a thousand and one." *Collected Works,* III, 312. A Jefferson County Revolutionary War veteran expressed the sentiment of many who had migrated to Kentucky: "I Philip Graham . . . being conscious to myself that the practice of holding slaves in perpetual slavery is repugnant to the Golden Law of God and the inalienable rights of mankind, as well as to the very principle of the late glory of our Revolution. . . . emancipate all my negroes." Jefferson County (Ky.), Power of Attorney Register, I, 243.

53. Herndon claimed that "[Thomas] Lincoln left Kentucky to take his wife away from . . . bad influences." Herndon to Lamon, February 25, 1870, Herndon-Weik MSS, microfilm copies in Lincoln National Life Foundation of original manuscripts in the Library of Congress and the Huntington Library, San Marino, California. See "The Paternity Myth," in *The Lincoln Kinsman,* No. 31 (January, 1941).

CHAPTER II

1. Vincennes *Western Sun,* October 5, 1816.
2. A widely accepted tradition relating to the preliminary trip Thomas Lincoln is supposed to have made to Indiana is related in a book by William M. Thayer entitled *The Pioneer Boy and How He Became President,* published in Boston in 1864. This purely apocryphal story tells that Thomas sold his Knob Creek farm to a fictitious person for ten barrels of whiskey and built a flatboat to transport it and the heavy wares belonging to the family—his carpenter's tools, furniture, kitchen utensils—to Posey's landing in Indiana, whence it was hauled by wagon sixteen miles through the wilderness to the homesite. Thomas Lincoln's Knob Creek land was in litigation at the time, an ejectment suit having been brought against him, which would make a title to his land almost worthless, and certainly not negotiable.
3. Hardin County (Ky.) Tax Book, 1815. John G. Nicolay and John Hay in their *Abraham Lincoln, a History* (10 volumes. New York, 1890), I, 28, state that ". . . the backs of two borrowed horses sufficed for the load." For variations of this tradition see Eleanor Atkinson, *The Boyhood of Lincoln* (New York, 1908), pp. 14–15, and Carl Sandburg, *Abe Lincoln Grows Up* (New York, 1926), pp. 67–68.
4. A neighbor in Kentucky purchased a wagon and gears on January 2, 1815, which indicates vehicles were available at that time. Hardin County (Ky.) Deed Book E, p. 265.
5. Statement of Christopher Columbus Graham in Durrett Collection, University of Chicago.
6. Hardin County (Ky.) Circuit Court: Kennedy *vs.* Lincoln, Bundle 82.
7. Hardin County (Ky.) Will Book B, p. 183.
8. "Mr. Lincoln remembered to have visited the now unmarked grave of this little one, along with his mother, before leaving Kentucky." Joseph H. Barrett, *Life of Abraham Lincoln* . . . (New York, 1865), pp. 16–17. Barrett had two conferences with Lincoln and recalled that "he received me kindly and showed no unusual reserve in talking of either his earlier or mature life . . . he readily gave me such facts as my

inquiry invited or suggested." Joseph H. Barrett, *Abraham Lincoln and His Presidency* (2 volumes. Cincinnati, 1904), I, iii–iv.

9. As early as 1804 Daniel Lewis established a ferry from his farm on the Kentucky side of the Ohio River to the mouth of Crooked Creek two miles south of Troy on the Indiana side. Breckinridge County (Ky.) Order Book, February 16, 1804. By 1816 this ferry was in possession of Hugh Thompson and numerous references to the Thompson Ferry are to be found in the Breckinridge County records. All early Lincoln biographers including Barrett, Brockett, Herndon, Holland, Lamon, and Raymond, as well as later writers such as Barton, Nicolay and Hay, and Tarbell mention the crossing of the Ohio at the mouth of Anderson River. Raymond claims that Lincoln mentioned Thompson's Ferry as the place of crossing. Henry J. Raymond, *The Life and Public Service of Abraham Lincoln . . .* (New York, 1865), p. 19.

10. Breckinridge County (Ky.) Court, Minute Book 2, p. 96.

11. Vincennes *Western Sun & General Advertiser,* November 23, 1816.

12. *Ibid.,* and June 16, 1827, and Henry A. and Kate B. Ford, *History of Cincinnati, Ohio . . .* (Cincinnati, 1881), pp. 349–50.

13. Thomas Lincoln was in Kentucky as late as November 11, 1816, when his name appears on a court document. Hardin County (Ky.) Circuit Court, November 11, 1816: Lincoln *vs.* Bush, Equity Bundle No. 24.

14. Perry County (Ind.) Circuit Court, Order Book, October Term, 1815.

15. Nathaniel Grigsby to William Herndon, September 12, 1865, Herndon-Weik MSS.

16. Raymond, *The Life and Public Service of Abraham Lincoln,* p. 19.

17. There were a dozen or more of these saline deposits north of the Lincoln home on Little Pigeon Creek, which were well known to hunters. Ward H. Lamon, *The Life of Abraham Lincoln; from His Birth to His Inauguration as President* (Boston, 1872), p. 21.

18. The land on which Thomas Lincoln settled was in Section 32, T 4 S, R 5 W. See Record of Field Notes South and West of the Second Principal Meridian, in Archives Division, Indiana State Library.

19. Observations made by George R. Wilson from surveyors' original field notes, in possession of Mr. Wilson's sister, Margaret Wilson, Jasper, Indiana. Dennis Hanks is responsible for the confusion about the water supply on the Lincoln farm. He wrote Herndon that Thomas Lincoln " 'riddled his land like a honeycomb' in search of good water." Quoted in Lamon, *The Life of Abraham Lincoln,* p. 21. Yet when Hanks was interviewed by Eleanor Atkinson he said that the site of the home was "on a crick with a deer-lick handy, an' a spring o' good water." Atkinson, *The Boyhood of Lincoln,* p. 15. Beveridge states: ". . . the supply of drinking water nearest the knoll selected by him was a spring more than a mile away; and no brook ran closer. Little Pigeon Creek was slightly less distant, but not so accessible as the spring. . . ." Beveridge, *Abraham Lincoln,* I, 41. However, another wrote, "The particular site of his dwelling was doubtless determined, as usual, by the discovery of a living spring of water, after fixing on his selection of a farm." Barrett, *Life of Abraham Lincoln,* p. 22.

In 1925 the author made a visit to the Lincoln farmsite for the primary purpose of investigating the water supply. The first local citizen interviewed was David Enlow, an aged man who laughed heartily when questioned about the lack of water on the Lincoln farm. He recalled that one summer, before all the timber was cut, he had watered forty head of steers at the spring. An elderly neighbor lady, whose family for a long time had been using the spring as a source of water, said she could not remember it ever having run dry. Also, three homes located within three hundred feet of the Lincoln cabin secured their water from three private wells, one of them within fifty feet of the site.

20. The erroneous story that the Lincolns lived one winter in a half-face camp may be attributed to Thayer's *The Pioneer Boy,* pp. 88–90.

21. Hardin County (Ky.) Court, Judgments and Other Papers, 1808–1809: Thomas Lincoln *vs.* Denton Geoghegan.

22. For an excellent account of how log cabins were built see *A Home in the Woods. Oliver Johnson's Reminiscences of Early Marion County* (Indianapolis, Indiana Historical Society, 1951), pp. 149–51. The cabin which the Lincoln family built in Macon County, Illinois, fourteen years later "was begun March 30, 1830, and four days were spent in building it." Phebe A. C. Hanaford, *Abraham Lincoln: His Life and Public Service* (Boston, 1865), p. 24.

23. Mattresses or feather beds were put on the loft floor and here the children slept. As they mounted the crude ladder, the pegs creaked and squeeked under their feet. Lincoln mentioned this loft "bedroom" in his interview with Dr. John Putnam Gulliver, March 10, 1860. See *Lincoln Lore, No. 1076* (November 21, 1949).

24. Vincennes *Western Sun & General Advertiser,* December 30 [28], 1816.

25. Scripps, *Life of Abraham Lincoln* (1900 ed.), p. 16.

26. *Ibid.,* p. 17. Mentor Graham who claimed to have helped Abraham study grammar stated to William Herndon that, "Lincoln told him that the way he learned to write so well and so distinctly and precisely was that many people who came with them from Kentucky and different sections after they moved to Indiana say his perceptions were sharpened and he learned to see other people's thoughts and feelings and ideas by writing their friendly confidential letters." Herndon-Weik MSS, no date.

27. "When . . . acceleration of development is accompanied by an intensified, well-integrated behavior organization, it is a normal symptom of giftedness." Arnold Gesell, *Studies in Child Development* (New York, 1948), p. 143.

CHAPTER III

1. "Autobiography," in *Collected Works,* IV, 62.

2. J. S. Duss, *George Rapp and His Associates* (*The Harmony Society*) (Indianapolis, 1914), pp. 11–12.

3. Vincennes *Western Sun & General Advertiser,* July 26, 1828.

4. David D. Banta, *A Historical Sketch of Johnson County Indiana* (Chicago, J. H. Beers & Co., 1881), p. 50.

5. In the course of his speech in Indianapolis in September, 1859, Lincoln remarked that "the scenes he passed through today are wonderfully different from the first scenes he witnessed in the State of Indiana where he was raised, in Spencer County, on the Ohio River. There

was an unbroken wilderness there then, and an axe was put in his hand; and with the trees and logs and grubs he fought until he reached his twentieth year." *Collected Works*, III, 463.

6. *History of Warrick, Spencer and Perry Counties, Indiana* . . . (Chicago, Goodspeed Bros. & Co., 1885), p. 260. Lincoln must have recalled this scene when in a speech in 1838, eight years after he left Indiana, in commenting on the passing of the Revolutionary soldiers, he said, "They are gone. They *were* a forest of giant oaks; but the all-restless hurricane has swept over them, and left only here and there a lonely trunk, despoiled of its verdure, shorn of its foliage; unshading and unshaded, to murmur in a few more breezes, and to contact with its mutilated limbs, a few more ruder storms, then to sink, and be no more." Address before the Young Men's Lyceum of Springfield, Illinois, January 27, 1838, in *Collected Works*, I, 115.

7. Scripps (*Life of Abraham Lincoln* [1900 ed.], pp. 19–20), lists books which Lincoln read as a boy in the order in which he may have read them, a very valuable bit of information. The first book in the list is Dilworth's Speller. The title page reads: Dilworth's Spelling-Book, Improved. | A | New Guide | to the | English Tongue: | Containing, [thirty-three lines of contents in two columns] | To the whole is prefixed, | Forms of Prayer, for the Use of Schools. | By Thomas Dilworth, | Author of the Schoolmaster's Assistant; Young Book-keepers | Assistant, &c. and Schoolmaster in Wapping. | A New American Edition; with many | Additions and Alterations. | Philadelphia: | Printed and sold by John M'Culloch No. 1. | North Third-street.—1796.

8. *Dilworth's Spelling-Book*, p. 9.

9. *Ibid.*, p. 29.

10. *Ibid.*, p. 78.

11. *Ibid.*, p. 88.

12. *Ibid.*, p. 112.

13. A deputation of colored folk visited Abraham Lincoln at the White House on September 7, 1864, and presented him with a copy of the Bible. In his reply of acceptance the President said, "In regard to this Great Book, I have but to say, it is the best gift God has given to man." *Collected Works*, VII, 542.

14. Scripps, *Life of Abraham Lincoln*, p. 18. Lincoln, when reviewing the Scripps manuscript, allowed the following statements to stand: "The practice [Bible reading], continued faithfully through a series of years, could not fail to produce certain effects. Among other things, its tendency was to impart an active acquaintance with Bible history and Bible teachings; and it must also have been largely instrumental in developing the religious element in the character of the younger members of the family. . . . There are few men in public life so familiar with the Scriptures as Mr. Lincoln, while to those pious labors of his mother in his early childhood are doubtless to be attributed much of that purity of life, that elevation of moral character, that exquisite sense of justice, and that sentiment of humanity which now form distinguishing traits of his character."

Beveridge, citing Dennis Hanks, says that there was no Bible in the Lincoln home until 1819. *Abraham Lincoln*, I, 70.

15. This Bible is in Visitor's Center, at Lincoln's birthplace, Hodgenville.

The author has had the privilege of carefully studying the preliminaries and expository features of it. The signature "Abraham Lincoln," which appears on the back of the front cover, is said to have been written "When but nine years of age."

Following is the title page of the Lincoln Bible: The Holy Bible | containing | The Old and New | Testaments | with Arguments | prefixed to the different books and | moral and theological | Observations | illustrating each chapter | Composed by | The Reverend Mr. Ostervald, Professor of | Divinity and One of the Ministers at | Neufchatel in Switzerland | Translated at the Direction of and Rec | ommended by the Society for Propa- | gating Christian Knowledge. | And sold by all book dealers in | Great Britain | MDCCXCIX.

16. Lincoln students are agreed that the beauty and simplicity of his literary style traces its origin to his reading of the Bible. The Gettysburg Address is set in a framework remindful of the Bethlehem nativity story. The Second Inaugural makes fourteen references to deity, three to prayer, and contains three quotations from the Bible. An editorial in the *British Standard* characterized this Inaugural as "the most remarkable thing ever produced by any President of the United States from the first day until now. Its Alpha and Omega is Almighty God, the God of justice and the father of Mercies. . . . there is in fact much of the old prophet about it." Undated clipping, Lincoln National Life Foundation, Fort Wayne.

17. Rankin, *Personal Recollections of Abraham Lincoln*, p. 321. This volume records the reminiscences of the author's mother, Arminda Rankin, of Petersburg, Illinois, in whose home Lincoln often visited. Mrs. Rankin related that Lincoln stated "that his instruction by [his mother] . . . in letters and morals, and especially the Bible stories, and the interest and love he acquired in reading the Bible through this teaching of his mother, had been the strongest and most influential experience in his life." *Ibid.*, p. 320.

18. Abraham Lincoln to Jesse Lincoln, April 1, 1854, in *Collected Works*, II, 217.

19. James L. Nall to W. H. Sweeney, 1881, in "James L. Nall. The Biographical Notes of a Descendant of Abraham Lincoln's Grandfather," in *The Lincoln Kinsman*, No. 44 (February, 1942), pp. 2–3. Mr. Nall was a great-grandson of the pioneer Abraham Lincoln.

20. Draper Manuscripts, 12CC-4b, State Historical Society of Wisconsin. See also Louis A. Warren, "Abraham Lincoln Senior, Grandfather of the President," in *The Filson Club Quarterly*, V, No. 3 (July, 1931), p. 146.

21. This is the story as related by Mitchell Thompson, a son of Sarah Mitchell Thompson, and printed in the Louisville *Courier-Journal*, January 5, 1881.

22. Durrett MSS, Chronological Files, 1795, University of Chicago Library. "In the week evenings Thomas Lincoln would entertain his family with stories, many of which related to the Adventures of Daniel Boone and other pioneers of Kentucky." See also David D. Thompson, *Abraham Lincoln, the First American* (Cincinnati, 1894), pp. 9–10.

23. George R. Wilson, *Early Indiana Trails and Surveys* (Indiana Historical Society *Publications*, VI, No. 3, Indianapolis, 1919), p. 388.

24. James H. Kellar, *An Archaeological Survey of Spencer County* (Indianapolis, Indiana Historical Bureau, 1956).
25. *History of Warrick, Spencer and Perry Counties*, pp. 251–54. Variant accounts given in Will Fortune (ed.), *Warrick and Its Prominent People* (Evansville, 1881), pp. 10–13, and Arvil S. Barr, "Warrick County Prior to 1818," in *Indiana Magazine of History,* XIV (1918), 320–22. In the Rockport (Ind.) *Democrat,* March 17, 1860, there is an account by William Kellums, who was born in 1785. His recollections differ considerably from the other accounts cited.
26. Rockport *Democrat,* March 17, 1860.
27. *History of Warrick, Spencer and Perry Counties,* pp. 586–87.
28. Josiah G. Holland, *The Life of Abraham Lincoln* (Springfield, Mass., 1866), p. 23.
29. "Autobiography," in *Collected Works,* IV, 62. Senator Daniel W. Voorhees recalled that during the Civil War Lincoln once said to him, "Voorhees, doesn't it seem strange to you that I should be here? Doesn't it strike you as queer that I, who couldn't cut the head off of a chicken, and who was sick at the sight of blood, should be cast into the middle of a great war, with blood flowing all about me?" Undated clipping in the Lincoln National Life Foundation.
30. The Indiana Historical Society Library has a rare elephant folio edition of the *Birds of America* (London, 1827–38).

    One wonders if an episode which occurred in the White House when Lincoln's own son Tad was about the age Abraham was at the time of the turkey incident, might not have brought back some vivid memories to the President. A live turkey had been sent to the White House to be used during the holidays. Tad immediately made friends with the bird which followed him about the grounds. It was named Jack, and Tad fed him and made a great pet of him. When it came time to prepare the turkey for the table, Tad, in great alarm, rushed to his father who was in a cabinet meeting. One author recreates the episode thus: "Tad burst into the room like a bombshell, sobbing and crying with rage and indignation. The turkey was about to be killed. Tad had procured from the executioner a stay of proceedings while he hurried to lay the case before the President. 'Jack must not be killed; it is wicked.' 'But,' said the President, 'Jack was sent here to be killed, and eaten. . . .' 'I can't help it,' roared Tad between his sobs, 'He's a good turkey, and I don't want him killed.' The President of the United States pausing in the midst of his business took a card and on it wrote an order of reprieve. The turkey's life was spared, and Tad, seizing the precious bit of paper, fled to set him at liberty." Ralph Bradford, *Reprieve. A Christmas Story of 1863* (Washington, D. C., 1940).
31. There is a tradition that Audubon and Ferdinand Rozier were in business in Elizabethtown in 1807 and 1808, before Audubon moved to Henderson. If this is true, Thomas Lincoln probably met him. Samuel Haycraft, *History of Elizabethtown* (Elizabethtown, Ky., 1921), p. 108; Francis H. Herrick, *Audubon the Naturalist* (2 volumes. New York, 1917), Chronology, I, xxvi–xxviii.

    Audubon listed for taxation in the year 1816 three slaves and five town lots with a valuation of $3,495.00. Henderson County (Ky.)

Commissioners Tax Book. He purchased his first town lot on December 22, 1812. Henderson County Deed Book A, p. 57. On October 15, 1819, Audubon and his wife Lucy, "of the town of Henderson," sold their remaining lots. *Ibid.*, D, p. 228. Between the two above dates, there are twenty-five real estate deals recorded in which Audubon was one of the parties. A bronze tablet has been placed on a business block at Henderson bearing this inscription: "On this corner stood the general merchandise store of John J. Audubon, 1810–1820."

32. Maximilian, Prince of Wied, *Travels in the Interior of North America,* in Reuben Gold Thwaites (ed.), *Early Western Travels* (32 volumes. Cleveland, 1904–7), pp. 168–69, 194–95.
33. William Hebert, quoted in Harlow Lindley (comp.), *Indiana as Seen by Early Travelers* (*Indiana Historical Collections,* I, Indianapolis, 1916), p. 337.
34. Quoted in Mrs. Horace St. John, *Audubon, The Naturalist of the New World* (Boston, 1861), p. 33.
35. Quoted in Lindley (comp.), *Indiana as Seen by Early Travelers,* p. 510.
36. On this point see Warren, *Lincoln's Parentage and Childhood,* pp. 176–79.
37. Sarah Bush Lincoln to Herndon, September 8, 1865. Herndon-Weik MSS.
38. Cited in Duss, *George Rapp and His Associates,* p. 12.
39. *History of Warrick, Spencer and Perry Counties,* p. 557.
40. *Collected Works,* I, 386–88. Lincoln concluded this poem, which he composed in 1846, with the following stanzas which contain a moral similar to the morals found in *Æsop's Fables.*

> And now a dinsome clamor rose,
> 'Bout who should have his skin;
> Who first draws blood, each hunter knows,
> This prize must always win.
>
> But who did this, and how to trace
> What's true from what's a lie,
> Like lawyers, in a murder case
> They stoutly *argufy.*
>
> Aforesaid fice, of blustering mood,
> Behind, and quite forgot,
> Just now emerging from the wood,
> Arrives upon the spot.
>
> With grinning teeth, and up-turned hair—
> Brim full of spunk and wrath,
> He growls, and seizes on dead bear,
> And shakes for life and death.
>
> And swells as if his skin would tear,
> And growls and shakes again;
> And swears, as plain as dog can swear,
> That he has won the skin.

Conceited whelp! we laugh at thee—
Nor mind, that not a few
Of pompous, two-legged dogs there be,
Conceited quite as you.

41. William M. Cockrum, *A Pioneer History of Indiana* (Oakland City, Ind., 1907), pp. 464–65.
42. Tract Book, Vincennes District, No. VI, vol. II, p. 296, in Archives Division, Indiana State Library. Here Lincoln is spelled Linkern.
43. *Ibid.*
44. National Archives, Records of the General Land Office, Receipt No. 9205. In this receipt Lincoln is again spelled Linkern.

CHAPTER IV

1. *Indiana Boundaries. Territory, State, and County* (*Indiana Historical Collections,* XIX, Indianapolis, 1933), p. 742.
2. Vincennes *Western Sun & General Advertiser,* July 12, 1817.
3. Perry County (Ind.) Circuit Court Order Book, 1815. For sketch of the Joseph Hanks family see *The Lincoln Kinsman,* No. 22 (April, 1940).
4. Perry County Order Book, 1815; *Executive Proceedings of the State of Indiana 1816–1836,* edited by Dorothy Riker (*Indiana Historical Collections,* XXIX, Indianapolis, 1947), pp. 256, 602. Thomas Lincoln was the last of the five children of the pioneer Abraham to move westward. As noted above Josiah was living in Harrison County, Indiana; Mordecai had moved into Grayson County, Kentucky; Mary, the wife of Ralph Crume, was in Breckinridge County, and Nancy, wife of William Brumfield, was in western Hardin County. For information on these migrations see *The Lincoln Kinsman,* No. 38 (August, 1941); No. 39 (September, 1941); No. 41 (November, 1941), and No. 42 (December, 1941).
5. Undated newspaper clipping in possession of Ora Brown, Dale, Indiana.
6. Jonathan T. Hobson, *Footprints of Abraham Lincoln . . .* (Dayton, Ohio, 1909), p. 19.
7. "Autobiography," in *Collected Works,* IV, 62.
8. Holland, *Life of Abraham Lincoln,* p. 34.
9. See Herndon and Weik, *Herndon's Life of Lincoln* (1930 ed.), p. 51. Lamon says that "he did not recover for many minutes." *Life of Abraham Lincoln,* p. 68. See also "The Concussive Head Injury," in *Lincoln's Emotional Life,* by Milton H. Shutes (Philadelphia, 1957), p. 194.
10. Account by Estwick Evans in Thwaites (ed.), *Early Western Travels,* VIII, 270.
11. According to Scripps, *Life of Abraham Lincoln* (1900 ed.), p. 19, after the Bible, in Abe's reading list came "Esop's Fables, which he read with great zest, and so often as to commit the whole to memory. After that he obtained a copy of The Pilgrim's Progress."
12. David Turnham to Herndon, n. d., Herndon-Weik MSS.
13. "When a boy, the owner of a bow and arrow, I found one must let up on the bow, if the arrow is to have force." Lincoln to Josiah B. Grinnell, quoted in Grinnell, *Men and Events of Forty Years . . .*

(Boston, 1891), p. 171. One of Lincoln's boyhood friends recalled that he "was figurative in his speeches, talks & conversation. He argued much from analogy and explained things hard for us to understand by stories, maxims, tales and figures." Nathaniel Grigsby to Herndon, September 12, 1865, Herndon-Weik MSS.

14. Lincoln wrote to Dr. Sunderland, chaplain of the Senate, a few days before he issued the Emancipation Proclamation: "As for the negroes . . . what is to become of them. . . . it made me think of a story I read in one of my first books, 'Æsop's Fables.' It was an old edition and had curious rough wood-cuts, one of which showed four white men scrubbing a negro in a potash kettle filled with cold water. The text explained that the men thought that by scrubbing the negro they could make him white. . . ." Emanuel Hertz, *Abraham Lincoln. A New Portrait* (2 volumes. New York, 1931), II, 898.

15. Elias Nason, *Eulogy on Abraham Lincoln* (William V. Spencer, Boston, 1865), p. 10.

16. Thompson, *Abraham Lincoln, the First American*, p. 16.

17. Rev. Chauncey Hobart, *Recollections of My Life. Fifty Years of Itineracy in the Northwest* (Red Wing Printing Co., 1885), p. 57. The Rockport *Journal* of February 19, 1897, published an article submitting a list of the ten best works for children. The first four named were: *Æsop's Fables, Robinson Crusoe, Swiss Family Robinson,* and *The Pilgrim's Progress.*

18. The title page of the copy in hand reads: The | Pilgrim's Progress | from | This World | To That Which Is to Come. | Delivered | Under the Similitude of a Dream | By John Bunyan. | In Three Parts. | A New Edition, Divided into Chapters. | To which are added, | Explanatory and Practical Notes, | By Messrs. Mason, Scott, and Burder. | Embellished with Elegant Engravings. | Philadelphia: | Published by Jonathan Pounder, 134 N. Fourth Street | and William W. Woodward, 52 S. Second Street. | Griggs & Co. Printers. | 1817.

19. *Ibid.,* p. vi.

20. *Ibid.,* p. 9.

21. *Ibid.,* pp. 32–33.

22. Dennis Sparrow, *et al., vs.* Robert Alexander, Hardin County (Ky.) Circuit Court, Equity Bundle 32. The plaintiff in the suit claimed that Thomas Sparrow was "defrauded out of his land." For Dennis Hanks's relationship see below, p. 252, note 20.

23. This assumption is supported by a suit brought against Thomas Sparrow and his brother-in-law, Jesse Friend, by Mrs. Nancy Ashcraft for "a broken covenant." Sparrow and Friend had agreed in March, 1798, to work Mrs. Ashcraft's land "for one-third of what should be raised." Apparently they did no work whatsoever. Hardin County (Ky.) Court, Ashcraft *vs.* Friend and Sparrow, Ordinary Bundle 4.

24. Evansville *Journal* (wkly), October 14, 1840.

25. On September 16, 1950, when the author delivered an address at Nancy Hanks Lincoln's grave, he noticed several of these plants growing close by.

26. James Fitton Couch, a chemist with the Pathological Division of the Bureau of Animal Industry, after several years of research, determined that milk sickness was caused by "tremetol," active in richweed or white

snakeroot *(Eupatorium urticaefolium). Journal of the American Chemical Society,* LI, No. 12 (December, 1929), pp. 3617–19.

27. For other articles on milk sickness see *Journal of Agricultural Research,* XXXV, No. 6 (December 15, 1927); *The Outlook,* November 3, 1926, p. 297; *American Review of Reviews,* June, 1923, p. 657; *American Forests and Forest Life,* March, 1924; *Hoard's Dairyman,* May 2, 1924; and Philip D. Jordan, "The Death of Nancy Hanks Lincoln," in *Indiana Magazine of History,* XL (June, 1944), 103–10.

28. Spencer County (Ind.) Wills, 1818.

29. Hobson, *Footprints of Abraham Lincoln,* p. 18.

30. Dennis Hanks to Herndon, June 13, 1865, Herndon-Weik MSS; lecture by Joshua Speed, undated clipping in Lincoln National Life Foundation.

31. Biographical notes on leaf excerpted from the Lincoln family Bible. *Collected Works,* II, 95. William Wood, a neighbor of the Lincolns, stated many years later, "Mrs. Thomas Lincoln, Abe's mother, was sick about one and a half years after she came. . . . I do not think she absolutely died of the milk sickness entirely. Probably this helped to seal her fate." Wood to Herndon, September 15, 1865, Herndon-Weik MSS.

32. For the origin of "angel mother," see *Lincoln Lore,* No. 832 (March 19, 1945).

33. The burial plot was on land owned by John Carter in Clay Township, in the northeast quarter of Section 5.

34. Hobson, *Footprints of Abraham Lincoln,* p. 18.

35. The headstone apparently was broken and carried away by souvenir hunters, and the grave of Nancy Hanks Lincoln was for many years unmarked. In 1879 P. E. Studebaker of South Bend, Indiana, had a beautiful but simple stone placed at her grave, inscribed: "Nancy Hanks | Lincoln | Mother of President | Lincoln | Died October 5, A.D. 1818 | Aged 35 Years | Erected by a friend of her martyred son 1879.

    Allen Brooner, son of Henry Brooner, assisted in the location of Nancy's grave when the stone was placed. J. Edward Murr, "Lincoln in Indiana," in *Indiana Magazine of History,* XIV (1918), 177–79; Ida M. Tarbell, *The Early Life of Abraham Lincoln* (New York, 1896), p. 75.

    On October 1, 1892, a more elaborate stone was placed at the grave, but this was later removed and the Studebaker stone retained. Under the direction of the Indiana State Department of Conservation, assisted by the Indiana Lincoln Union, a beautiful memorial structure has been erected south of the grave. One of the buildings is named The Nancy Hanks Lincoln Hall. A marker placed at the entrance of the approach to the burial place is inscribed: "You are facing the wooded knoll on which sleeps Nancy Hanks Lincoln, mother of the President who lived in this Hoosier environment during the formative years of his life from 1816 to 1830. Beyond, to the north, is marked the humble log cabin where she led him for a little while along the path to greatness."

36. The author has interviewed Elkin's descendants and they generally claim such a letter was written, and one aged member of the family even

said that she had seen it and stated that it was last possessed by Bert Aitken. Author's notes.

37. Warren, *Lincoln's Parentage and Childhood*, pp. 244–48.
38. Quoted from an undated clipping from a Louisville newspaper, in the Lincoln National Life Foundation. Also see Holland, *The Life of Abraham Lincoln*, p. 29.
39. Isaac N. Arnold, *The Life of Abraham Lincoln* (Chicago, 1885), p. 19.
40. William Wood to Herndon, September 15, 1865, Herndon-Weik MSS.
41. Nathaniel Grigsby to Herndon, September 12, 1865, in *ibid.*
42. Dennis Hanks to Herndon, June 13, 1865, in *ibid.*

CHAPTER V

1. John Hanks, half brother of Dennis, described Nancy Lincoln as being "by nature refined, and of far more than ordinary intellect. Her friends spoke of her as being a person of marked and decided character. . . ." Arnold, *The Life of Abraham Lincoln*, p. 19. John Hanks never knew Nancy Hanks Lincoln personally, but knew those who had known her very well.
2. "It is certain that Lincoln cherished, with just pride, a family repute for native ability, and alluded to it in after life, when he felt his first impulse of ambition and began in earnest his struggle with the accidents of ignorance and poverty." William Dean Howells, *Life of Abraham Lincoln* (Abraham Lincoln Association, Springfield, Ill., 1938), p. 20. The little volume carries on its title page this statement: "This campaign biography corrected by the hand of Abraham Lincoln in the summer of 1860 is reproduced here with careful attention to the appearance of the original volume." In correcting the biography Lincoln let the "family repute" statement stand. In an autobiographical sketch Lincoln prepared for Jesse Fell he said that his parents were "of undistinguished families. . . . Any effort to identify them with the New England family of the same name indeed is nothing more definite than a similarity of Christian names in both families such as Enoch, Levi, Mordecai, Solomon, Abraham. . . ." *Collected Works*, III, 511. However, as seen in Chapter I, the New England Lincolns and Kentucky-Indiana Lincolns were branches of the same family.
3. Quoted in Atkinson, *The Boyhood of Lincoln*, p. 19.
4. Rankin, *Personal Recollections of Abraham Lincoln*, p. 320.
5. Nelson County (Ky.) Court, Possessioners' Report Book, 1781; Hardin County (Ky.) Commissioners Tax Book, 1793.
6. Hardin County (Ky.) Court, Order Book B, p. 13.
7. Haycraft, *History of Elizabethtown*, pp. 16, 53.
8. Bleakley & Montgomery Day Book, May 27, June 4, 1806.
9. Hardin County (Ky.) Marriage Bonds, 1806.
10. Newman *vs.* Johnston and Bush, Hardin County (Ky.) Circuit Court, Ordinary Bundle 5, 1811.
11. Reed *vs.* Johnston and Bush, in *ibid.*, Ordinary Bundle 5, 1811.
12. Bleakley & Montgomery Day Book, September 17, 1805. Facsimile in possession of the Lincoln National Life Foundation.
13. Christopher Bush, father of Sally, made his will on February 24, 1812, signing with his mark. He stated, "I have already given to my children

except Christopher and John their full share of my estate both real and personal and being decided that my two sons, Christopher and John, shall share in my estate equally to what I have given the rest of the children who have left me. . . ." So it appears that as early as 1812, with Sally's share of the estate already received, Johnston is noted on the court records as being "Without funds." Hardin County (Ky.) Will Book B, p. 75.

Christopher Bush and Hannah his wife conveyed to Elijah Bush and Daniel Johnston on July 1, 1809, 730 acres of land in Breckinridge County. (Hardin County, Ky., Deed Book D, p. 192.) The same day Elijah Bush and Nancy his wife sold their share in the above tract to Daniel Johnston. (*Ibid.*, p. 309.) On February 26, 1811, Daniel Johnston and Sarah his wife sold the entire tract to James Crutcher, both Daniel and Sarah signing the deed by making their marks. (*Ibid.*, p. 520.)

14. Hardin County (Ky.) Court, Judgments and Other Papers, 1812.
15. Hardin County (Ky.) Court, Order Book C, p. 192.
16. Haycraft, *History of Elizabethtown*, p. 29.
17. Hardin County (Ky.) Court, Order Book C, p. 315.
18. *Ibid.*, p. 368.
19. The agreement read: "This shall oblige me or my executor to convey to Sarah Johnston a certain lot of land containing an acre and one-fourth lying and situated near Elizabethtown and adjoining to Ben Helm lot and garden and beginning about four feet northwest of the southeast corner of said Helm's lot running thence north thirty and west twenty-two poles to a stake, thence with the line of said Helm to the beginning—The said conveyance to be made when it will be thought more practicable. Witness my hand and Seal 12th Day of February 1817.

    "Test.
    "Ich'd Radley   Samuel Haycraft"

    Ichabod Radley was Sally's brother-in-law. On the back of this document there are two endorsements. The first states: "I do assign over the one half of the within lot to Ich'd Radley, the end next to the Mill Race, as witness my hand and seal February 12, 1818. Sarah **X** Bush, witness Christopher Bush." The second endorsement reveals that Radley sold the half of the original lot he had purchased from Sally to George L. Rogers on March 17, 1819.

    The document is in the possession of George E. Merrifield.
20. Hardin County (Ky.) Deed Book G, p. 213.
21. Affidavit of Squire H. Bush in possession of the author. On November 11, 1816, Thomas Lincoln paid to Samuel Carpenter, a justice of the peace of Nelson County, the sum of $2.50 for the printing of a "Cross Bill" against Isaac Bush to collect the $200.00 which the court had decreed Bush should pay Lincoln in the litigation over the farm which Lincoln had purchased from Bush in 1808. In 1818 the court ordered that Bush should pay Lincoln the $200.00 and costs which amounted to $8.40. Mather *vs.* Vance, Bush, and Lincoln, Hardin County (Ky.) Circuit Court, Equity Bundle 12. Possibly Thomas Lincoln was able to collect some of this money from Bush with which to pay Sally Bush Johnston's debt.

22. Hardin County (Ky.) Marriage Bonds, 1819; Marriage Register, December 2, 1819.

In 1921, during a three-year residence in Elizabethtown, the author observed that an old building about to be razed was the residence of the Rev. George Rogers. It was here, according to Squire Bush, that Thomas Lincoln and Sally Bush Johnston were married. The author acquired the studding of the roof and had it cut into small blocks about three inches square. These were presented to the Elizabethtown Woman's Club to sell. When the clapboards which covered the old brick chimney were removed, a large block of stone, bearing the initials S. P. and the date 1806, was discovered. The initials were those of Samuel Patton who built the home. It is possible that Thomas Lincoln, then doing carpentry work in the town, might have helped build the structure in which he and Sally were married.

For pictures of the cabin in process of demolition, the marriage bond, Squire Bush, and his statement concerning Thomas Lincoln's proposal quoted above, see *Sarah Bush Lincoln* (Elizabethtown Woman's Club, 1922).

23. The relative social and economic status of the Lincolns and Bushes has been discussed at some length by various authors. Herndon wrote that Sally's social status was fixed by the comparison of a neighbor who observed that "life among the Hankses, the Lincolns, and the Enlows was a long way below life among the Bushes." Herndon and Weik, *Herndon's Life of Lincoln* (1930 ed.), p. 28. This would be hard to prove. Comparison of the economic backgrounds of the Lincolns and Bushes reveals that the pioneer Abraham Lincoln entered over five thousand acres of land. This was a much larger acreage than Christopher Bush ever possessed. Intellectually, too, the Lincolns compared very favorably. See Waldo Lincoln, *History of the Lincoln Family.*

24. Sally Bush Lincoln to William Herndon, September 8, 1865, Herndon-Weik MSS.

25. Atkinson, *The Boyhood of Lincoln,* p. 22.

26. Dennis Hanks to Herndon, June 13, 1865, Herndon-Weik MSS.

27. Atkinson, *The Boyhood of Lincoln,* p. 21.

28. Vincennes *Western Sun,* January 31, 1829.

29. The title page of the copy in hand follows: The | American | Spelling Book; | Containing, | The Rudiments | of the | English Language | for the | Use of Schools | in the | United States. | By Noah Webster Esq. | The revised impression. | Hartford: | Printed by Hudson & Goodwin. 1809.

30. The title page of the copy in hand follows: The | Life | and Most | Surprising Adventures | of | Robinson Crusoe, | of York, Mariner, | Who Lived Eight and Twenty Years | in an Uninhabited Island, | on the Coast of America, near the Mouth of | Great River Oroonoque. With an | Account of His Deliverance Thence; | and His After | Surprising Adventures. | A new edition, complete in One Volume; | with plates, descriptive of the subject. | London: | Published and sold by the book-sellers; | and by T. Wilson and Son, Printers, | High-house gate, York. | 1810.

31. Daniel Defoe, though trained for the ministry, entered into business. While in London he organized a dissenting congregation to which he sometimes preached. "Defoe has been called the father of the modern English novel. . . . Like Bunyan his aim was moral. . . . Crusoe's thoughts upon religion and the need for repentance might have been written by the author of *Pilgrim's Progress.*"

32. An interesting parallel is found in the next to last paragraph of Lincoln's Second Inaugural Address, March 4, 1865: "If we shall suppose that American Slavery is one of those offences which, in the providence of God, must needs come, but which, having continued through His appointed time, He now wills to remove, and that He gives to both North and South, this terrible war, as the evil due to those by whom the offence came, shall we discern therein any departure from those divine attributes which the believers in a living God always ascribe to Him? Fondly do we hope—fervently do we pray—that this mighty scourge of war may speedily pass away. But if God wills that it continue, until all the wealth piled by the bond-man's two hundred and fifty years of unrequited toil shall be sunk, and until every drop of blood drawn with the lash, shall be paid by another drawn with the sword, as was said three thousand years ago, so it must be said 'the judgments of the Lord, are true and righteous altogether.'" *Collected Works,* VIII, 333.

33. Lincoln used many figures of speech that apparently reached back to his early reading. In the debate with Douglas at Alton, on October 15, 1858, he said, "In every speech you heard Judge Douglas make, until he got into this 'imbroglio,' as they call it, with the Administration about the Lecompton Constitution, every speech on the Nebraska bill was full of his felicitations that we were *just at the end* of the slavery agitation. The last tip of the last joint of the old serpent's tail was just drawing out of view." [Author's italics] *Collected Works,* III, 306.

34. Atkinson, *The Boyhood of Lincoln,* p. 24.

35. *Ibid.,* pp. 24, 25. David Turnham states that a copy of "Sinbad the Sailor" was brought by his family from Kentucky and that Abe read it in their home. Turnham to Herndon, October 12, 1866, Herndon-Weik MSS.

36. Quoted in Gesell, *Studies in Child Development,* pp. 145–46.

CHAPTER VI

1. Minutes of the Board of Trustees of Elizabethtown (Ky.), No. 1.

2. Once during his Presidency when he was being pressured to hand out military commissions, Lincoln sent this message to Richard Yates and William Butler: ". . . you must know that Major Generalships in the Regular Army are not as plenty as blackberries." April 10, 1862, in *Collected Works,* V, 186.

3. See Logan Esarey, *The Indiana Home* (R. E. Banta, Crawfordsville, Ind., 1943), pp. 34 ff.

4. Nathaniel Grigsby to Herndon, September 12, 1865, Herndon-Weik MSS. Lincoln is said to have told Peter Smith: "In my young days I frequently went barefooted. . . . never in cold weather." Smith to J. Warren Keifer, July 17, 1860, in Lincoln National Life Foundation.

5. Leonard Swett, a friend of Lincoln in his later years, quoted in Indianapolis *Journal*, February 10, 1879. Swett went on to say that Lincoln related the story of his childhood as a happy one. "There was nothing sad or pinched, and nothing of want and no allusion to want in any part of it. His own description of his youth was that of a happy joyous boyhood. It was told with mirth and glee and illustrated by pointed anecdotes, often interrupted by his jocund laugh."

There is a picture of the traditional swimming hole of the neighborhood in Ida M. Tarbell's *Early Life of Abraham Lincoln*, p. 55.

6. Bleakley and Montgomery, Day Book, May 27, 1806.

7. The title page reads: Lessons in Elocution: | or, a | Selection of Pieces, | in | Prose and Verse, | for the Improvement of Youth | in Reading and Speaking. | by William Scott. | The ninth American, from the fifth British, edition. | To which are prefixed, | Elements of Gesture, Illustrated by four Elegant Copper-plates; also, Rules | for expressing, with propriety, the various Passions and Emotions of the Mind. | Whitehall: | Printed for William Young, Bookseller and | Stationer, No. 52, South Second Street, Philadelphia. | 1801.

8. Lincoln stated that a single line in Gray's Elegy, "The short and simple annals of the poor," contained the substance of his early life. Herndon and Weik, *Herndon's Life of Lincoln* (1930 ed.), p. 2.

9. There is a tradition that Abraham secured a copy of Scott's *Lessons* from David Turnham. If so it may have been a later edition than the one Sally brought with her. David Turnham to Herndon, October 12, 1866, in Herndon-Weik MSS.

10. Dennis Hanks to Herndon, June 13, 1865, Herndon-Weik MSS.

11. Sally Bush Lincoln to Herndon, September 8, 1865, in *ibid*.

12. John Romine to Herndon, n. d., in *ibid*.

13. Quoted in Hobson, *Footprints of Abraham Lincoln*, p. 19.

14. John Hanks to Herndon, n. d., Herndon-Weik MSS.

15. Sally Bush Lincoln to Herndon, September 8, 1865, in *ibid*.

16. Allen Thorndike Rice (comp.), *Reminiscences of Abraham Lincoln* . . . (New York, 1888), p. 485; Sally Bush Lincoln to Herndon, September 8, 1865, in Herndon-Weik MSS.

17. "Autobiography," in *Collected Works*, IV, 62.

There are many unsupported traditions concerning schools attended by Abraham Lincoln and the teachers who taught them. According to a history of Spencer County, "The first school taught in Carter Township [where Thomas Lincoln's farm was located] was in 1820–21, by Joab Hungate in a rude log-cabin which stood near the present site of Dale. . . . This house was used for several years, and it is said Abraham attended here one or more terms. . . . Another early school cabin stood on Section 32, near the Lincoln home. Dorsey, Bryant, Price and others taught there. It is probable Abe Lincoln went to all of them. . . .

"School was taught in the old Pigeon Baptist Church as soon as it was built by James Bryant. . . . He taught all through this portion of the county, and Abe Lincoln was one of his pupils." John Prosser taught a school near Grandview, and there is a tradition that Abraham Lincoln credited Prosser with being of much help to him. Also, there was a school at Troy which Lincoln was supposed to have attended. *History of Warrick, Spencer and Perry Counties*, pp. 409–12.

18. Herndon's visit to Indiana, September 14, 1865, in Herndon-Weik MSS.
19. *Executive Proceedings of Indiana, 1816–1836*, p. 69. He resigned as justice in 1821. *Ibid.*, p. 176.
20. Photostats of returns in Genealogy Division, Indiana State Library.
21. Warrick County (Ind.) Marriage Records. This would indicate that the wife listed in the census had died or that the census return was taken later than November 2 and that Crawford had been single and married a widow with two children.
22. The first marriage Crawford performed as justice of the peace was that of Joseph C. Wright and Diana Pierce, on January 20, 1819. During 1819 he married Fayette Parker and Diana Wright, William Gordon and Lucinda Randle, George Angel and Elizabeth Turnham, and Emanuel Seyson and Phoebe Smith. The following year he married David M. Hutcherson and Polly Mason, Robert Zans and Ann Jones, and Isaiah Thorpe and Nancy Lamar. On March 14, 1821, he married Robert Angel and Polly Richardson. Spencer County (Ind.) Marriage Records.
23. Nathaniel Grigsby thought it was in the winter of 1818–19. Grigsby to Herndon, September 12, 1865, Herndon-Weik MSS, "The Crawford school was attended by Abraham 'about the time of his father's second marriage.'" Nason, *Eulogy on Abraham Lincoln*, p. 11.
24. Autobiographical sketch prepared by Lincoln for Jesse W. Fell, December 20, 1859, in *Collected Works*, III, 511.
25. Grigsby to Herndon, September 12, 1865, in Herndon-Weik MSS.
26. Herndon and Weik, *Herndon's Life of Lincoln* (1930 ed.), p. 35. Since Lincoln is also supposed to have helped Hannah Gentry to spell "defied" in the same manner, the story may be completely apocryphal. See below, p. 245.
27. Abraham Lincoln told this story to Senator John Brooks Henderson of Missouri, when he saw Thaddeus Stevens, Charles Sumner, and Henry Wilson coming into the White House. These three men had been pressuring the President to hasten emancipation. Anthony Gross (ed.), *Lincoln's Own Stories* (New York and London, 1912), pp. 113–15.

CHAPTER VII

1. Spencer County (Ind.) Marriage Register. The ceremony was performed by the Rev. Samuel Bristow.
2. Sally Bush Lincoln to Herndon, September 8, 1865, Herndon-Weik MSS. William Herndon who questioned that Thomas Lincoln was the father of Abraham, also tried to show that the relationship between father and son was not a friendly and congenial one. Herndon and Weik, *Herndon's Life of Lincoln* (1930 ed.), pp. 7, 24, 60.

Beveridge wrote, "Between Thomas Lincoln and his son, so different in intellect, character and appearance, there was little sympathy or understanding; and for some reason the father treated Abraham roughly." Beveridge, *Abraham Lincoln*, I, 65–66, 67, citing Dennis Hanks and A. H. Chapman, son-in-law of Hanks.

See "Lincoln's Respect for His Father," in *Lincoln Lore*, No. 197

(January 16, 1933), and "The Filial Relation of Thomas and Abraham Lincoln," in *ibid.*, No. 1263 (June 22, 1953).

3. Dennis Hanks to Herndon, June 13, 1865, in Herndon-Weik MSS.

4. Henry C. Whitney, *Life of Lincoln* (2 volumes. New York, 1908), I, 10; Nathaniel Grigsby to Herndon, September 12, 1865, in Herndon-Weik MSS.

5. Whitney, *Life of Lincoln*, I, 10.

6. Statement of John Hanks in Herndon-Weik MSS.

7. John J. Hall, son of Matilda Johnston Hall, quoted in St. Louis *Globe Democrat*, September 29, 1895.

8. Atkinson, *The Boyhood of Lincoln*, pp. 44–45.

9. W. H. Doak, in Terre Haute *Star*, February 11, 1923.

10. The proceedings relative to building the meetinghouse may be found in the Little Pigeon Church, Minute Book, Illinois State Historical Society. A transcription of this is in the Indiana State Library.

11. Scripps, *Life of Abraham Lincoln* (1900 ed.), p. 19.

12. *One Hundred Influential American Books Printed before 1900 . . .* (The Grolier Club, New York, 1947), p. 58.

13. *Ibid.*, pp. 58–59.

14. The volume Abe read may have been: The | Life | of | Dr. Benjamin Franklin | written by himself | Montpelier | Printed by Samuel Goss | for Josiah Parks | 1809. 202 pp.

15. Franklin to Benjamin Vaughn, October 24, 1788, in *The Works of Benjamin Franklin . . .* , edited by Jared Sparks (10 volumes. Boston, 1840), X, 304.

16. In his address at Cooper Institute, February 27, 1860, Lincoln listed Franklin as one of "the most noted anti-slavery men of those times." *Collected Works*, III, 531.

17. *One Hundred Influential American Books*, p. 64.
    While addressing the New Jersey Senate on February 21, 1861, Lincoln said, "May I be pardoned, if, upon this occasion, I mention that away back in my childhood, the earliest days of my being able to read, I got hold of a small book, such a one as few of the younger members have ever seen, 'Weems' Life of Washington.'" *Collected Works*, IV, 235.

18. A likely edition for Lincoln to have read is: The | Life of | George Washington | with | Curious Anecdotes, | Equally Honourable to Himself | and exemplary to his young country men. | [4 lines of verse] | Ninth edition—greatly improved. | Embellished with seven engravings. | by M. W. Weems, | formerly rector of Mount-Vernon Parish. | [8-line endorsement by H. Lee, Maj. Gen. Army U. S.] | Philadelphia: | Printed for Mathew Carey. | 1809.

19. Scripps, *Life of Abraham Lincoln* (1900 ed.), p. 19.

20. Weems, *Life of George Washington*, pp. 23, 26.

21. *Ibid.*, pp. 12–14.

22. *Ibid.*, p. 87. In a speech made at Virginia, Illinois, on February 22, 1844, Lincoln, according to a reporter, "labored hard to prove that Washington never done [*sic*] a wrong thing in his life." *Collected Works*, I, 332.

23. Weems, *Life of George Washington*, pp. 84–86. In addressing the New

236

Jersey Senate (see note 17 above) Lincoln continued: "I remember all the accounts there [in Weems's *Washington*] given of the battle fields and struggles for the liberty of the country, and none fixed themselves upon my imagination so deeply as the struggle here at Trenton, New-Jersey. The crossing of the river; the contest with the Hessians; the great hardships endured at that time, all fixed themselves on my memory more than any single revolutionary event; and you all know, for you have all been boys, how these early impressions last longer than any others. I recollect thinking then, boy even though I was, that there must have been something more than common that these men struggled for." *Collected Works*, IV, 235–36.

In Lincoln's writing and speaking we find passages with diction reminiscent of Weems. The latter frequently used the adverb "so" associated with an adjective or other adverb: "so brutish a practice," "so great their ambition," "so keen was their passion," "so uncommon for war," "so well deserved," "so great were his fears," "so confident of success," "so great was the dread," "so harassed my heart," "so dignified with virtue," "so quickly tarnished," "so wonderful a manner," "so heartily beloved," "so powerful an armament."

In Lincoln's writing we observe the same thing. In his First Inaugural Address we find "so grave a matter," "so desperate a step," "so fearful a mistake." In the Gettysburg Address he said "any nation so conceived and so dedicated," "so nobly advanced." In two letters which President Lincoln wrote on November 21, 1864, one to John Phillips and the other to the Widow Bixby he used these expressions: "so honored a part," "a citizen so venerable," "served so long and so *well*," "a loss so overwhelming," "so costly a sacrifice." *Collected Works*, IV, 255; VII, 23; VIII, 117, 118. See also "Lincoln's Unique Phraseology," in *Lincoln Lore*, No. 1299 (March 1, 1954).

The eulogy which Lincoln pronounced upon the death of Gen. Zachary Taylor, on July 25, 1850, contains this account of the relief of Fort Brown in 1845, the dramatic style of which is certainly remindful of Weems: "And now the din of battle nears the fort and sweeps obliquely by; a gleam of hope flies through the half imprisoned few: they fly to the wall; every eye is strained; it is—it is—the stars and stripes are still aloft! Anon the anxious brethren meet; and while hand strikes hand, the heavens are rent with a loud, long, glorious, gushing cry of victory! victory!! victory!!!" *Collected Works*, II, 85.

24. Lincoln's address to the New Jersey Senate, February 21, 1861, in *Collected Works*, IV, 236.

25. Weems, *Life of George Washington*, p. 85.

26. Lincoln concluded his address before the Springfield Washingtonian Temperance Society at Springfield, Illinois, February 22, 1842, by saying: "Washington is the mightiest name of earth—*long since* mightiest in the cause of civil liberty; *still* mightiest in moral reformation. On that name, an eulogy is expected. It cannot be. To add brightness to the sun, or glory to the name of Washington, is alike impossible. Let none attempt it. In solemn awe pronounce the name, and in its naked deathless splendor leave it shining on." *Collected Works*, I, 279.

27. Nason, *Eulogy on Abraham Lincoln*, p. 11.

CHAPTER VIII

1. Nathaniel Grigsby to Herndon, September 12, 1865, in Herndon-Weik MSS.
2. Sally Bush Lincoln to Herndon, September 8, 1865, in *ibid*. She had cooked for Abe for fifteen years. Primitive methods of cooking prevailed in withdrawn areas in southern Indiana for fifty years after the Lincolns left. George R. Wilson, of Dubois County, recalled that in the eighties he "ate Johnny cake baked on a clean ash board set before an open fireplace and bacon fried on the blade of a garden hoe."
3. Statement of John Hanks in Herndon-Weik MSS.
4. Atkinson, *The Boyhood of Lincoln*, pp. 44–45.
5. John Morgan to his wife, August 5, 1822, photostat in Lincoln National Life Foundation.
6. Undated clipping from Louisville *Courier-Journal*, in Lincoln National Life Foundation.
7. Joseph C. Richardson to Herndon, September 14, 1865, in Herndon-Weik MSS.
8. Individual land entries may be found in the Tract Books in the Archives Division of the Indiana State Library. Photostat copies of the 1820 census records are in the Genealogy Division of the library. Of course, a land entry does not necessarily mean that the person making the entry moved with his family onto the land entered. See also *History of Warrick, Spencer and Perry Counties*, pp. 32–33, 270–74.
9. Colonel Durrett Day Book, in Durrett Collection, University of Chicago Library.
10. Warrick County (Ind.) Probate Court, Order Book, A, p. 1.
11. Charlott Swaney married Charles Meyers on January 21, 1821. Spencer County (Ind.) Marriage Register.
12. Perhaps Swaney was as well prepared as many who attempted to teach in the short-term, short-lived subscription schools of that day. See p. 82, above. On May 4, 1822, the Louisville *Advertiser* carried an announcement that "Joseph Buchanon wishes to establish himself at some place where the local population and wealth could support a reputable seminary. He teaches English literature, the Sciences, and the Latin Language. Address him at Yellow Banks, Kentucky." Yellow Banks was down river from Rockport, county seat of Spencer County, about ten miles. It is regrettable that the patrons of the Little Pigeon school were not financially able to hire him.
13. Hoskins entered land in section 23, T 5 S, R 4 W, in Jackson Township, Spencer County, on September 2, 1818. This location was about four and a half miles from the Lincoln home.
14. Lamon, *Life of Abraham Lincoln*, pp. 35–36.
15. *Ibid.*, p. 36. There is no doubt that Abraham went, however briefly, to this school taught by Swaney. In his autobiography prepared for Scripps he wrote: "While here [Indiana] A. went to A. B. C. schools by littles, kept successively by Andrew Crawford, —— Sweeney, and Azel W. Dorsey." *Collected Works*, IV, 62. The name Swaney often appears as "Sweeney" in records and histories, but the former seems to be correct. Also, herein, the author has assumed that Lincoln's first teacher in

Indiana was Andrew Crawford, then Swaney, and finally Dorsey, since Abraham himself lists them thus "successively."

According to Leonard Swett, Thomas Lincoln had endorsed a note for a neighbor which fell due about this time, the payment of which caused him financial distress and young Abe had to drop out of school. Rice (comp.), *Reminiscences of Abraham Lincoln,* p. 458.

On December 18, 1825, James Swaney married Sarah Jane Cranmore, and by 1830 he had acquired two tracts of land in Spencer County. According to the 1830 census he was then living in Rockport and had one child under five years. Spencer County (Ind.) Marriage Register; photostat of 1830 census in Genealogy Division, Indiana State Library.

16. Herndon wrote, "Mr. Lincoln told me in later years that Murray's English Reader was the best school-book ever put into the hands of an American youth." Herndon and Weik, *Herndon's Life of Lincoln* (1930 ed.), p. 34.

17. The *Reader* should not be confused with the English grammar which was compiled by the same author. A possible edition of the *Reader* for Abraham to have read was: The | English Reader | or | Pieces in Prose and Poetry | selected from | The Best Writers. | Designed to Assist Young Persons, | To Read with Propriety and Effect; | To Improve Their | Language and Sentiments, | and to inculcate | some of the most important principles | of piety and virtue. | With a few preliminary observations | on the principles of good reading. | By Lindley Murray, | Author of "English Grammar adapted to the different classes of learners," &c. | From the latest English edition, | New-York: | Published by Evert Duyckinck, | 102 Pearl Street. | John C. Totten, Printer. | 1815.

18. *Ibid.,* iii.

19. *Ibid.,* pp. 19–22.

20. *Ibid.,* pp. 156–58.

21. *Ibid.,* pp. 145–47.

22. *Ibid.,* pp. 105–7. Lincoln wrote a letter to Gen. Robert H. Milroy on June 29, 1863, in which he said, "You have constantly urged that you were persecuted because you did not come from West Point. . . . this my dear General is the rock on which you split." *Collected Works,* V, 368.

23. Murray, *English Reader,* p. 204.

24. *Ibid.,* p. 208.

25. *Ibid.,* p. 222.

26. Lincoln often has been called the most quoted American. For more than four hundred axioms, aphorisms, etc., see *Lincoln Lore,* Nos. 289, 334, 350, 364, 366, 372, 435, 489, 492, 501, and 1012.

27. The complete title reads: An Authentic Narrative | of the loss of the | American Brig Commerce, | Wrecked on the Western Coast of Africa, in the Month | of August, 1815. | With | An Account of the Sufferings | of her | Surviving officers and crew, | who were enslaved by the wandering Arabs on the great | African Desart, or Zahahrah, | and | Observations Historical, Geographical, &c. | Made during the travels of the author, while a slave to | the Arabs, and in the empire of Morocco. | By James Riley, | Late master and supercargo. | Preceded by a brief sketch of the author's life; and concluded by | a description of the famous city of Tombuctoo, on the river Niger, | and of another large city, far south of

it, on the same river, call- | ed Wassanah; narrated to the author at Mogadore, by Sidi Ha- | Met, the Arabian Merchant. | With an Arabic and English vocabulary. | Illustrated and embellished with ten hand- some copperplate engravings. | New-York: | Printed and published for the author, | by T. & W. Mercein, No. 93 Gold Street. | 1817.

28. Scripps, *Life of Lincoln* (1900 ed.), p. 19. See also *John Locke Scripps' 1860 Campaign Life of Abraham Lincoln Annotated . . .* , foreword and notes by M. L. Houser (Peoria, Ill., 1931), p. 14n.

29. Riley, *Narrative*, vii.

30. *Ibid.*, p. 2.

31. *Ibid.*, pp. 4–5.

32. *Ibid.*, pp. 473 ff., and 495 ff.

33. *Ibid.*, pp. 531–32.

CHAPTER IX

1. Transcription of Minute Book in Indiana State Library from original in Illinois State Historical Society Library, Springfield.

2. J. H. Spencer, *A History of Kentucky Baptists from 1769 to 1885 . . .* (2 volumes. Cincinnati, 1885), I, 164; II, 570–71.

3. The census reveals that in 1820, Bristow was between twenty-six and forty-five years of age with four boys and three girls in his family. It was he who united Dennis Hanks and Elizabeth Johnston in marriage in 1821.

4. Little Pigeon Association of United Baptists, Minutes, in Franklin College Library, Franklin, Indiana.

5. For a statement of the differences between the Regular and Separate Bap- tists see Spencer, *History of Kentucky Baptists*, I, 104–7.

6. The minutes of the Little Pigeon Church for June 7, 1823, read:
   "The chirch met and after prayer proceeded to busyness.
   1st. Inquired for fellowship.
   2nd. Invited members of Sister Churches to Seats with us.
   3rd. Opend a dore for the Reception of Members.
   4th. Receivd Brother Thomas Linkhon by letter and
   5th. The case of Sister Elizabeth White calld for . . .
   6th. The church appoints thair Messengers to Represent them . . .
   7th. Receivd Brother John Wire by Relation And Sister Linkhon and Thomas Carter by Experance."
   Dennis Hanks's statement in an article in the *American Magazine*, February, 1908, that Sally Lincoln "set some kind of trap fur him and got Tom to join the Baptist church," is completely unfounded. Appar- ently it was Thomas who persuaded his wife to join the church.

7. Atkinson, *The Boyhood of Lincoln*, pp. 44–45.

8. Terre Haute *Star*, February 11, 1923.

9. Herndon and Weik, *Herndon's Life of Lincoln* (1930 ed.), p. 24.

10. Dennis Hanks to Herndon, April 2, 1866, and Turnham to Herndon, n.d., in Herndon-Weik MSS.

11. Spencer, *History of Kentucky Baptists*, I, 170, 347–48.

12. Scripps, *Life of Lincoln* (1900 ed.), pp. 21–22.

13. Lincoln is reported to have said: "I don't like to hear cut and dried ser- mons. When I hear a man preach I like to see him act as if he were fight-

ing bees." Charles T. White, *Lincoln the Athlete and Other Stories* (New York, 1930), p. 24.

14. In a speech at Cincinnati on September 17, 1859, Lincoln said, "The good old maxims of the Bible are applicable, and truly applicable to human affairs, and in this as in other things, we may say here that he who is not for us is against us; he who gathereth not with us scattereth," Paraphrase of Matthew 12:30. *Collected Works*, III, 462. See also "Lincoln Quotes Scripture," in *Lincoln Lore*, No. 1393 (December 19, 1955).

15. The early antislavery influence is seen in the following statement of Lincoln in a letter to A. C. Hodges, April 4, 1864: "I am naturally anti-slavery. If slavery is not wrong nothing is wrong. I cannot remember the day when I did not so think and feel." *Collected Works*, VII, 281.

16. Spencer, *History of Kentucky Baptists*, I, 336; Dennis Hanks to Herndon, June 13, 1865, in Herndon-Weik MSS.

17. Spencer, *History of Kentucky Baptists*, I, 164.

18. *Ibid.*, II, 572.

19. Spencer County (Ind.) Marriage Register, 1821.

20. Beveridge, *Abraham Lincoln*, I, 53n.

21. *History of Warrick, Spencer and Perry Counties*, pp. 589, 725.

22. Spencer, *History of Kentucky Baptists*, I, 328, 330.

23. *Ibid.*, II, 68.

24. John Morgan to his wife, August 5, 1822, photostat in Lincoln National Life Foundation.

25. Spencer, *History of Kentucky Baptists*, II, 63; *History of Warrick, Spencer and Perry Counties*, p. 489. When Lincoln was in Indianapolis on September 19, 1859, he was introduced to James C. Veatch of Spencer County, a candidate for the state legislature, and upon hearing his name, asked, "Your name sounds familiar to me, was your grandfather a Baptist preacher?" Upon an affirmative reply, Lincoln said, "Oh! I have often heard him preach." Isaac Veatch was the father, not the grandfather, of James C. Undated clipping from the Indianapolis *News* in the Lincoln National Life Foundation.

26. William T. Stott, *Indiana Baptist History 1798–1908* (Franklin, Ind., 1908), p. 122.

27. Little Pigeon Creek Baptist Church, Minute Book.

28. Sally Bush Lincoln to Herndon, September 7, 1865, in Herndon-Weik MSS.

29. Dennis Hanks in Shelbyville (Ill.) *Shelby County Leader*, 1892, clipping in Lincoln National Life Foundation.

30. "I have knowledge of an incident which I have never seen in print. In the year 1866 while a teacher in Rockport academy at Rockport in the southern part of Indiana, I was invited by the Methodist presiding elder, the Rev. J. J. Stallard of the Rockport district, Indiana conference, to attend and assist him in conducting a quarterly meeting to be held near Gentryville, Ind. The meeting was near where Mr. Lincoln's mother lies buried. . . . we visited the grave of Mr. Lincoln's mother and were taken to the log cabin where the Lincoln family had lived. We then visited an old log church standing probably a quarter of a mile distant from either the cabin or the grave, an old log Baptist church not then in use, but where my guide told me the Lincoln family had formerly worshiped.

"While in the old church I climbed up into the loft to familiarize myself with the building and discovered in a crevice between two of the upper logs an old faded memorandum book that had been used in other years. Opening it and scanning its contents I found this entry where the church was charged

'Dr. To 1 broom

"To ½ doz. tallow candles.'

and signed 'ABE LINCOLN, Sexton.'

"To me it was an interesting discovery but I did not then realize the value of that little entry in Lincoln's own handwriting as I have realized it since. So after noting it carefully I placed the book yellow with age back in the crevice where I had found it.

"I have never seen it referred to or in fact in print that Mr. Lincoln was the sexton in an old log Baptist church. . . .

"May it not be that while he ministered at the altar in that old church and listening to the man of God that occupied the pulpit of that primitive sanctuary, Abraham Lincoln caught some of the inspiration and learned some of the principles that were manifested in his remarkable life in after years?"

Statement of Caleb A. Obenshain, pastor, Memorial Baptist Church, Dewey, Oklahoma, January 18, 1909, in Kansas City *Journal,* January 22, 1909.

31. Original Schedules, Census of Manufactures, 1820, Indiana, microfilm in Archives Division, Indiana State Library.

32. Duss, *George Rapp and His Associates,* p. 21.

33. *Ibid.,* p. 19.

34. Vincennes *Western Sun & General Advertiser,* April 5, 1828. Arthur E. Bestor, Jr., New Harmony historian, states that Owen paid $135,000 for 25,000 acres. Indiana Historical Bureau files.

35. *The Diaries of Donald Macdonald, 1824–1826* (Indiana Historical Society *Publications,* XIV, No. 2, Indianapolis, 1942), pp. 249–50.

CHAPTER X

1. Lincoln kept track of the Dorsey family. In the autobiography he prepared for Scripps in 1860 he wrote, "The family of Mr. Dorsey now resides in Schuyler Co. Illinois." *Collected Works,* IV, 62.

2. Going way back one finds that Nancy Hanks Lincoln's grandfather, Robert Shipley, Jr., married a Sarah Dorsey, in Ann Arundel County, October 9, 1713. Records of Christ Church, Queen Caroline Parish, Ann Arundel (now Howard) County, Maryland, Book I.

3. His tombstone inscription reads, "Azel W. Dorsey Died Sept. 13, 1858, aged 73 yrs. 10 mos. 8 ds." The headstone has been made a part of a cobblestone monument erected at Dorsey's grave which is on the farm of Arthur King, one-half mile south of Huntsville, Illinois.

4. Hardin County (Ky.) Court of Quarter Sessions, Minute Book, October 18, 1803.

5. Bleakley & Montgomery, Day Book, June 12, 1806.

6. Nelson County (Ky.) Marriage Register. Azel's wedding must have exhausted his finances, for three days later he and his brother Greenberry signed a note for $92.25 due the following December 23. The brothers

were unable to make payment when due, and it was May before any payment thereon was made. Finally Jacob Van Meter, the holder of the note, sued the brothers for the remainder due on December 3, 1813. Hardin County (Ky.) Circuit Court, Ordinary Bundle 9.

7. Hardin County (Ky.) Circuit Court, Book C. September 14, 1809.

8. Hardin County (Ky.) Tax Book, 1813.

9. Hardin County (Ky.) Court, Order Book C, p. 58.

10. *History of Warrick, Spencer and Perry Counties*, p. 22.

11. *Ibid.*, p. 327.

12. *Ibid.*, pp. 278, 280.

13. *Ibid.*, pp. 278, 281; *Executive Proceedings of Indiana, 1816–1836*, p. 61.

14. Spencer County (Ind.) Deed Book A, p. 16.

15. *Ibid.*, p. 82.

16. *Ibid.*, pp. 32, 118.

17. *History of Warrick, Spencer and Perry Counties*, p. 413.

18. Lamon, *Life of Abraham Lincoln*, p. 32.

19. Raymond, *The Life and Public Service of Abraham Lincoln*, p. 21. The Rev. Chauncey Hobart, in his *Recollections of My Life*, p. 71, writes that Dorsey remembered young Lincoln kindly, spoke of him as "one of the noblest boys I ever knew and . . . certain to become noted if he lives."

   Dorsey migrated to Illinois two years before the Lincolns, and taught a term of school in the winter of 1828–29. See J. B. Oakleaf, "Azel W. Dorsey, Lincoln's Teacher in Indiana, Buried in Illinois," in Illinois State Historical Society, *Journal*, XXII, No. 2 (October, 1929), pp. 447–51. In 1840 Dorsey entered two tracts of land, which according to Oakleaf, were military grants in recognition of his service in the War of 1812.

20. "We had an old dog-eared arithmetic in our house, and father determined that somehow, or somehow else, I should cipher clear through that book." Lincoln to Leonard Swett, in Rice (comp.), *Reminiscences of Abraham Lincoln*, p. 458. "At the age of forty-five Lincoln told Swett that the *summum bonum* of his father's ambition was to give his boy a first-rate education, and that his *ne plus ultra* of such an education was to 'learn to cipher clean through the 'rithmetic.'" Whitney, *Life of Lincoln*, I, 23.

21. According to Nathaniel Grigsby, "Lincoln ciphered at Crawfords School, Dorseys and Swaneys. He used Pikes Arithmetic. Rays was sometimes used." Grigsby to Herndon, September 12, 1865, in Herndon-Weik MSS.

22. A copy of the 1788 edition is in the Lincoln National Life Foundation.

23. The title page reads: The | New Complete System | of | Arithmetick, | composed for | the use of the citizens of the | United States. | By Nicholas Pike, A. M. | Member of the American Academy of Arts and Sciences. | Abridged for the use of schools. | Fifth edition. | Boston: | Printed by J. T. Buckingham, | for Thomas & Andrews. | Sold at their book-store, No. 45 Newbury-Street, and by the booksellers | throughout the United States. | Oct. 1804.

24. In the Lincoln National Life Foundation.

25. Pike, *The New Complete System of Arithmetick*, p. 339.

26. The title page reads: Daboll's | Schoolmaster's Assistant: | improved and enlarged, | being a plain practical system | of | Arithmetic: Adapted to the United States. | Stereotype Edition. | By Nathan Daboll |

Albany: Printed and published by E. & E. Hosford, | By permission of the proprietor of the Copy Right. | 1817.

When Elias Nason delivered a eulogy on Abraham Lincoln in Boston on May 3, 1865, before the New England Genealogical Society, he stated: "It is true that young Lincoln in his buckskin clothes and racoon skin cap did pick up a little of Daboll's Arithmetic." Nason, *Eulogy on Abraham Lincoln,* p. 11.

27. Dennis Hanks stated that he bought the paper with which Abraham made the book, but inasmuch as he was already married with a family of his own, this may be another of Hanks's unfounded boasts. When Herndon first saw the book (Septemper, 1865), then in possession of Abe's stepmother, there were only "ten or twelve sheets of this rudely bound volume." The stepmother said "originally it contained many more leaves but that the greater number has been lost or destroyed." There were probably as many as fifty sheets in the original book. There is a tradition that Thomas Johnston, son of Lincoln's stepbrother, "sold part of it at least, page by page during the war." Herndon took back to Springfield all that was left of the book. Thomas Dilworth's *The Schoolmaster's Assistant* . . . (Wilmington, 1796), appears to have been a primary source for the problems in this copybook.

28. The compilers of the *Collected Works of Abraham Lincoln* valued these ten surviving sheets so highly that they reproduced them in the preliminary pages of Volume I.

29. Reproduced in *Collected Works,* I, sheet [c]. The sheet is now in the Indiana University Library.

30. Reproduced in *ibid.*, I, sheet [i]. The probable source is Dilworth's *The Schoolmaster's Assistant,* p. 24. This sheet is now in the Herndon-Weik Collection.

31. Reproduced in *ibid.*, I, sheet [e]. This sheet is now in the Columbia University Library.

32. Reproduced in *ibid.*, I, sheet [a]. This sheet is now in the possession of Justin G. Turner.

33. Reproduced in *ibid.*, I, sheet [b]. This sheet is now in the Indiana Historical Society Library. A problem on this sheet resembles one given in Daboll's *Arithmetic,* p. 52.

34. Reproduced in *Collected Works,* I, sheet [g]. This sheet is now in the possession of A. Conger Goodyear.

35. Reproduced in *ibid.*, I, sheet [f]. This sheet is now in the Foreman M. Lebold estate.

36. Reproduced in *ibid.*, I, sheet [j]. This sheet is now in possession of Peter H. Brandt.

37. Reproduced in *ibid.*, I, sheet [h]. This sheet is now in the Chicago Historical Society.

38. Reproduced in *ibid.*, I, sheet [d]. This sheet is now in the Brown University Library.

39. Nathaniel Grigsby to Herndon, September 12, 1865, in Herndon-Weik MSS.

40. David Turnham to Herndon, September 15, 1865, in *ibid.*

41. Nathaniel Grigsby to Herndon, September 12, 1865, in *ibid.*

42. Sally Bush Lincoln to Herndon, September 8, 1865, in *ibid.*

43. *Ibid*. Of interest in connection with this observation of Abe's stepmother is the report of the interview that the Rev. John P. Gulliver had with Lincoln on March 10, 1860. Gulliver had heard Lincoln speak at Norwich, Connecticut, on March 9. The next morning he met him at the depot and they boarded the same train. Gulliver said that he asked the future President: "I want very much to know, Mr. Lincoln how you got this unusual power of 'putting things.' It must have been a matter of education. No man has it by nature alone. What has your education been?" This was Lincoln's answer: "I have been putting the question you ask me, to myself, while you have been talking. I can say this, that among my earliest recollections, I remember how, when a mere child, I used to get irritated when anybody talked to me in a way I could not understand. I don't think I ever got angry at any thing else in my life. But that always disturbed my temper, and has ever since. I can remember going to my little bedroom, after hearing the neighbors talk, of an evening, with my father, and spending no small part of the night walking up and down, and trying to make out what was the exact meaning of some of their, to me, dark sayings. I could not sleep, though I often tried to, when I got on such a hunt after an idea, until I had caught it; and when I thought I had got it, I was not satisfied until I had repeated it over and over, until I had put it in language plain enough, as I thought, for any boy I knew to comprehend. This was a kind of passion with me, and it has stuck by me; for I am never easy now, when I am handling a thought, till I have bounded it north and bounded it south, and bounded it east, and bounded it west. Perhaps that accounts for the characteristic you observe in my speeches, though I never put the things together before." John P. Gulliver in *The Independent* (New York), September 1, 1864. See also "Lincoln's 'Unusual Power of Putting Things,'" in *Lincoln Lore*, No. 1076 (November 21, 1949).

44. Sally Bush Lincoln to Herndon, September 8, 1865, in Herndon-Weik MSS.

45. Ohio County (Ky.) Marriage Register.

46. Hannah Gentry according to a family story received the same aid from Abe that Ann Roby did in helping spell the word "defied." In this story, however, Abe missed the word, spelling it with a "y" instead of "i." While the word was passing down the line, Abe then "stepped out when the teacher's eyes were turned," and came up to a window near which Hannah was standing. "When the word came to her she was about to give up when her attention was suddenly drawn to the window. There stood Lincoln jabbing his finger in his eye." She caught the meaning of the gesture, spelled the word correctly, and was complimented by the teacher. Bess V. Ehrmann, "Lincoln and His Neighbors," in Rockport *Democrat*, October 3, 1947.

47. On September 6, 1846, Lincoln sent this poem to Andrew Johnston, a practicing lawyer of Quincy, Illinois. The covering letter gave some background details and the final sentence read, "When, as I told you in my other letter I visited my old home in the fall of 1844, I found him [Matthew Gentry] still lingering in the wretched condition. In my

poetizing mood I could not forget the impression his case made upon me." *Collected Works,* I, 384–86.

> But here's an object more of dread
>   Than ought the grave contains—
> A human form with reason fled,
>   While wretched life remains.
>
> Poor Matthew! Once of genius bright,
>   A fortune-favored child—
> Now locked for aye, in mental night,
>   A haggard mad-man wild.
>
> Poor Matthew! I have ne'er forgot,
>   When first, with maddened will,
> Yourself you maimed, your father fought,
>   And mother strove to kill;
>
> When terror spread, and neighbours ran,
>   Your dange'rous strength to bind;
> And soon, a howling crazyman
>   Your limbs were fast confined.
>
> How then you strove and shrieked aloud,
>   Your bones and sinews bared;
> And fiendish on the gazing crowd,
>   With burning eye-balls glared—
>
> And begged, and swore, and wept and prayed,
>   With maniac laugh[ter?] joined—
> How fearful were those signs displayed
>   By pangs that killed thy mind!
>
> And when at length, tho' drear and long,
>   Time soothed thy fiercer woes,
> How plaintively thy mournful song
>   Upon the still night rose.
>
> I've heard it oft, as if I dreamed,
>   Far distant, sweet, and lone—
> The funeral dirge, it ever seemed
>   Of reason dead and gone.
>
> To drink it's strains, I've stole away,
>   All stealthily and still,
> Ere yet the rising God of day
>   Had streaked the Eastern hill.
>
> Air held his breath; trees, with the spell,
>   Seemed sorrowing angels round,
> Whose swelling tears in dew-drops fell
>   Upon the listening ground.

But this is past; and nought remains,
  That raised thee o'er the brute.
Thy piercing shrieks, and soothing strains,
  Are like, forever mute.

Now fare thee well—more thou the *cause,*
  Than *subject* now of woe.
All mental pangs, by time's kind laws,
  Hast lost the power to know.

O death! Thou awe-inspiring prince,
  That keepst the world in fear;
Why dost thou tear more blest ones hence,
  And leave him ling'ring here?

48. Scripps, *Life of Abraham Lincoln* (1900 ed.), p. 22.
49. Joseph C. Richardson to Herndon, September 14, 1865, in Herndon-Weik MSS; White, *Lincoln the Athlete,* p. 7.
50. Guardian contract, Spencer County (Ind.) Will Book A, p. 28.
51. Lucius C. Embree, "Morris Birkbeck's Estimate of the People of Princeton in 1817," in *Indiana Magazine of History,* XXI (1925), 292–93; *Lincoln Lore,* No. 1193 (February 18, 1953).
52. Jesse W. Weik, in Indianapolis *Star,* February 7, 1909.
53. When Lincoln was on his way to his first inauguration, he was introduced at Lafayette, Indiana, to a man named Stockwell, to whom he told the following incident: "When I was a boy about fifteen years of age, I took some wool to Princeton to be carded. As I entered the village I was struck with a quaint sign on the corner of the public square. It stood out in bold relief, Robert Stockwell merchant. It was the first time in my life I had seen gold lettering on a sign and hence I was strongly impressed. I have never forgotten it." Lincoln then asked Stockwell if he might be related to Robert Stockwell, to which he replied, "I am the man." Evansville *Journal,* July 11, 1890.
54. Evansville *Journal,* July 11, 1890. See also David Thomas, *Travels Through the Western Country in the Summer of 1816,* in Lindley (comp.), *Indiana As Seen by Early Travelers,* p. 113.

CHAPTER XI

1. Statement of Christopher C. Graham, Durrett Collection, University of Chicago Library, quoted in Tarbell, *Early Life of Abraham Lincoln,* p. 233.
2. Whitney, *Life of Lincoln,* I, 10n.
3. Haycraft letter, in Louisville *Democrat,* July 9, 1865.
4. Haycraft, *History of Elizabethtown,* p. 55.
5. John Romine to Herndon, September 14, 1865, in Herndon-Weik MSS. Romine added that Thomas Lincoln, as a farmer, "didn't raise more than enough for family and stock."
6. Atkinson, *The Boyhood of Lincoln,* p. 16.
7. William Wood to Herndon, September 15, 1865, in Herndon-Weik MSS.

8. Turnham to Herndon, September 15, 1865, Herndon-Weik MSS.

9. These eight corner cupboards, six of which the author has seen, may be identified by recording the name of the earliest known owner and the present location of each piece:

J. O. Dever—Speed Museum, Louisville, Kentucky

John T. Cowley—R. Gerald McMurtry residence, Fort Wayne, Indiana

David Turnham—Museum of Fine Arts and History, Evansville, Indiana

Reuben Grigsby—R. T. Savage residence, Mt. Vernon, Illinois

Josiah Crawford—Edison Institute, Dearborn, Michigan

Elizabeth Crawford—Spencer County Courthouse, Rockport, Indiana

—— Crooks—Townsend Taylor residence, South Bend, Indiana

Aaron Grigsby—William L. Clements Library, University of Michigan, Ann Arbor

See also article by R. Gerald McMurtry, in *Lincoln Herald*, XLV, No. 1 and 2 (February and June, 1943).

10. Ida M. Tarbell, *In the Footsteps of the Lincolns* (New York and London, 1924), p. 133.

11. Nathaniel Grigsby to Herndon, September 12, 1865, in Herndon-Weik MSS.

12. In the "Autobiography" which he prepared for Jesse Fell, Lincoln wrote: "I was raised to farm work, which I continued till I was twenty two." *Collected Works*, III, 511–12.

13. Dennis Hanks to Herndon, June 26, 1865, in Herndon-Weik MSS.

14. Cockrum, *Pioneer History of Indiana*, pp. 318–21.

15. Frank B. Carpenter, *Six Months at the White House with Abraham Lincoln* . . . (New York, 1866), p. 129.

16. Romine to Herndon, September 14, 1865, in Herndon-Weik MSS. Lincoln sent a note to Major George D. Ramsay, on October 17, 1861, in which he wrote: "The lady bearer of this says she has two sons who want to work. Wanting to work is so rare a want that it should be encouraged." *Collected Works*, IV, 556.

17. Romine to Herndon, September 14, 1865, in Herndon-Weik MSS.

18. Mrs. Josiah Crawford to Herndon, September 16, 1865, in Herndon-Weik MSS.

19. William Smith, in Indianapolis *Star*, February 6, 1921.

20. *Collected Works*, IV, 62. Ward Lamon says that when he was a young man contemplating the study of law he was introduced to Lincoln, who said to him, "Going to try your hand at the law, are you? I should know at a glance that you are a Virginian; but I don't think you would succeed at splitting rails. That was my occupation at your age, but I don't think I have taken as much pleasure in anything else from that day to this." Ward H. Lamon, *Recollections of Abraham Lincoln, 1847–1865* (Chicago, 1895), pp. 14–15.

R. Y. Bush, nephew of Sally Bush Lincoln, visited the President in Washington a short time before his assassination and wrote: "Tell Aunt that they are working him very hard at Washington, & if he had not been raised to *maul rails,* he could never stand the hard labor

at the White house." Letter to John F. Hall, April 5, 1865, in Carl
Sandburg, *Lincoln Collector. The Story of Oliver R. Barrett's Great
Private Collection* (New York, 1950), p. 109.

21. Francis F. Browne, *The Every-Day Life of Abraham Lincoln* . . . (New
York and St. Louis, 1886), p. 53.

   In 1862 some experiments with a new gun called Lincoln to the
Washington Navy Yard. Taking up an ax that was hanging outside the
cabin door on the steamer he and his party had boarded, he remarked,
"Gentlemen, you may talk about your 'Raphael repeaters' and 'eleven-
inch Dahlgrens;' but *here* is an institution which I guess I understand
better than either of you." Thereupon, "he held the axe out at arm's
length by the end of the handle, or 'helve,' as the wood-cutters call it—
a feat not another person of the party could perform." James B.
McClure, *Lincoln's Stories and Speeches* (Chicago, 1885), p. 162.

22. William Smith, in Indianapolis *Star,* February 6, 1921.

23. *Revised Laws of Indiana,* 1831, p. 225.

24. William Adams of Rockport, grandson of Josiah Crawford, said:
"Grandfather employed young Abe to make rails for pens. These rails
were longer than the ordinary ten-foot rails and larger. Abe notched
the rails at the ends to make them fit close together." Adams recalled
that as a boy of eight in 1860, when there was a demand for rails split
by Lincoln, he went "over the farm with grandfather . . . searching
for these rails. They were easily identified by their length and size
and notches in the ends." Quoted in paper read before the Perry County
(Ind.) Historical Society, February 1, 1925. See also Evansville *Daily
Journal,* June 2, 1860.

   An 1860 campaign riddle went thus: Question: "What are Lincoln
rails made of?" Answer: "Appears to be pop[u]lar." *Ibid.,* May 30,
1860.

25. About this same time Joseph Lane, who was eight years older than
Abraham, was operating a woodyard down river in Vanderburgh
County. Lane was to be the vice-presidential candidate on the Demo-
cratic ticket of Breckinridge and Lane in 1860. Evansville *Daily Journal,*
July 2, 1860. See also address by William Fortune quoted in *The
Missing Chapter in the Life of Abraham Lincoln* . . . , by Bess V.
Ehrmann (Chicago, 1938), pp. 66–67.

26. Weik, *The Real Lincoln,* p. 25.

27. See Joseph C. Richardson's statement to Herndon, n. d., in Herndon-Weik
MSS, Library of Congress. Indiana law required that licensed ferry
keepers (or their deputies) should be on hand "from day-light in the
morning until dark in the evening, so that no unnecessary delay may
happen to persons having occasion to pass said ferry: and all licensed
ferry keepers shall be obliged, at any hour of the night if required,
except in cases of evident danger, to give passage to all expresses
above recited, and to all other persons requiring the same, on their
tendering and paying double the rate of ferriage allowed to be taken
during the day time; and it shall be the duty of all ferry keepers within
this state, to cause the banks of the river or creek to be dug sufficiently
low, and kept in good passable order for the passage of man and horse
and loaded wagons." *Revised Laws of Indiana,* 1831, p. 262.

28. Mrs. K. Evans, cited in clipping from the Minneapolis *Journal* in Lincoln National Life Foundation.
29. Capt. W. H. Daniel recalled that at Taylor's, Abraham "used to play marbles, mumblety peg, etc.," with the children. He also recalled that Abe kept "a pet deer called Roxey that followed him wherever he might go." Jasper (Ind.) *Herald*, June 6, 1900. See also George R. Wilson's notebooks, XIX, 657, in possession of Margaret Wilson, Jasper, Indiana.
30. Grandview *Monitor*, November 22, 1928; Anna C. O'Flynn's interview with Green B. Taylor in 1895, in Southwestern Indiana Historical Society Papers; Ehrmann, *The Missing Chapter in the Life of Abraham Lincoln*, pp. 99–100.
31. Abraham Lincoln is supposed to have related this story to Secretary of State William Seward, adding, "You may think it was a very little thing, but it was a most important incident in my life." Holland, *Life of Abraham Lincoln*, p. 34.
    Leonard Swett claims that Lincoln told him the story also, and adds a sequel to the effect that while Abe was playing at the end of a flatboat he lost one of the half dollars in the river. Years later he told Swett, "I can see the quivering and shivering of that half dollar yet." Rice (comp.), *Recollections of Abraham Lincoln*, p. 458.
    On October 1, 1939, the State of Indiana dedicated Lincoln Ferry Park, an area of three acres at the mouth of Anderson River, a part of the original Taylor farm. Evansville *Courier*, September 29, 1939.
32. Louisville *Courier-Journal*, February 16, 1913; William Littell and Jacob Swigert, *A Digest of the Statute Law of Kentucky* . . . (2 volumes. Frankfort, 1822), I, 589–90; American Bar Association *Journal*, XIV, No. 2 (February, 1928), p. 82.
33. Karl Postel, *Americans as They Are*, quoted in Lindley (comp.), *Indiana as Seen by Early Travelers*, p. 527.
34. *History of Warrick, Spencer and Perry Counties*, p. 592.
35. *Ibid.*, pp. 668, 671; Index of Indiana Post Offices, Indiana Division, Indiana State Library.
36. *Appleton's Cyclopædia of American Biography* (6 volumes. New York, 1888–89), II, 471–72. The will of John Fitch is recorded in the Nelson County (Ky.) Will Book A, p. 351. This volume also contains the inventory of the estate of Abraham Lincoln, grandfather of the President.
37. Vincennes *Western Sun*, June 16, 1827.
38. Charles N. Thompson, "General La Fayette in Indiana," in *Indiana Magazine of History*, XXIV (1928), 67–69.

CHAPTER XII

1. There is a tradition that the daughter of Thomas and Nancy Hanks Lincoln was named Nancy and that she changed her name to Sarah after her father's marriage to Sally Bush Johnston, but there is no factual evidence to support this. Nicolay and Hay, *Abraham Lincoln, a History*, I, 27.
2. Hobson, *Footprints of Abraham lincoln*, p. 21.
3. Sarah Lincoln was born February 10, 1807. Pages from Lincoln family Bible record, in *Collected Works*, II, 94.

4. Sally Bush Lincoln to Herndon, September 8, 1865, in Herndon-Weik MSS.
5. John Hanks to Herndon, n. d., in *ibid.*
6. Browne (comp.), *Every-day Life of Abraham Lincoln,* p. 71. Many years after Sarah's death and the Lincolns' departure from Indiana, an editor of a southern Indiana paper wrote that Sarah was "considered a great beauty." Grandview *Monitor,* February 16, 1928. Abraham would have enjoyed this statement inasmuch as she was said to have looked like him.
7. Little Pigeon Creek Baptist Church, Minute Book.
8. Severns Valley (Ky.) Baptist Church Record Book, November 21, 1789, in Baptist Theological Seminary, Louisville, Kentucky.
9. Spencer County (Ind.) Will Book A, p. 120. Will dated February 10, 1833.
10. Tarbell, *Early Life of Abraham Lincoln,* p. 67.
11. Spencer County (Ind.) Marriage Register, August 2, 1826. The record bears this note signed by Charles Harper: "I married these on the same within."
12. J. Edward Murr claimed that the wedding took place in the home of Reuben Grigsby and that Abraham was not invited. We doubt that Sarah would have stood for this. "Lincoln in Indiana," in *Indiana Magazine of History,* XIV, 39–40.
13. Those desiring to read other stanzas of the poem may find them in Herndon and Weik, *Herndon's Life of Lincoln* (1930 ed.), I, 43. A footnote in Barrett, *Abraham Lincoln and His Presidency,* p. 23, referring to this poem, reads, "an old and yellow manuscript agreeing substantially with the document as far as the latter goes, but of greater length, is in possession of the present writer, to whom it came as a family relic handed down from generation to generation since the date August 21, 1786, written in Massachusetts but origin remote."

   See also a discussion of the authorship of this poem by John E. Iglehart, in Southwestern Indiana Historical Society, *Proceedings,* February 28, 1923 (Indiana Historical Commission, *Bulletin No. 18,* Indianapolis, October, 1923), pp. 83 ff. Iglehart agreed that Lincoln may have recited the poem but the claim that he wrote it "involves evidence which Herndon does not produce."
14. Warrick County (Ind.) Probate Court Order Book, A, p. 1.
15. Nathaniel Grigsby to Herndon, September 12, 1865, in Herndon-Weik MSS.
16. Mrs. Matilda Johnston Hall Moore to Herndon, September 8, 1865, in Herndon-Weik MSS.
17. *Ibid.;* Emanuel Hertz, *The Hidden Lincoln, from the Letters and Papers of William H. Herndon* (New York, 1938), pp. 422–23.
18. Hardin County (Ky.) Commissioners Tax Book, 1800; U. S. census, Hardin County, Kentucky, 1810, 1820. Levi Hall was one of five children of James and Elizabeth Hall. The other children were Henry, Elizabeth, William, and Benjamin. After James's death his widow married Caleb Hazel, Abe's Kentucky schoolteacher. Hazel promised, at the time of the marriage, to give each of James Hall's five children the value of five pounds in stock or produce when they came of age. Nelson County (Ky.) Deed Book, November 17, 1788.
19. The ceremony was performed by the Rev. Young Lamar. Spencer County Marriage Register.

There has been preserved this memento of Squire and Matilda Hall, a small undated card addressed to Squire Hall:

	Present this Complement
M^{ss} H. Watkins	to Squire hall and Lady
J Rose—	to attend a ball held at
managers	Jasper littles on the 19 of
	this instant p m

Sandburg, *Lincoln Collector*, p. 90.

20. The property acquired by Dennis Hanks was in the southeastern quarter of section 32, T 4 S, R 5 W, in Carter Township, assigned to him by Thomas Barrett. Herndon mentions visiting "Dennis Hanks old place" on September 14, 1865. Herndon-Weik MSS.

The relationship of Dennis Hanks and Squire Hall is shown by the following data:

Joseph Hanks (wife Nancy), of Virginia, later Kentucky, made his will on January 8, 1793, naming "all my children:" Thomas, Joshua, William, Charles, Joseph, Elizabeth, Polly (Mary), and Nancy. Another son James had died, probably in Virginia.

James Hanks married Lucy Shipley. They had one child, Nancy, who married Thomas Lincoln. Lucy married (2d) Henry Sparrow April 30, 1791.

William Hanks married Elizabeth Hall, September 12, 1793.

Elizabeth Hanks married Thomas Sparrow, brother of Henry, October 17, 1796.

Mary Hanks married Jesse Friend, December 10, 1795.

Nancy Hanks gave birth out of wedlock (by Charles Friend, brother of Jesse Friend) to a son, Dennis Friend Hanks, who was brought up by Thomas and Elizabeth Sparrow. Nancy was married, by the Rev. Alexander McDougal, to Levi Hall, brother of Elizabeth Hall, and among several children was one named Squire.

Therefore, Dennis Hanks and Squire Hall were sons of Nancy Hanks Hall, daughter of Joseph Hanks. Nancy Hanks Lincoln was the daughter of James Hanks, a brother of William, Elizabeth, Mary, and Nancy.

The claim that Levi and Nancy Hanks Hall came to Indiana and lie buried in the same lot with Nancy Hanks Lincoln lacks confirmation. Beveridge, *Abraham Lincoln*, I, 73n.

21. Atkinson, *The Boyhood of Lincoln*, p. 38.

22. Quoted in Murr, "Lincoln in Indiana," in *Indiana Magazine of History*, XIV, 15.

23. See statement of Dennis Franklin Johnston, son of John D. Johnston, in an undated clipping from a Los Angeles newspaper in the Lincoln National Life Foundation. Dennis Johnston also said, "My father was better looking than Uncle Abe when they were young fellows and he tried to cut Uncle Abe out with the girls, but he [Abe] didn't care."

24. Statement of John Hanks to Herndon, n. d., in Herndon-Weik MSS.

25. Statement of Turnham to Herndon, n. d., in *ibid*.

26. Ida M. Tarbell, *The Life of Abraham Lincoln* . . . (2 volumes. New York, 1902), I, 26–27.

27. Polly further commented: "If I had known he was to be President some day I'd a' took him." Murr, "Lincoln in Indiana," in *Indiana Magazine*

of History, XIV, pp. 53–58; Spencer County (Ind.) Marriage Register.

28. Thomas James de la Hunt, in Evansville *Courier and Journal,* February 12, 1928.
29. Jacob Grigsby, in Grandview *Monitor,* April 19, 1935; Spencer County (Ind.) Marriage Register.
30. Dr. William E. Barton refers to Caroline Meeker as one of Abraham's seven sweethearts. *The Women Lincoln Loved* (Indianapolis, 1927), p. 141 ff.
31. William Herndon twisted the testimony of Matilda Johnston so as to make it appear that there was something more than a wholesome relationship between her and Abraham. In fact, Herndon tried to involve Abraham in three Indiana love affairs. Herndon and Weik, *Herndon's Life of Lincoln* (1930 ed.), pp. 30–31; Herndon's interview with Matilda Johnston Hall Moore, September 8, 1865, in Herndon-Weik MSS.
32. Herndon tried to manufacture a romance between Abe and Elizabeth and wrote to Turnham about it. Turnham to Herndon, September 5, 1866, in Herndon-Weik MSS.
33. Spencer County (Ind.) Marriage Register.
34. Ida D. Armstrong, "The Lincolns in Spencer County," in Southwestern Indiana Historical Society, *Proceedings,* February 28, 1923 (Indiana Historical Commission, *Bulletin No. 18,* October, 1923), p. 59.
35. Grandview *Monitor,* February 22, 1934; clipping from the Evansville *Journal,* July, 1860, in Lincoln National Life Foundation; Lucius C. Embree, "Morris Birkbeck's Estimate of the People of Princeton in 1817," in *Indiana Magazine of History,* XXI (1925), 293.
36. Herndon and Weik, *Herndon's Life of Lincoln* (1930 ed.), p. 35. See above, pp. 178–79.
37. Many of the traditions about Abraham's early love affairs were first related after he became President, and any attention he had paid to a young girl in his youth was greatly magnified.

    Apparently Abraham Lincoln, as an eligible young bachelor living in the Illinois state capital and a member of the legislature at that, did not do much courting and did not attract the young ladies of the town, as this statement affirms: "I have been spoken to by but one woman since I've been here [six weeks], and should not have been by her, if she could have avoided it." Letter to Mary Owens, May 27, 1837, in *Collected Works,* I, 78.
38. Receipts Nos. 8499 and 9205, General Land Office Records, National Archives. See above, pp. 41–42.
39. Records of Vincennes Land Office, Relinquishments, T 4 S, R 5 W (Spencer County), in Archives Division, Indiana State Library.
40. Beveridge, *Abraham Lincoln,* I, 95. Abraham must have been recalling his father's land problems when he commented: "Knowing, as I well do, the difficulty that poor people *now* encounter in procuring homes, I hesitate not to say, that when the price of the public lands shall be doubled or trebled . . . it will be little less than impossible for them to procure those homes at all." Speech on the Sub-Treasury, December [26], 1839, in *Collected Works,* I, 163.
41. James Gentry to Joseph Gentry, March 11, 1834, in Spencer County (Ind.) Deed Book 2, p. 419.
42. The following statement of Dennis Hanks reveals how little he actually

knew about Thomas Lincoln's financial affairs: "This was an eighty-acre tract, and Mr. Lincoln, not being able to pay for it, lost his $80. which he paid to the government and which the government kept and has today . . . . Mr. Lincoln never owned the land, more than kind of pre-emption right, and sold it when he moved to Illinois." Hanks to Herndon, June 13, 1865, in Herndon-Weik MSS.

43. Herndon's report on his visit to the Lincoln farm, September 14, 1865, in *ibid.*

CHAPTER XIII

1. Elizabeth Crawford to Herndon, May 3, 1866, in Herndon-Weik MSS.
2. Statement of Elizabeth Crawford to Herndon, September 16, 1865, in *ibid.*
3. "This [the wardrobe] was a fine piece of furniture proving that Thomas Lincoln was a splendid carpenter. . . . In the center of the panels were the initials 'J. C.' for Josiah Crawford and 'E. C.' for Elizabeth Crawford." Elizabeth Crawford's statement to Anna O'Flynn quoted in Ehrmann, *The Missing Chapter in the Life of Abraham Lincoln*, p. 100.
4. In the fall of 1844 Lincoln returned to southern Indiana to participate in the political campaign. Following a speech in his neighborhood he went home with Josiah Crawford. He asked his host about the old sawpit. It was still there, partly fallen down, but Lincoln remarked, "This looks more natural than I thought it would." Louisville *Courier-Journal*, August 20, 1902.
5. In an interview regarding the Lincoln family in 1881, Mrs. Crawford stated that the Lincolns "had little of even the comforts of that time in their home. Life in the Lincoln home was so hard that she had invited Sarah, Abraham's sister, to come and live in the Crawford home and pay for her board by helping with the housework." In her interview with Herndon she said, "Sarah . . . worked for me." Ehrmann, *The Missing Chapter in the Life of Abraham Lincoln*, pp. 72–73; statement of Elizabeth Crawford to Herndon, September 16, 1865, in Herndon-Weik MSS.
6. Statement of Elizabeth Crawford to Herndon, September 16, 1865, *loc. cit.*; see also Evansville *Enquirer*, May 23, 1860.
7. Tarbell, *Early Life of Abraham Lincoln*, p. 62.
8. Scripps, *Life of Abraham Lincoln* (1900 ed.), p. 20.
9. Herndon and Weik, *Herndon's Life of Lincoln* (1930 ed.), p. 53.
10. Statement of Elizabeth Crawford to Herndon, September 16, 1865, in Herndon-Weik MSS.

There is no evidence that the injured book caused a rift between the Crawfords and Abe. Herndon, in recording his interview with Elizabeth Crawford in 1865, says that she showed him a picture of her husband, and Herndon observed, "and I say a cruel hard husband judging from his looks." This statement may have been responsible for the variation of the story in Lamon's *Life of Abraham Lincoln*. Lamon wrote that Crawford was "a sour and churlish fellow at best, and flatly refused to take the damaged book again. He said, that if Abe had no money to pay for it, he could work it out." Lamon continued this theme, saying Abe in return leveled his wit at Crawford's nose, "a monstrosity," and was responsible for Josiah being labeled "Old Bluenose." See pp. 38, 51.

254

11. On April 1, 1835, about a dozen years after first seeing this picture Abraham Lincoln wrote in a letter to Mrs. O. H. Browning: "I was fixed 'firm as the surge repelling rock' in my resolution." *Collected Works,* I, 118.

12. The title page reads: The | Life | of | George Washington, | Commander in Chief | of | Armies of the United States of America, throughout | the War which established their | independence | and First President of the United States | By David Ramsay, M. D. | Author of the History of the American Revolution. | Second Edition. | Boston | Published by D. Mallory and Co. | Sold by them, and B. B. Hopkins and Co. W. W. Woodward, and A. Finlay and Co., Philadel- | phia; P. H. Nicklin, Baltimore; D. W. Farrand and Greene, Albany; Biers and Howe | and I. Cook and Co. New Haven; O. D. Cook. Hartford; A. Lyman and Co. | Portland; Swift and Chapman, Middlebury, Vermont. | 1811. | S. Etheridge, Jun. Printer.

13. Rice (comp.), *Reminiscences of Abraham Lincoln,* p. 71.

14. Charles T. Baker, in *Grandview Monitor,* September 29, 1938.

15. Spencer County (Ind.) Will and Probate records.

16. *History of Warrick, Spencer and Perry Counties,* pp. 273, 288; Ida D. Armstrong, "The Lincolns in Spencer County," in Southwestern Indiana Historical Society, *Proceedings,* February 28, 1923 (Indiana Historical Commission, *Bulletin No. 18,* Indianapolis, October, 1923), p. 56.

17. Turnham to Herndon, September 15, 1865, in Herndon-Weik MSS; Nicolay and Hay, *Abraham Lincoln,* I, 36.

18. The Life | of | Gen. Francis Marion, | A Celebrated Partisan Officer | in the | Revolutionary War | against the British and Tories | in South Carolina and Georgia | By Brig. Gen. P. Horry, of Marion's Brigade: and | M. L. Weems. |
    "On Vernon's Chief, why lavish all our lays?
    "Come, honest Muse, and sing great Marion's praise."
    Eighth Edition. | Philadelphia: | M. Carey & Sons—Chestnut Street. | 1822.

19. Herndon noted that when he interviewed Mrs. Crawford on September 16, 1865, she gave him her husband's copy of *The Kentucky Preceptor.* Herndon-Weik MSS. Herndon then wrote in the book: "This book was given to me by Mrs. Elizabeth Crawford. . . . it is the one out of which Mr. Lincoln learned his speeches." The book became part of the great Lincoln collection assembled by Oliver R. Barrett, which was sold at auction at New York in 1952. The volume now is owned by Indiana University.
    The title page reads: The | Kentucky Preceptor, | containing | a number of useful lessons | for reading and speaking. | Compiled for the use of schools. | By a teacher. | [4 lines of verse] | Third edition, revised, with considerable additions. | Copy-right secured according to law. | Lexington, (Ky.) | Published by Maccoun, Tilford & Co. | 1812.

20. This is the title of the thirtieth edition, Glasgow, 1802. The copy of Bailey's *Dictionary* discovered in 1879 in the old home of Mordecai Lincoln could hardly be the copy used by Abe. See Beveridge, *Abraham Lincoln,* I, 21, 73. Mordecai had a son Abraham Lincoln.

21. Nicolay and Hay, *Abraham Lincoln,* I, 35. When Herndon interviewed

Abe's stepmother on September 8, 1865, she produced a copy of James Barclay's *Dictionary* saying, "Here is Barclay's Dictionary dated 1799; it has Abe's name in it . . . [a] boyish scrawl." Herndon-Weik MSS. Dennis Hanks also referred to a copy of Barclay: "He [Abe] then some [how] had or got Barclay's English Dictionary, a part of which I have now and which can be seen now at my house and which I am to give to W. H. Herndon. . . ." Hanks to Herndon, June 13, 1865, in *ibid*. The whereabouts of this volume today is not known to the author. Barclay's *Dictionary* contained "I. A full explanation of difficult words and technical terms . . . II. A pronouncing dictionary . . . III. The origin of each word . . . to which are prefixed, a free enquiry into the origin and antiquity of letters . . . A new compendious grammar . . . and to the whole is added, an outline of ancient and modern history. . . ."

22. They are listed in the Vincennes *Western Sun,* November 18, 1826.
23. Sally Bush Lincoln to Herndon, September 8, 1865, in Herndon-Weik MSS; Atkinson, *The Boyhood of Lincoln,* p. 25.
24. John Romine to Herndon, September 14, 1865, in Herndon-Weik MSS.
25. President Lincoln mentioned this strange coincidence in a speech which might be called "The Preliminary Gettysburg Address," which he delivered from the White House in response to a serenade on July 7, 1863: "The two most distinguished men in the framing and support of the Declaration were Thomas Jefferson and John Adams—the one having penned it and the other sustained it the most forcibly in debate—the only two of the fifty-five who signed it being elected President of the United States. Precisely fifty years after they put their hands to the paper it pleased Almighty God to take both from the stage of action. This was indeed an extraordinary and remarkable event in our history." *Collected Works,* VI, pp. 319–20.
26. Wood to Herndon, September 15, 1865, in Herndon-Weik MSS.
27. Sally Bush Lincoln to Herndon, September 8, 1865, in *ibid*.
28. Grigsby's statement to Herndon, September 12, 1865, in Herndon-Weik MSS; Lamon, *Life of Abraham Lincoln,* p. 35.
29. This scrapbook is owned by Ora Brown, of Dale, Indiana.
30. Tarbell, *The Early Life of Abraham Lincoln,* p. 84.
31. Wood to Herndon, September 15, 1865, in Herndon-Weik MSS. All efforts to find the article by Lincoln have proved fruitless. The Rev. Aaron Farmer, minister of the United Brethren Church, began publishing the *Zion's Advocate,* a denominational paper, in Salem, Indiana, in 1829. It was short-lived, and no copy is known to have survived. Donald F. Carmony, "Kingdom Church," in *Indiana Magazine of History,* XXIX (1933), 106. See also Hobson, *Footprints of Abraham Lincoln,* pp. 51–52.
32. Wood to Herndon, September 15, 1865, and Sally Bush Lincoln to Herndon, September 8, 1865, in Herndon-Weik MSS; Murr, "Lincoln in Indiana," in *Indiana Magazine of History,* XIV, 39.

While a member of Congress, Lincoln is supposed to have told a colleague, "I promised my precious mother only a few days before she died that I would never use anything intoxicating as a beverage, and I consider that promise as binding to-day as it was on the day I made it." Hobson, *Footprints of Abraham Lincoln,* p. 51.

In the course of an address to the Sons of Temperance on the twenty-first anniversary of their organization, September 29, 1863, Lincoln said, "When I was a young man, long ago, before the Sons of Temperance as an organization, had an existence, I in an humble way, made temperance speeches, and I think I may say that to this day I have never, by my example, belied what I then said." *Collected Works*, VI, 487.

33. Turnham to Herndon, September 15, 1865, in Herndon-Weik MSS. Dennis Hanks did not remember this incident when he wrote to Herndon on June 13, 1865: "The story about his carrying home a drunken man is not true as I think or recollect. He was good enough and tender enough and kind enough to have saved any man from evil, wrong, difficulties, or damnation. Let him claim nothing but what is true." *Ibid.*

34. Hobson, *Footprints of Abraham Lincoln*, p. 80. Lincoln in the debate with Douglas at Ottawa, Illinois, said: "It is true that Lincoln did work the latter part of one winter in a small still house, up at the head of a hollow." *Collected Works*, III, 16.

Henry C. Whitney wrote that John D. Johnston "grew up to be one of the laziest and most shiftless of mortals. He constantly appealed to Lincoln for aid for himself and his progeny." *Life of Lincoln*, I, 37.

35. *New-Harmony Gazette*, October 1, 1825.

36. Both Atkinson and Vannest make extravagant claims that young Lincoln was largely influenced by Owen and the New Harmonists. Both rely on the testimony given by Dennis Hanks when nearly ninety years old to the effect that Abe heard of a boarding school at New Harmony. Hanks said that "Abe'd a broke his back to go, and it nigh about broke his heart when he couldn't. . . . He said, 'Denny thar's a school an thousand o' books thar an' fellars that know everything in creation.'" Charles G. Vannest, *Lincoln the Hoosier. Abraham Lincoln's Life in Indiana* (St. Louis and Chicago, 1928), pp. 117–22; Atkinson, *Boyhood of Lincoln*, p. 31.

CHAPTER XIV

1. Paper by Nancy Grigsby Inco, niece of Aaron Grigsby, in Southwestern Indiana Historical Society, *Proceedings*, February 28, 1923 (Indiana Historical Commission, *Bulletin No. 18*, October, 1923), p. 91.

2. Mrs. John W. Lamar quoted in Hobson, *Footprints of Abraham Lincoln*, p. 22.

3. Newspaper clipping, no name and undated, in Lincoln National Life Foundation.

4. Hobson, *Footprints of Abraham Lincoln*, p. 24.

5. Illinois State Historical Society, *Transactions*, 1907 (Springfield, 1908), pp. 166–67. After Lincoln's election to Congress, he saw Dr. Moore in Jacksonville, Illinois, and asked him if he did not remember his former patient. Moore was born in Ireland on May 26, 1798, and while an infant brought to Frankfort, Kentucky, and later to Bloomfield in Nelson County. He studied medicine under Dr. Bemis at Bardstown and attended medical lectures at Louisville.

6. Dr. Allen was practicing near Troy as early as 1827, as evidenced by

bills for medical service which he rendered to Henry C. Acton covering
the period from 1827 to 1830. Perry County (Ind.) Probate Court
record.
7. Minute Book of the Little Pigeon Baptist Church.
8. *Ibid.*
9. Evansville *Courier and Journal,* February 2, 1933.
10. Nancy Grigsby Inco stated that "she (Sarah) was given the best kind
    of burial that could be given and my father erected a sand stone
    marker to the graves of both her and her husband, and always looked
    after these graves as well as others of our family as long as he lived."
    Paper in Southwestern Indiana Historical Society, *Proceedings,*
    February 28, 1923, p. 91.

    The grave of Sarah Lincoln in the Little Pigeon Church Cemetery
    is now marked by a fine monument dedicated on May 30, 1916. It bears
    this inscription:

    Sarah Lincoln
    Wife of
    Aaron Grigsby
    Feb. 10, 1807
    Jan. 20, 1828

11. Whether or not there was any controversy over the place of burial is
    not known, but at the following meeting of the Board of Trustees of
    the Little Pigeon Church Thomas Lincoln submitted his resignation
    as trustee. Minute Book of Little Pigeon Church.

    On September 11, 1830, Aaron Grigsby married Margaret Miller.
    The ceremony was performed by John B. Greathouse, justice of the
    peace. Spencer County (Ind.) Marriage Register. There was one child,
    Elsa, born to this union. The inscription on Aaron's tombstone which
    stands beside Sarah's, reads: "Aaron Grigsby Born 1801 Died 1831."
    Below is this verse: "Farewell my friends, weep not for me, for we
    shall meet in eternity." See Dale (Ind.) *Weekly Reporter,* June 23,
    1916.

    Aaron's will was probated February 10, 1833. Josiah Crawford was
    one of the appraisers of the estate, which was valued at $269.78, plus
    a note for $16.97. The items of appraisal were: 1 lot of cupboard ware,
    2 butcher knives, 2 beds and bedding, 1 bundle of table cloths and
    pillow slips, 1 bed and bedding, 1 pair cards and slate, 1 lot of wool
    and rolls, 1 lot of bed clothing, 1 lot of thread, 1 looking glass, 1 lot of
    books, 1 razor, case and shaving instruments, 6 chairs, 1 table, 1 cradle,
    1 wheel and reel, 1 tray and service, 2 saddles, 1 lot of salt, soap, 1
    lot of flax, 1 stable horse, 2 cows and calves, 3 yearling calves, 8 sheep,
    1 mare, 1 lot of stock hogs, 1 colt, 15 geese, 12 chickens, 10 hogs,
    stack of wheat. Spencer County (Ind.) Will Book, p. 120.
12. Statement of Joseph C. Richardson to Herndon, September 14, 1865,
    Herndon-Weik MSS.
13. Herndon asked: "What gave him that peculiar melancholy? What cancer
    had he inside?" Herndon and Weik, *Herndon's Life of Lincoln* (1900
    ed.), vi. Herndon answered his questions to his own satisfaction by
    shaking Lincoln's genealogical tree under which he claimed he found
    spoiled fruit. He concluded without grounds that Lincoln pined for the
    sins of his forebears.

14. Lincoln to Andrew Johnston, September 6, 1840, enclosing verses written upon a visit to his old home and his recollection of the madness of his friend. *Collected Works*, I, 384–85. See above, pp. 246–47.
15. Gladstone was moved by Lincoln's Second Inaugural Address to say: "I am taken captive by so striking an utterance as this. I see in it the effect of sharp trial when rightly borne to raise men to a higher level of thought and feeling. It is by cruel suffering that nations are sometimes borne to a better life: so it is with individual men. Mr. Lincoln's words show that upon him anxiety and sorrow wrought their true effect. The address gives evidence of a moral elevation most rare in a statesman, or indeed in any man." *Lincoln Lore*, No. 1212 (June 30, 1952).
16. In the "Autobiography" he prepared for Scripps, Lincoln wrote, "When he was nineteen, still residing in Indiana, he made his first trip upon a flatboat to New-Orleans. He was a hired hand merely; and he and a son of the owner, without other assistance, made the trip." *Collected Works*, IV, 62. Here Lincoln specifically says this was his "first trip," and thus nullifies the story told by William Forsythe, of Grandview, that he had made a flatboat trip to New Orleans with Jefferson Ray two years earlier. Murr, "Lincoln in Indiana," in *Indiana Magazine of History*, XIV, 19. Some historians have stated the trip was made in the spring of 1828. For evidence supporting the winter trip see Ehrmann, *The Missing Chapter in the Life of Abraham Lincoln*, pp. 7–8.
17. Article by Bess V. Ehrmann in the Evansville *Courier and Journal*, February 9, 1936.
18. A tract of land of one hundred acres had been acquired on the river at Rockport by James Gentry from Daniel Grass in 1825. Spencer County (Ind.) Deed Book A, pp. 140, 154, 155.
19. See above, p. 5.
20. Hobson, *Footprints of Abraham Lincoln*, p. 25, quoting Capt. John W. Lamar.
21. Ehrmann, *The Missing Chapter in the Life of Abraham Lincoln*, p. 21.
22. Lincoln wrote to Cassius M. Clay, July 20, 1860. "In passing let me say, that at Rockport you will be in the county within which I was brought up from my eighth year. . . ." *Collected Works*, IV, 85. Lincoln spoke at Rockport on October 30, 1844, during a speaking tour of southern Indiana in behalf of Henry Clay. *Ibid.*, I, 341–42. He was a guest at the Rockport Tavern, no longer standing. A "pioneer village" was dedicated at Rockport on July 4, 1935, which contains replicas of many buildings associated with Lincoln.
23. Spencer County (Ind.) Deed Book 3, p. 220. The fact that Jones intended to start loading his goods by December 1 confirms that flatboats went down river in the winter. The claim that Abe had some experience in boat building before reaching Illinois is supported by John E. Roll who helped Lincoln build a flatboat at Sangamon Town, Illinois, in 1831. He recalled: "It took about a month as I remember it to build the boat, and during that time a number were employed, some of them just for a day or two, in helping Lincoln. . . . I can testify that Lincoln bossed the job well and that the boat was well built." Springfield (Ill.) *Globe Democrat*, May 7, 1892.
    The Estray Books of old Hardin County, Kentucky, which bordered

on the Ohio, give a good description of flatboats found adrift in the river. Here are dimensions of a few: 51 by 18 feet; 50 by 12 feet; 58 by 18 feet; 63 by 15 feet; 70 by 16 feet; 60 by 16 feet; 60 by 17 feet; 82 by 20 feet. The average measurements were 65 by 16 feet, the dimensions of the boat commissioned by William Jones.

24. Whitney, *Life of Lincoln*, I, 49–50.
25. Among the names of Kentucky flatboats launched about the time Thomas Lincoln made his trip in 1806 were *Happy Return, Experiment, Nancy, Lovely Nan, Necessity, Good Hope, Hard Times, Slipeasy, Swift Safety, Hard Fortune.*
26. Hobson, *Footprints of Abraham Lincoln*, p. 24.
27. Statement of John Romine to Herndon, September 14, 1865, Herndon-Weik MSS.
28. Spencer County (Ind.) Marriage Register. The ceremony was performed by Charles Pierce, a justice of the peace.
29. This story is related in Browne, *The Every-day Life of Abraham Lincoln*, p. 78.
30. Ehrmann, *The Missing Chapter in the Life of Abraham Lincoln*, p. 8.
31. Whitney, *Life of Lincoln*, I, 51–52.
32. [John Baillie], "An Englishman's Pocket Note-Book in 1828," in *Magazine of American History*, XIX (January-June, 1888), 336–37.
33. *Ibid.*, XIX, 425.
34. *Ibid.*, XIX, 424.
35. *Ibid.*
36. *Ibid.*, XIX, 425.
37. *Ibid.*
38. *Ibid.*, XIX, 425–26. Lincoln in an address delivered January 27, 1838, referred to "the native Spanish moss of the country, as a drapery of the forest." *Collected Works*, I, 110.
39. Baillie, *op. cit.*, XIX, 426–27.
40. *Ibid.*, XIX, 427.
41. *Ibid.*, XIX, 511, 512.
42. *Ibid.*, XX, 61.
43. New Orleans *Argus*, December 5, 1828. A manifesto dated at Baltimore October 2, 1828, listing a cargo of 201 slaves shipped from Norfolk and arriving in New Orleans about the time the Gentry flatboat reached there, gives the height, age, and sex of each slave, and also his color, whether black, brown, copper, mulatto, or yellow. Lincoln National Life Foundation.
44. This letter is in the Lincoln National Life Foundation.
45. Scripps, *Life of Abraham Lincoln* (1900 ed.), p. 22. In the Autobiography that he prepared for Scripps, Lincoln wrote: "The nature of part of the cargo-load, as it was called—made it necessary for them to linger and trade along the Sugar coast—and one night they were attacked by seven negroes with intent to kill and rob them. They were hurt some in the melee, but succeeded in driving the negroes from the boat, and then 'cut cable' 'weighed anchor' and left." *Collected Works*, IV, 62. A story that lacks confirmation states that Abe put off "on the innocent folk along the river some counterfeit money," which a shrewd fellow had imposed upon Allen. Lamon, *Life of Abraham Lincoln*, p. 71n.

46. Thayer, *Pioneer Boy*, p. 97; Ehrmann, *The Missing Chapter in the Life of Abraham Lincoln*, p. 8.
47. Issue of April 26, 1828.
48. This statement was reported by Absalom Gentry, a son of Allen, who heard his father make the remark, and claimed that Abe said at this time, "If I ever get a chance to hit this thing I'll hit it hard." Related to Mrs. Bess V. Ehrmann and reported by her in a letter in the Lincoln National Life Foundation. The same remark is alleged to have been made by Abe on viewing the slave markets on his second New Orleans trip.
49. New Orleans *Louisiana Advertiser*, December 10, 1828.
50. *Ibid.*, December 9, 1828.
51. For a list of steamboats built and operated on the western waters from 1812 to 1836, with place and date of construction, tonnage, and date of loss and how destroyed, see Ethel C. Leahy (comp.), *Who's Who on the Ohio River and Its Tributaries* . . . (Cincinnati, 1931), pp. 370–81. The data included here are from James Hall's *Statistics of the West* (1837).
52. *Ibid.*, p. 370.
53. Col. W. D. Ferguson, who operated a woodyard at Greenock, Arkansas (since washed away), stated that about 1828, Abraham Lincoln, in need of funds to return to Indiana after his trip to New Orleans, worked for him for several weeks until he had earned enough to pay his way back. Ferguson is said to have renewed his acquaintance with Lincoln in Washington while he was President. Richard C. Rippin to author, October 20, 1939. No further evidence to support this has been found.

CHAPTER XV

1. Index of Indiana post offices, Indiana State Library.
2. Spencer County (Ind.) Deed Book A, p. 227.
3. Spencer County (Ind.) Marriage Register.
4. Index of Indiana post offices, Indiana State Library.
5. The name of the post office was not changed to Gentryville until 1835. In 1837 it was changed to Jonesboro, and then in 1844 back to Gentryville. *Ibid.* See also record of land transactions, Whittinghill to Jones, Spencer County (Ind.) Deed Book 2, p. 62; Evansville *Sunday Courier and Journal*, February 9, 1930.
6. The grandson was Otis E Jones. See article by Bess V. Ehrmann in Rockport *Democrat*, October 24, 1947.
7. Grigsby to Herndon, September 16, 1865, in Herndon-Weik MSS.
8. In the autobiographical sketch he prepared for Jesse W. Fell, Lincoln wrote, "Always a whig in politics." *Collected Works*, III, 512.
9. John Hanks to Herndon, n. d., in Herndon-Weik MSS.
10. John P. Gulliver's account of a conversation with Lincoln in *The Independent* (New York), September 1, 1864, reprinted in Carpenter, *Six Months at the White House*, pp. 312–13.
11. In the Presidential election of 1832, in Carter Township, Clay polled eighteen votes and Jackson thirteen. Spencer County, however, gave 191 to Jackson and 106 to Clay. In 1844 when Abraham visited his

old home and made some speeches, the vote in Carter Township was Clay seventy-four, Polk fourteen. Spencer County as a whole gave Clay 586 to 494 for Polk. In the national election in 1860 the Carter Township vote was 124 for Lincoln, 76 for Douglas, nine for Breckinridge, and none for Bell. The Spencer County vote was Lincoln 1,296, Douglas 1,108, Breckinridge 175, and Bell 172. The 1864 election in Carter Township resulted in 145 votes for Lincoln to 96 for McClellan. The county vote was 1,558 for Lincoln to 1,417 for McClellan. *History of Warrick, Spencer and Perry Counties,* pp. 299–305. These returns do not bear out Nathaniel Grigsby's statement: "We were all Jackson boys and men at this time in Indiana." Grigsby to Herndon, September 12, 1865, in Herndon-Weik MSS.

12. Atkinson, *The Boyhood of Lincoln,* p. 40.
13. Vincennes *Western Sun & General Advertiser,* May 29 through July 3, 1824.
14. *Ibid.,* February 9 and 16, 1828. Expressing thanks for a medallion of Clay, Lincoln referred to him as one "whom, during my whole political life, I have loved and revered as a teacher and leader." Lincoln to Daniel Ullmann, February 1, 1861, in *Collected Works,* IV, 184. In a speech at Carlinville, Illinois, on August 3, 1854, Lincoln said, "I can express all my views on the slavery question by quotations from Henry Clay. Doesn't this look like we are akin." *Collected Works,* III, 79.
15. Sketch of Boon in *Journals of the General Assembly of Indiana Territory, 1805–1815* (*Indiana Historical Collections,* XXXII, Indianapolis, 1950), pp. 960–61.
16. Vincennes *Western Sun & General Advertiser,* May 8, 1819. In concluding a communication "to the people of Sangamo County," March 9, 1832, when he was running for a seat in the Illinois House of Representatives, Lincoln wrote, "I was born and have ever remained in the most humble walks of life. I have no wealthy or popular relations to recommend me. My case is thrown exclusively upon the independent voters of this county, and if elected they will have conferred a favor upon me, for which I shall be unremitting in my labors to compensate. But if the good people in their wisdom shall see fit to keep me in the background, I have been too familiar with disappointments to be very much chagrined." *Collected Works,* I, 8–9.
17. *History of Warrick, Spencer and Perry Counties,* p. 272.
18. Grandview *Monitor,* April 27, 1933; December 22, 1938.
19. Herndon and Weik, *Herndon's Life of Lincoln* (1930 ed.), p. 50.
20. Lamon, *Life of Abraham Lincoln,* pp. 57–58.
21. *Sketch of the Life of Abraham Lincoln and a Catalogue of Articles Once Owned and Used by Him. Now Owned by the Lincoln Memorial Collection* (Chicago [1887]), p. 15.
22. Dennis Hanks to Herndon, June 13, 1865, in Herndon-Weik MSS.
23. Howells, *Life of Abraham Lincoln,* p. 20.
24. About the origin of his stories Lincoln once said, "I remember a good story when I hear it, but I never invented anything original." Quoted in Carpenter, *Six Months at the White House,* p. 235. Lincoln often introduced a story by saying, "As my old father used to say," or "My old father used to tell a story. . . ."
25. Grandview *Monitor,* October 14, 1926. There is a tradition that Abraham

once worked at this tannery. A marker has been erected at the site bearing this inscription: Hammond Farm | Site of Hammond Tannery | Visited by Abe Lincoln | during his Residence in | Spencer County 1816–1830 | July 1936.

26. Sandburg, *Lincoln Collector,* p. 109.
27. Atkinson, *The Boyhood of Lincoln,* pp. 35–36.
28. The title page reads: Quin's Jests | or, the | Facetious Man's | Pocket-Companion. | Containing Every Species of | Wit, Humour, and Repartee with a Compleat Collection of Epigrams, Bon-Mots &c., &c. | London | Printed for S. Bladon, in Pater-Noster Row | MDCCLXVI. Microfilm copy in Lincoln National Life Foundation from copy in the Huntington Library, San Marino, California. See also article of William Fortune in Ehrmann, *The Missing Chapter in the Life of Abraham Lincoln,* p. 76.
29. Herndon and Weik, *Herndon's Life of Lincoln* (1930 ed.), pp. 45–47.
30. Spencer County and Dubois County (Ind.) Marriage Records. J. Edward Murr claims that the double wedding which caused the writing of "The Chronicles" occurred in 1826, and that Sarah Lincoln was one of the brides and that a daughter of Reuben Grigsby the other. "Lincoln in Indiana," in *Indiana Magazine of History,* XIV, 39–41.
31. Rockport *Journal,* February 12, 1897.
32. Hobson, *Footprints of Abraham Lincoln,* p. 27.
33. Murr, "Lincoln in Indiana," in *Indiana Magazine of History,* XIV, 38–39.
34. John Ginley, in Chicago *Tribune,* September 23, 1890; John O. Chewing, in Louisville *Courier-Journal,* August 20, 1902.
35. Eldora Minor Raleigh, "John A. Brackenridge," in Southwestern Indiana Historical Society, *Proceedings,* January 31, 1922 (Indiana Historical Commission, *Bulletin No. 16,* Indianapolis, October, 1922), pp. 60–62.
36. Warrick County (Ind.) Marriage Register; U. S. Census returns, 1830, photostats in Genealogy Division, Indiana State Library. At Rockport he is listed as between twenty and thirty years of age, his wife between fifteen and twenty, and they had one male child under five years of age. John Pitcher signed as to the correctness of the census schedule, November 10, 1830, with John B. Greathouse and John A. Brackenridge as witnesses.
37. *History of Warrick, Spencer and Perry Counties,* p. 66.
38. Herndon-Weik MSS.
39. Beveridge, *Abraham Lincoln,* I, 91.
40. Johnston's statement to Herndon, September 14, 1865, in Herndon-Weik MSS.
41. Arnold, *Life of Abraham Lincoln,* p. 25; Browne, *Every-day Life of Abraham Lincoln,* pp. 73–74; Murr, "Lincoln in Indiana," in *Indiana Magazine of History,* XIV, 161; Vannest, *Lincoln the Hoosier,* p. 105.
    There is no point in reviewing the story that Lincoln met either Lawyer Breckinridge of Kentucky or Lawyer Brackenridge of Indiana in Washington, except to repeat what Lincoln is supposed to have said about the argument used by the lawyer at the trial: "It was the best speech that I, up to that time, ever heard. If I could, as I then thought, make as good a speech as that, my soul would be satisfied." See Johnston's statement, September 14, 1865, in Herndon-Weik MSS.
42. Murr, "Lincoln in Indiana," in *Indiana Magazine of History,* XIV, 159.

43. *History of Warrick, Spencer and Perry Counties,* p. 74.
44. When Lincoln visited Boonville in 1844, campaigning for Clay, he must have met Brackenridge. Both were condidates for elector on the Clay ticket. In the Evansville *Daily Journal,* June 7, 1860, there is the statement that "Mr. Lincoln passed through the town [Boonville] some years ago and made a speech at our court house. All who heard him (without distinction of party) concur in saying he made one of the best speeches ever delivered in this place." There is no record of Lincoln meeting Brackenridge at this time, or paying him a personal or a public compliment.
45. Kate Pitcher Schultz, "General Thomas Gamble Pitcher," in Southwestern Indiana Historical Society, *Proceedings During Its Sixth Year (Indiana History Bulletin,* December, 1925), pp. 37–38.
46. A second John Pitcher appears in the 1820 census as a resident of Vincennes. However, he and his wife were both over forty-five years of age and had a son and daughter. See photostats of 1820 census returns in Genealogy Division, Indiana State Library. Apparently this John Pitcher remained in Vincennes at least for a decade. On May 21, 1825, he advertised in the Vincennes *Western Sun* for a horse that had strayed, and there was an announcement in that paper that John Pitcher's household goods would be "on sale at his home on September 12, 1829."
47. Pike County (Ind.) Court Order Book A, p. 119.
48. *Ibid.,* B, p. 123.
49. Spencer County (Ind.) Deed Book A, pp. 232, 239, 245.
50. Spencer County (Ind.) Marriage Register.
51. U. S. Census returns, 1830, photostats in Genealogy Division, Indiana State Library.
52. *History of Warrick, Spencer and Perry Counties,* pp. 312–13.
53. Beveridge, *Abraham Lincoln,* I, 91n.
54. Weik, *The Real Lincoln,* p. 130.
55. Alice L. Harper Hanby, "John Pitcher," in Southwestern Indiana Historical Society, *Proceedings,* January 31, 1922 (Indiana Historical Commission, *Bulletin No. 16,* October, 1922), p. 55.
56. Weik, *The Real Lincoln,* p. 130.
57. Hanby, "John Pitcher," in Southwestern Indiana Historical Society, *Proceedings,* January 31, 1922, p. 55.
58. William E. Barton stated that Squire Pate of Kentucky lent Lincoln law books as early as 1826 when he was working at Troy. *The Women Lincoln Loved,* p. 149.
59. According to David Turnham, his own father, Thomas Turnham, and Abe's father, Thomas Lincoln, "were acquaintances in Kentucky." The names of Thomas Turnham and Bathsheba Lincoln, mother of Thomas, appear in the same Nelson County (Ky.) Commissioners Tax Book, 1789.

On October 23, 1860, Abraham Lincoln, candidate for President of the United States, wrote to David Turnham:
"My dear old friend:
"Your kind letter of the 17th is received. I am indeed very glad to learn that you are still living and well. I well remember when you and I last met, after a separation of fourteen years, at the crossroad voting

place, in the fall of 1844. It is now sixteen years more and we are both no longer young men. I suppose that you are a grandfather; and I, though married much later in life, have a son nearly grown.

"I would much like to visit the old home, and old friends of my boyhood, but I feel the chance of doing so soon, is not very good.

"Your friend & Sincere well-wisher, A. Lincoln."

Collected Works, IV, 130–31.

60. The book was published in Corydon, printed by Carpenter and Douglass. The copy read by Abraham is now in the Indiana University Library at Bloomington. In 1865 Turnham gave it to William Herndon as the latter tells in the statement pasted inside the front cover of the volume:

"In the year 1865 I was in Spencer County, Indiana, Lincoln's old home, gathering up the facts of young Abraham's life. I then and there became acquainted with David Turnham, merchant and man of integrity, a playmate, schoolfellow, associate, and firm friend of Mr. Lincoln, who gave me at that time and place, a good history of young Lincoln. I took the history down in his presence at the time. At the conclusion of our business, he asked me if I would like to have some relic of Mr. Lincoln, and to which I said I should like to have such relic very much; he then gave me this book, stating to me that it was the first law book that Lincoln ever read." Herndon presented the volume to the Lincoln Memorial Collection of Chicago in 1886. In 1894 it was purchased by William H. Winters, librarian of the New York Law Institute. After his death it was acquired by William H. Townsend. American Bar Association, *Journal*, XIV, No. 2 (February, 1928), p. 82.

61. In a speech delivered in Independence Hall in Philadelphia, on February 22, 1861, when he was on his way to Washington for the Inauguration, Lincoln said: "I am filled with deep emotion at finding myself standing here in the place where were collected together the wisdom, the patriotism, the devotion to principle, from which sprang the institutions under which we live . . . all the political sentiments I have entertained have been drawn, so far as I have been able to draw them, from the sentiments which originated, and were given to the world from this hall. . . ." *Collected Works*, IV, 240.

62. Grandview *Monitor*, November 14, 1926.

63. J. Edward Murr, in Ehrmann, *The Missing Chapter in the Life of Abraham Lincoln*, pp. 89–90.

64. In 1856, in Decatur, Illinois, Abraham Lincoln stopped by the courthouse, at the "exact spot where I stood by our wagon when we moved from Indiana. . . ." Henry C. Whitney who was with him asked him if, at that time, he "had expected to be a lawyer and practise law in that courthouse." To which Lincoln replied, "No; I didn't know I had sense enough to be a lawyer then." Related in Tarbell, *The Early Life of Abraham Lincoln*, pp. 99–100.

CHAPTER XVI

1. William Wood's statement to Herndon, September 15, 1865, in Herndon-Weik MSS.

2. William Wood said that the new house "was not completed until after

Lincoln left for Illinois. The house that Lincoln lived in is gone."
Ibid.

3. For John Hanks' contacts with the Lincolns in Indiana see Lincoln to Hanks, August 24, 1860, in *Collected Works*, IV, 100–1.
4. Dennis Hanks to Herndon, March 7, 1866, in Herndon-Weik MSS.
5. Herndon and Weik, *Herndon's Life of Lincoln* (1930 ed.), p. 57. Dennis Hanks claimed that the recurrence of the milk sickness in the Little Pigeon Creek community was a contributing factor to the removal. Hanks to Herndon, March 7, 1866, in Herndon-Weik MSS.
6. Thomas and Sarah Lincoln to Thomas J. Wathen, Hardin County (Ky.) Deed Book C, p. 19.
7. Dennis Hanks to Herndon, June 13, 1865, in Herndon-Weik MSS.
8. Spencer County (Ind.) Deed Book B, p. 63. Also Hanks to Herndon, June 13, 1865, in Herndon-Weik MSS.
9. Spencer County Deed Book B, p. 419: James Gentry to Joseph Gentry.
10. David Turnham, September 15, 1865; in Herndon-Weik MSS.
11. Thomas Lincoln had been in Illinois but a year when he decided to return to Spencer County. He, Squire Hall, and Dennis Hanks, with their wives and children, retraced their steps as far as Coles County where they were persuaded to settle by some of Sally Lincoln's relatives. Abraham and John D. Johnston did not accompany them, but stayed on the Sangamon River. Charles H. Coleman, *Abraham Lincoln and Coles County, Illinois* (New Brunswick, N. J., 1955), p. 19.
12. Quoted in Stott, *Indiana Baptist History*, p. 64.
13. John A. Cady, in Grandview *Monitor*, April 11, 1935.
14. "Autobiography," prepared for Scripps, in *Collected Works*, IV, 63. John Hanks stated that when Thomas Lincoln came to Macon County he owned "four yoke of oxen." Statement to Herndon, n. d., in Herndon-Weik MSS. Mrs. Harriet Chapman, daughter of Dennis and Elizabeth Hanks, who made the trip as a four-year-old girl, testified late in her life, that the party had "three covered wagons, two drawn by oxen, and one by horses, and two saddle horses." *The Lincoln Way. Report of the Board of Trustees of the Illinois State Historical Library on the Investigations Made by C. M. Thompson* [Springfield, 1913], pp. 18–22.
15. Evansville *Daily Journal*, May 28, 1860. Nicolay and Hay stated that Thomas Lincoln "packed his household goods and those of his children and sons-in-law into a single wagon drawn by two yoke of oxen. . . ." *Abraham Lincoln, a History*, I, 45.
16. Paducah (Ky.) *Journal*, May 26, 1860. A campaign poem of 1860 was based on the wagon-building enterprise. The first stanza reads:
      "I made a little wagon when we moved to Illinois
      To haul my good old parents, and the little girls and boys
      I drove a yoke of oxen, walking barefoot by their side
      So wait for the wagon and we'll take a ride."
   Evansville *Daily Journal*, July 17, 1860.
17. Tarbell, *The Early Life of Abraham Lincoln*, p. 99; Vannest, *Lincoln the Hoosier*, p. 205; Murr, "Lincoln in Indiana," in *Indiana Magazine of History*, XIV, 166; Hobson, *Footprints of Abraham Lincoln*, p. 34.
18. J. Edward Murr, in Ehrmann, *The Missing Chapter in the Life of Abraham Lincoln*, p. 93.

266

19. The "pen" phase of the story apparently originated with a Rockport correspondent of the Evansville *Enquirer,* who, in a story published in that paper on September 2, 1860, stated that "Abe slid off" without paying for the pens which he purchased from Jones, and added that "the people expected it." Jones came back with a reply in the paper of September 5, saying that he had read this story and "can say that there is not one word of truth in the assertion. . . ."

20. Upon closing the genealogical story of the Lincolns this comment coming from one who interviewed Abraham should be exhibited: "Recognizing that his parents were of humble life, and ranking himself with plain people, he distinctly claimed to be of a stock, which though it had produced no man of great eminence, had always been of good repute in general as to both character and capacity." Barrett, *Abraham Lincoln and His Presidency,* I, iii.

21. Vannest, *Lincoln the Hoosier,* p. 207.

22. Cockrum, *Pioneer History of Indiana,* pp. 320–21.

23. Arthur F. Hall, *The Lincoln Memorial Way through Indiana* (Indianapolis, 1932), p. 63.

24. Tarbell, *The Early Life of Abraham Lincoln,* p. 87.

25. Luke 2:52.

26. "Autobiography," in *Collected Works,* IV, 62.

27. Atkinson, *The Boyhood of Lincoln,* p. 35.

28. Stevens Point (Wis.) *The Wisconsin Pinery,* September 29, 1895.

29. According to an account of a speech which Lincoln made in Indianapolis on September 19, 1859, he said that "Away back in the fall of 1816, when he was in his eighth year, his father brought him over from the neighboring State of Kentucky, and settled in the State of Indiana, and he grew up to his present enormous height on our own good soil of Indiana." *Collected Works,* III, 563.

30. Sally Bush Lincoln to Herndon, September 8, 1865, in Herndon-Weik MSS.

31. Frank Moore, *Anecdotes, Poetry and Incidents of the War: North and South, 1860–1865* (New York, 1866), p. 524. Frank B. Carpenter, the artist who lived in the White House for six weeks in 1863, wrote: "Mr. Lincoln's height was six feet three and three-quarters inches 'in his stocking-feet.' He stood up, one day, at the right of my large canvas, while I marked his exact height upon it." *Six Months at the White House,* p. 217. The measurement agrees with Lincoln's own statement in 1859: "I am, in height, six feet, four inches, nearly. . . ." *Collected Works,* III, 512.

32. Sally Bush Lincoln to Herndon, September 8, 1865, in Herndon-Weik MSS.

33. "Autobiography," prepared for Scripps, in *Collected Works,* IV, 62. In the autobiographical note prepared for Jesse W. Fell, Lincoln wrote, "Of course when I came of age I did not know much." Yet two years later he announced as candidate for the Illinois legislature. He further advised Fell, "I have not been to school, since. The little advance I now have upon this store of education, I have picked up from time to time under the pressure of necessity." *Ibid.,* III, 511.

Just two years after Lincoln left Indiana he was writing, "Upon the subject of education, not presuming to dictate any plan or system respecting it, I can only say that I view it as the most important subject which we as a people can be engaged in. That every man may receive at least, a moderate education, and thereby be enabled to read the histories of his own and other countries, by which he may duly appreciate the value of our free institutions, appears to be an object of vital importance, even on this account alone, to say nothing of the advantages and satisfaction to be derived from all being able to read the scriptures, and other works, both of a religious and moral nature, for themselves." "Communication to the People of Sangamo County," March 9, 1832, in *ibid.*, I, 8.

34. Stephen T. Logan, who later took Lincoln into partnership, heard him speak in August, 1832, when he was running for the legislature. "He made a very sensible speech," Logan recalled. "His manner was very much the same as in after life; that is, the same peculiar characteristics were apparent then, though of course in after years he evinced more knowledge and experience. But he had the same novelty and same peculiarity in presenting his ideas. He had the same individuality that he kept through all his life." Nicolay and Hay, *Abraham Lincoln, a History*, I, 108.

35. After reaching Illinois, but while he was still but twenty-one years of age, Abraham Lincoln gave a political speech, the subject of which was the navigation of the Sangamon River. A candidate for the state legislature preceded him, and Abe "beat him to death" in political oratory. Two years later he was running for the legislature himself. Lamon, *Life of Abraham Lincoln*, p. 78.

36. Rankin, *Personal Recollections of Abraham Lincoln*, p. 321. Lincoln then added, "The fundamental truths reported in the four gospels as from the lips of Jesus Christ and that I first heard from the lips of my mother, are settled and fixed moral precepts with me." *Ibid.*, p. 325.

37. Rockport *Journal*, October 3, 1902.

38. Thomas Shoaff, in Lerna (Ill.) *Eagle*, November 17, 1920.

39. Herndon and Weik, *Herndon's Life of Lincoln* (1930 ed.), p. 39.

40. Lucius E. Chittenden, *Personal Reminiscences 1840–1890* . . . (New York, 1893), p. 347.

41. Sally Bush Lincoln to Herndon, September 8, 1865, in Herndon-Weik MSS.

42. Severns Valley Church Record Book, November 21, 1789, in the Baptist Theological Seminary, Louisville, Kentucky.

43. A conversation which the Hon. Henry C. Deming, congressman from Connecticut, had with Abraham Lincoln, while he was President, with respect to his attitude towards church membership, has been preserved as follows:

"He said, he had never united himself to any church, because he found difficulty in giving his assent, without mental reservation to the long complicated statements of Christian doctrine, which characterize their Articles of Belief and Confession of Faith. 'When any church,' he continued, 'will inscribe over its altar, as its sole qualification for membership the Saviour's condensed statement of the substance of both law and Gospel, "Thou shalt love the Lord thy God with all thy heart, and with all thy soul and with all thy mind, and thy neighbor as thyself," that church will I join with all my heart and all my soul.'"

Henry C. Deming, *Eulogy of Abraham Lincoln . . . June 8, 1865* (Hartford, Conn., 1865), p. 42.

44. Lincoln referred to Henry Clay as "my beau ideal of a statesman," in his opening debate with Douglas, at Ottawa, Illinois, August 21, 1858. *Collected Works,* III, 29.
45. Atkinson, *The Boyhood of Lincoln,* p. 45.
46. John Hanks cited in Evansville *Daily Journal,* July 12, 1860.
47. Joseph C. Richardson to Herndon, September 14, 1865, in Herndon-Weik MSS. After visiting in the Little Pigeon neighborhood and interviewing those who knew Abraham as a boy, William Herndon wrote: "Oh, what an admirable sweet, good boyish record 'Abe' has left behind, i.e., his childhood's life for the world to love and to imitate." Herndon to Charles H. Hart, April 13, 1866, in Herndon-Weik MSS.
48. Evansville *Daily Journal,* July 19, 1866.
49. Scripps, *Life of Abraham Lincoln* (1900 ed.), p. 22.
50. Sally Bush Lincoln to Herndon, September 8, 1865, in Herndon-Weik MSS.
51. See report of Lincoln's address at Indianapolis, September 19, 1859, in *Collected Works,* III, 463.

Upon his return from a visit to his old home in Indiana in 1844, Lincoln wrote a long poem of four "cantos." Numbers 2 and 4 have already been included in either the text or footnotes. See above, pp. 39–41, 226–27, 246–47. All of Number 1 and the first two stanzas of the unfinished Number 3 follow:

[Canto 1]

My childhood's home I see again,
  And sadden with the view;
And still, as memory crowds my brain,
  There's pleasure in it too.

O Memory! thou midway world
  'Twixt earth and paradise,
Where things decayed and loved ones lost
  In dreamy shadows rise,

And, freed from all that's earthly vile,
  Seem hallowed, pure, and bright,
Like scenes in some enchanted isle
  All bathed in liquid light.

As dusky mountains please the eye
  When twilight chases day;
As bugle-notes that, passing by,
  In distance die away;

As leaving some grand waterfall,
  We, lingering, list its roar—
So memory will hallow all
  We've known, but know no more.

Near twenty years have passed away
    Since here I bid farewell
To woods and fields, and scenes of play,
    And playmates loved so well.

Where many were, but few remain
    Of old familiar things;
But seeing them, to mind again
    The lost and absent brings.

The friends I left that parting day,
    How changed, as time has sped!
Young childhood grown, strong manhood gray,
    And half of all are dead.

I hear the loved survivors tell
    How nought from death could save,
Till every sound appears a knell,
    And every spot a grave.

I range the fields with pensive tread,
    And pace the hollow rooms,
And feel (companion of the dead)
    I'm living in the tombs.

            [Unfinished Canto 3]
And now away to seek some scene
    Less painful than the last—
With less of horror mingled in
    The present and the past.

The very spot where grew the bread
    That formed my bones, I see.
How strange, old field, on thee to tread,
    And feel I'm part of thee!

Collected Works, I, 370, 378–79

Sources

L Lincolniana
O Orientation book or pamphlet
B Book which Lincoln read in Indiana
P Periodical
N Newspaper

D Local, county, state, or federal document
D-P Printed document
MS Manuscript
T Transcription—by photostat, microfilm, or typescript

OVER A PERIOD OF THIRTY YEARS the author has gathered the largest collection of books and pamphlets exclusively about Abraham Lincoln that has ever been assembled. As the eight thousand items passed through his hands, he became familiar with their contents. The index to this collection which is in the Lincoln National Life Foundation at Fort Wayne offers a most exhaustive reference file.

Books and pamphlets concerning Lincoln published previous to 1940 are listed in *Lincoln Bibliography 1839–1939,* compiled by Jay Monaghan (2 volumes. Illinois State Historical Society, Springfield, 1943). For Lincolniana published since 1940 see *Lincoln Lore, passim.*

This compilation of sources includes only the items to which direct or indirect reference is made in the text.

Abraham Lincoln Association, *The Collected Works of Abraham Lincoln* (8 volumes plus index. Rutgers University Press, 1952–55) [L]
Æsop's Fables (Lancaster, 1804) [B]
American Bar Association, *Journal,* XIV, No. 2 (February, 1928) [P]
American Forests and Forest Life (Washington, D. C.), March, 1924 [P]
American Magazine (New York), February, 1908 [P]
American Review of Reviews (New York), June, 1923 [P]
Appleton's Cyclopædia of American Biography (6 volumes. New York, 1888–89) [O]

271

[The Arabian Nights] *The Oriental Moralist, or the Beauties of the Arabian Nights Entertainments* . . . (Boston, 1797) [B]

Arnold, Isaac N., *The Life of Abraham Lincoln* (Chicago, 1885) [L]

Atkinson, Eleanor, *The Boyhood of Lincoln* (New York, 1908) [L]

Audubon, John James, *The Birds of America* (London, 1827–38) [O]

Bailey, Nathan, *A Universal Etymological English Dictionary* . . . (Glasgow, 1802) [B]

[Baillie, John] "An Englishman's Pocket Note-Book in 1828," in *Magazine of American History*, XIX (January–June, 1888), 331–38, 424–28, 511–12; XX (July–December, 1888), 61–64 [O]

Banta, David D., *A Historical Sketch of Johnson County Indiana* (Chicago, J. H. Beers & Co., 1881) [O]

Baptist Theological Seminary, Louisville and Elizabethtown, Kentucky, Severns Valley (Ky.) Baptist Church Record Book, 1789 [MS]

Barrett, Joseph H., *Abraham Lincoln and His Presidency* (2 volumes. Cincinnati, 1904) [L]

_____, *Life of Abraham Lincoln* . . . (New York, 1865) [L]

Barton, William E., *The Women Lincoln Loved* (Indianapolis, 1927) [L]

Beveridge, Albert J., *Abraham Lincoln 1809–1858* (2 volumes. Boston and New York, 1928) [L]

Bingham, Caleb, *The American Preceptor* . . . (2d ed. Boston, 1795) [O]

Bradford, Ralph, *Reprieve. A Christmas Story of 1863* (Washington, D. C., 1940) [L]

Brocket, Linus P., *The Life and Times of Abraham Lincoln, Sixteenth President of the United States* . . . (Philadelphia, 1865) [L]

Brown, Ora, Collection of Lincolniana, Dale, Indiana. Collection is exhibited at Santa Claus (Ind.) Post Office Museum [O]

Browne, Francis F., *The Every-Day Life of Abraham Lincoln* . . . (New York and St. Louis, 1886) [L]

Browne, Robert H., *Abraham Lincoln and Men of His Times* (2 volumes. New York, 1901) [L]

Bunyan, John, *The Pilgrim's Progress* . . . (Philadelphia, 1817) [B]

Carpenter, Frank B., *Six Months at the White House with Abraham Lincoln* . . . (New York, 1866) [L]

Chicago *Tribune*, September 23, 1890 [N]

Chittenden, Lucius E., *Personal Reminiscences 1840–1890* . . . (New York, 1893) [L]

Christ Church, Queen Caroline Parish, Ann Arundel (now Howard) County, Maryland, Records, 1713 [MS]

Cockrum, William M., *A Pioneer History of Indiana* (Oakland City, Ind., 1907) [O]

Coleman, Charles H., *Abraham Lincoln and Coles County, Illinois* (New Brunswick, N. J., 1955) [L]

Collins, Lewis, *Historical Sketches of Kentucky* . . . (Cincinnati, 1848) [O]

Daboll, Nathan, *Daboll's Schoolmaster's Assistant . . . being a plain practical system of Arithmetic* . . . (Albany, 1817) [B]

Dale (Ind.) *Weekly Reporter,* June 23, 1916 [N]

[Defoe, Daniel], *The Life and Most Surprising Adventures of Robinson Crusoe* . . . (London, 1810) [B]

De la Hunt, Thomas J., *Perry County, a History* (Indianapolis, 1916) [O]

Deming, Henry C., *Eulogy of Abraham Lincoln . . . June 8, 1865* (Hartford, Conn., 1865) [L]

Dilworth, Thomas. *Dilworth's Spelling-Book, Improved* . . . (Philadelphia, 1796) [B]

_____, *The Schoolmaster's Assistant* . . . (Wilmington, 1796) [B]

Dupuy, Starke, *Hymns and Spiritual Songs* (Louisville, 1818) [B]

Duss, John S., *George Rapp and His Associates (The Harmony Society)* (Indianapolis, 1914) [O]

Ehrmann, Bess V., *The Missing Chapter in the Life of Abraham Lincoln* . . . (Chicago, 1938) [L]

Elizabethtown (Ky.), Minutes of the Board of Trustees, No. 1, Town Hall, Elizabethtown [D]

Elizabethtown (Ky.) Academy, Record Book I, Town Hall, Elizabethtown [MS]

Esarey, Logan, *The Indiana Home* (R. E. Banta, Crawfordsville, Ind., 1943) [O]

Evansville (Ind.) *Courier and Journal,* February 12, 1928; February 9, 1930; February 2, 1933; September 29, 1939 [N]

Evansville *Enquirer,* May 1, 1860–January 1, 1861 [N]

Evansville *Journal,* October 14, 1840; May 28, 30, 1860; June 2, 7, 1860; July 2, 1860–January 1, 1861; July 19, 1866; July 11, 1890 [N]

Executive Proceedings of the State of Indiana 1816–1836, edited by Dorothy Riker (*Indiana Historical Collections,* XXIX, Indianapolis, 1947) [O]

Fearing, Clarence W., *Contemporary Kindred of Abraham Lincoln* (Weymouth, Mass., 1928) [L]

The Filson Club Quarterly (Louisville, Ky.)
  Warren, Louis A., "Abraham Lincoln Senior, Grandfather of the President," in volume V, No. 3 (July, 1931), pp. [136] –52 [O]

Ford, Henry A. and Kate B., *A History of Cincinnati, Ohio* . . . (Cincinnati, 1881) [O]

Fortune, Will (ed.), *Warrick and Its Prominent People* (Evansville, 1881) [O]

Franklin, Benjamin. *The Life of Dr. Benjamin Franklin Written by Himself* (Montpelier, 1809) [B]

_____. *The Works of Benjamin Franklin.* . . , edited by Jared Sparks (10 volumes. Boston, 1840) [O]

Franklin College Library, Franklin, Indiana. Little Pigeon Association
of Separate Baptists, Minutes, 1822– [MS]

Gesell, Arnold, *Studies in Child Development* (New York, 1948) [O]

Grandview (Ind.) *Monitor,* October, 1926–December, 1938 [N]

Grinnell, Josiah B., *Men and Events of Forty Years . . .* (Boston, 1891)
[O]

Grolier Club. *One Hundred Influential American Books Printed before
1900 . . .* (The Grolier Club, New York, 1947) [O]

Gross, Anthony, *Lincoln's Own Stories* (New York and London, 1912)
[L]

Hall, Arthur F., *The Lincoln Memorial Way through Indiana* (Indianapolis, 1932) [L]

Hanaford, Phebe A. C., *Abraham Lincoln: His Life and Public Service*
(Boston, 1865) [L]

Haycraft, Samuel, *History of Elizabethtown* (Elizabethtown, Ky., 1921)
[O]

Herndon, William H., and Weik, Jesse W., *Herndon's Life of Lincoln
. . .,* with an introduction by Paul M. Angle (A. & C. Boni, New York,
1930) [L]

Herndon-Weik Papers [MS]

> During the month of June, 1865, William Herndon interviewed John
> and Dennis Hanks in Chicago, and later wrote down, from the
> notes he had made, what they had related to him in the first person
> but couched in his own words. The following September, Herndon
> visited in Coles County, Illinois, the stepmother of Abraham Lin-
> coln and also her daughter, Matilda Johnston Moore. On September
> 12 he reached Spencer County, Indiana, where he remained for
> four days and recorded the reminiscences of many people who had
> known Abraham when he lived there. Herndon later received
> several letters from these friends and relatives, which, with the
> records of the interviews, are in the Herndon-Weik collection of
> papers deposited in the Library of Congress, Washington, D.C.,
> and the Huntington Library, San Marino, California. A microfilm
> from the Library of Congress of the papers in both libraries is in
> the Lincoln National Life Foundation in Fort Wayne, Indiana. Most
> of the items in the collection of the Library of Congress appear in
> Emanuel Hertz, *The Hidden Lincoln . . .* (New York, 1938).

Herrick, Francis H., *Audubon the Naturalist* (2 volumes. New York,
1917) [O]

Hertz, Emanuel, *Abraham Lincoln, A New Portrait* (2 volumes. New
York, 1931) [L]

_____, *The Hidden Lincoln, from the Letters and Papers of Wil-
liam H. Herndon* (New York, 1938) [L]

History of Warrick, Spencer and Perry Counties, Indiana . . . (Chicago:
Goodspeed Bros. & Co., 1885) [O]

Hoard's Dairyman (Fort Atkinson, Wis.), May 2, 1924 [P]

Hobart, Chauncey, *Recollections of My Life, Fifty Years of Itineracy in the Northwest* (Red Wing Printing Co., 1885) [O]

Hobson, Jonathan T., *Footprints of Abraham Lincoln* . . . (Dayton, Ohio, 1909) [L]

Holland, Josiah G., *The Life of Abraham Lincoln* (Springfield, Mass., 1866) [L]

The Holy Bible. *Containing the Old and New Testaments with Arguments prefixed to the different books and moral and theological observations illustrating each chapter. Composed by the Reverend Mr. Ostervald* . . . (1799) [B]

Howells, William Dean, *Life of Abraham Lincoln* (Abraham Lincoln Association, Springfield, Ill., 1938) [L]

Illinois State Historical Library, Springfield
  Little Pigeon Church Minute Book, 1816–1840 [MS] A transcript of this is in the Indiana Division, Indiana State Library.

Illinois State Historical Society, *Journal* (Springfield) [P]
  Oakleaf, J. B., "Azel W. Dorsey, Lincoln's Teacher in Indiana, Buried in Illinois," in volume XXII, No. 2 (October, 1929), pp. 447–51
  _____, *Transactions*, 1907 (Springfield, 1908), pp. 165–67 [O]

Indiana, State of. *Revised Laws of Indiana*, 1824 [D-P, B]; 1831 [D-P]

Indiana Boundaries, Territory, State, and County (*Indiana Historical Collections*, XIX, Indianapolis, 1933) [O]

Indiana counties [D]
  Dubois, 1817 (county seat, Jasper): Marriage Register 1; Will Book A
  Gibson, 1813 (county seat, Princeton): Deed Book 1; Marriage Register 1; Will Book A
  Knox, 1790 (county seat, Vincennes): Deed Book A; Marriage Register 1; Court Order Books A, B
  Perry, 1814 (county seat, Cannelton): Circuit Court Order Books, 1815–1832; Deed Book, A, B, C; Marriage Register 1; Probate Court Record, 1813–30
  Pike, 1817 (county seat, Petersburg): Circuit Court Order Book, A, B; Court of Justice Books 1, 2; Marriage Register 1
  Spencer, 1818 (county seat, Rockport): Court Order Book, 1833, 1847; Deed Book A, B, 3, 4; Marriage Register 1; Will and Probate Record A
  Warrick, 1813 (county seat, Boonville): Circuit Court Order Book, 1818–1830; Commissioners Record, 1813; Complete Record Book, 1, 2; Deed Book, 1, 2, 5; Marriage Records 1; Probate Court Order Book A

Indiana Magazine of History (Bloomington) [P]
  Barr, Arvil S., "Warrick County Prior to 1818," in volume XIV (1918), 320–22
  Carmony, Donald F., "Kingdom Church," in volume XXIX (1933), 104–13

Embree, Lucius C., "Morris Birkbeck's Estimate of the People of Princeton in 1817," in volume XXI (1925), 289–99

Jordan, Philip D., "The Death of Nancy Hanks Lincoln," in volume XL (June, 1944), [103] –110

Murr, J. Edward, "Lincoln in Indiana," in volume XIII (1917), [307] –348; volume XIV (1918), 13–75, 148–82

Thompson, Charles N., "General La Fayette in Indiana," in volume XXIV (1928), 57–77

Warren, Louis A., "The Shipley Ancestry of Lincoln's Mother," in volume XXIX (1933), [203] –212

Indiana State Library, Indianapolis

Archives Division: Record of Field Notes South and West of the Second Principal Meridian, volume V [D]; Tract Book, Vincennes District, No. VI, volume II [D]; U. S. Census, 1820, Census of manufactures, microfilm of original returns in National Archives [T]; Vincennes Land Office Records, Relinquishments [D]

Genealogical Division: U. S. Census, 1820 and 1830, returns of heads of families for Indiana, photostats of original returns in National Archives [T]

Indiana Division: Index of Indiana Post Offices; Index to Indianapolis newspapers which includes over a thousand references to articles relating to Abraham Lincoln and the Lincoln family; Little Pigeon Church Minute Book, 1816–1840, transcript from original in Illinois State Historical Library [T]

Indiana Territory. *Journals of the General Assembly of Indiana Territory, 1805–1815* (*Indiana Historical Collections*, XXXII, Indianapolis, 1950) [O]

Indianapolis *Journal,* February 10, 1879 [N]

Indianapolis *News,* 1869–

Indianapolis *Star,* 1903–

Indianapolis *Times,* 1922–

Jasper (Ind.) *Herald,* June 6, 1900 [N]

Johnson, Howard, *A Home in the Woods. Oliver Johnson's Reminiscences of Early Marion County* (Indianapolis, Indiana Historical Society, 1951) [O]

Journal of Agricultural Research (Washington, D. C.,), XXXV, No. 6 (December 15, 1927) [P]

Journal of the American Chemical Society, LI, No. 12 (December, 1929)

Kansas City *Journal,* January 22, 1909 [N]

Kellar, James H., *An Archaeological Survey of Spencer County* (Indianapolis, Indiana Historical Bureau, 1956) [O]

Kentucky, State of. *A Digest of the Statute Law of Kentucky. . . ,* by William Littell and Jacob Swigert (2 volumes. Frankfort, 1822) [D-P]

Kentucky counties [D]

Breckinridge, 1799 (county seat, Hardinsburg): Circuit Court Deposition Book 1; County Court Minute Book 1, 2; Order Book 1, 2; Deed Book A, B, C; Marriage Register; Will Book, 1, 2

Green, 1792 (county seat, Greensburg): Deed Book, 7, 9, 15, 21; Marriage Register 1

Hardin, 1792 (county seat, Elizabethtown): Circuit Court, Equity Bundles, Order Book A; Court of Quarter Sessions, Minute Book, 1803, Order Book 1; County Court, Judgments and other papers, Order Book A, B, C, Ordinary Bundles; Deed Book A, B, C; Estray Book, 1806–15; Marriage Bonds; Marriage Register; Tax Book, 1792–1816

Henderson, 1798 (county seat, Henderson): Circuit Court, Ordinary and Equity Papers; Tax Books; Deed Book A, B, C, D

Jefferson, 1780 (county seat, Louisville): Deed Book U; Land Book A, B; Power of Attorney's Register 1; Surveyor's Book 1; Tax Book

Nelson, 1784 (county seat, Bardstown): Circuit Court Chancery Papers, Equity Bundles, Executions Book, District Fee Book, Judgments; County Court, Deposition Book 1 and Possessioners Report Book 1; Deed Book 1, 2; Marriage Register 1; Will Books A to F; Tax Books, 1785–1810

Mercer, 1785 (county seat, Harrodsburg): Deed Book 1, 2, 3, 7, 9; Surveyor's Book; Tax Books, 1789–1800; Will Book 1

Ohio, 1798 (county seat, Hartford): Marriage Register 1

Washington, 1792 (county seat, Springfield): Circuit Court Order Book A, B, Judgments and other Papers, Equity Bundles; County Court Order Book A, B; Deed Book A, B; Marriage Bonds; Marriage Register; Tax Book, 1792–1805; Will Book C

The Kentucky Preceptor . . . (Lexington, 1812) [B]

Lamon, Ward H., *The Life of Abraham Lincoln; from His Birth to His Inauguration as President* (Boston, 1872) [L]

——————, *Recollections of Abraham Lincoln, 1847–1865* (Chicago, 1895) [L]

Leahy, Ethel C. (comp.), *Who's Who on the Ohio River and Its Tributaries* . . . (Cincinnati, 1931) [O]

Lerna (Ill.) *Eagle*, November 17, 1920 [N]

Lincoln, Waldo, *History of the Lincoln Family: an Account of the Descendants of Samuel Lincoln of Hingham, Massachusetts, 1637–1920* (Worcester, Mass., 1923) [L]

Lincoln Herald (Harrogate, Tenn.) [P]

McMurtry, R. Gerald, "Thomas Lincoln's Corner Cupboard," in volume XLV, Nos. 1 and 2 (February and June, 1943), pp. 19–22, 32–33

The Lincoln Kinsman (Fort Wayne, Ind., Nos. 1–54, July, 1938–December, 1942) [P, L]

Lincoln Lore (Fort Wayne, Ind., April 15, 1929–   ) [P, L]

Lincoln Memorial Collection. *Sketch of the Life of Abraham Lincoln and a Catalogue of Articles Once Owned and Used by Him Now*

Owned by the Lincoln Memorial Collection (Chicago [1887]) [L]
Lincoln National Life Foundation, Fort Wayne, Indiana
  Bleakley, Robert, and Montgomery, William, Elizabethtown (Ky.)
    merchants, two Day Books and one Ledger, 1805–1809 [MS]
  Helm-Haycraft Collection, 1790–1830 [MS]
  Herndon-Weik Papers, microfilm from Library of Congress of Hern-
    don-Weik manuscripts in Library of Congress, Washington, D. C.,
    and the Huntington Library, San Marino, California (see note
    under Herndon-Weik Papers) [T]
  Letters: Simon Cameron to Dr. Sheldon Potter, December 20, 1831;
    John Morgan to wife, August 5, 1822; Peter Smith to J. Warren
    Keifer, July 17, 1860 [MS]
  Newspaper clippings [N]
  South Fork Baptist Church (Hardin County, Ky.) Record Book,
    photostat [T]
*The Lincoln Way. Report of the Board of Trustees of the Illinois State
Historical Library of the Investigations Made by C. M. Thompson*
  [Springfield, 1913] [L]
Lindley, Harlow (comp.), *Indiana as Seen by Early Travelers* (*Indiana
Historical Collections,* I, Indianapolis, 1916) [O]
Louisville *Advertiser,* May 4, 1822 [N]
Louisville *Courier-Journal,* February 20, 1874; January 5, 1881; Au-
  gust 20, 1902; February 16, 1913 [N]
Louisville *Democrat,* July 9, 1865 [N]
Lowe, Abraham T., *The Columbian Class Book* . . . (Worcester, Mass.,
  1824) [B]
Macdonald, Donald, *The Diaries of Donald Macdonald, 1824–1826*
  (Indiana Historical Society *Publications,* XIV, No. 2, Indianapolis,
  1942) [O]
McClure, James B., *Lincoln's Stories and Speeches* (Chicago, 1885) [L]
McMurtry, R. Gerald, *A Series of Monographs concerning the Lincolns
and Hardin County, Kentucky* (Elizabethtown, Ky., 1938) [L]
Maltby, Charles, *The Life and Public Services of Abraham Lincoln*
  (Stockton, Calif., 1884) [L]
Maryland, State of
  Annapolis Hall of Records, Land Grants, 1668 [D]
Moore, Frank, *Anecdotes, Poetry and Incidents of the War: North and
South* (New York, 1866) [O]
Murray, Lindley, *The English Reader* . . . (New York, 1815) [B]
Nason, Elias, *Eulogy on Abraham Lincoln* (William V. Spencer, Boston,
  1865) [L]
New-Harmony *Gazette,* October 1, 1825 [N]
New Orleans *Argus,* December 5, 1828 [N]
New Orleans *Louisiana Advertiser,* December 9, 10, 1828 [N]
New Orleans *Price Current and Commercial Intelligencer,* April 26,
  1828 [N]

Nicolay, John G., and Hay, John, *Abraham Lincoln, a History* (10 volumes. New York, 1890) [L]

The Outlook (New York), November 3, 1926 [P]

Paducah (Ky.) *Journal*, May 26, 1860 [N]

Pike, Nicholas, *The New Complete System of Arithmetick* . . . (Boston, 1804) [B]

Quin's Jests or, the Facetious Man's Pocket-Companion . . . (London, 1766) [B]

Ramsay, David, *The Life of George Washington* . . . (Boston, 1811) [B]

Rankin, Henry B., *Personal Recollections of Abraham Lincoln* (New York, 1916) [L]

Raymond, Henry J., *The Life and Public Service of Abraham Lincoln* . . . (New York, 1865) [L]

Rice, Allen Thorndike (comp.), *Reminiscences of Abraham Lincoln by Distinguished Men of His Times* (New York, 1888) [L]

Riley, James, *An Authentic Narrative of the Loss of the American Brig Commerce* . . . (New York, 1817) [B]

Rockport *Democrat*, March 17, 1860, September 12–November 17, 1947 [N]

Rockport (Ind.) *Journal*, February 12, 19, 1897, October 3, 1902 [N]

St. John, Mrs. Horace, *Audubon, The Naturalist of the New World* (Boston, 1861) [O]

St. Louis *Globe Democrat*, September 29, 1895 [N]

Sandburg, Carl, *Abe Lincoln Grows Up* (New York, 1926) [L]

_____, *Lincoln Collector. The Story of Oliver R. Barrett's Private Collection* (New York, 1950) [L]

Sarah Bush Lincoln (Elizabethtown Woman's Club, 1922) [L]

Scott, William, *Lessons in Elocution* . . . (Philadelphia, 1801) [B]

Scripps, John Locke, *The First Published Life of Abraham Lincoln, Written in the Year MDCCCLX* [Detroit, 1900] [L]

_____. *John Locke Scripps' 1860 Campaign Life of Abraham Lincoln Annotated*. . . , foreword and notes by M. L. Houser (Peoria, Ill., 1931) [L]

Shutes, Milton H., *Lincoln's Emotional Life* (Philadelphia, 1957) [L]

Southwestern Indiana Historical Society Papers [MS]

   Account of Anna C. O'Flynn's interview with G. B. Taylor [MS]

Southwestern Indiana Historical Society *Proceedings* (Indianapolis) [O]

   Armstrong, Ida D., "The Lincolns in Spencer County," in Indiana Historical Commission, *Bulletin No. 18*, October, 1923, pp. 54–62

   Iglehart, John E., "Some Correspondence between Lincoln Historians and This Society," in *ibid.*, pp. 63–88

   Inco, Nancy Grigsby, paper relating to the Lincolns and Grigsbys, in *ibid.*, pp. 91–92

   Hanby, Alice L. Harper, "John Pitcher," in Indiana Historical Commission, *Bulletin No. 16*, October, 1922, pp. 50–60

   Raleigh, Eldora Minor, "John A. Brackenridge," in *ibid.*, pp. 50–60

Schultz, Kate P. W., "General Thomas Gamble Pitcher," in *Indiana History Bulletin,* December, 1925, pp. 37–42

Spencer, J. H., *A History of Kentucky Baptists from 1796 to 1885 . . .* (2 volumes. Cincinnati, 1885) [O]

Springfield (Ill.) *Globe Democrat,* May 7, 1892 [N]

Stevens Point (Wis.) *The Wisconsin Pinery,* September 29, 1895 [N]

Stott, William T., *Indiana Baptist History 1798–1908* (Franklin, Ind., 1908) [O]

Tarbell, Ida M., *The Early Life of Abraham Lincoln* (New York, 1896) [L]

_____, *In the Footsteps of the Lincolns* (New York and London, 1924) [L]

_____, *The Life of Abraham Lincoln . . .* (2 volumes. New York, 1902) [O]

Terre Haute *Star,* February 11, 1923 [N]

Thayer, William M., *The Pioneer Boy and How He Became President* (Boston, 1864) [L]

Thompson, David D., *Abraham Lincoln, the First American* (Cincinnati, 1894) [L]

Thwaites, Reuben Gold (ed.), *Early Western Travels, 1784–1846 . . .* (32 volumes. Cleveland, 1904–7) [O]

Evans, Estwick, *A Pedestrious Tour . . .* 1818, volume VIII, 91–364

Maximillian, Prince of Wied, *Travels in the Interior of North America. . . ,* volumes XXII, XXIII, and XXIV

Townsend, William H., *Lincoln the Litigant . . .* (Boston and New York, 1925) [L]

U. S. National Archives

General Land Office, Receipts for sales of public lands, Nos. 8499, 9205 [D]

Census returns, *see under* Indiana State Library

University of Chicago, Chicago, Illinois

Durrett, R. T., Collection [MS]

Vannest, Charles G., *Lincoln the Hoosier. Abraham Lincoln's Life in Indiana* (St. Louis and Chicago, 1928) [L]

Vincennes (Ind.) *Western Sun & General Advertiser,* June, 1816–April, 1830 [N]

Warren, Louis A., *Lincoln's Parentage and Childhood* (New York, 1926) [L]

_____, *The Slavery Atmosphere of Lincoln's Youth* (Fort Wayne, Ind., 1933) [L]

_____, Transcription and Manuscript Collection [T, MS]: Helm-Haycraft Papers, 1790–1830; Hitchcock-Hanks Papers, Records and Correspondence

Webster, Noah, *The American Spelling Book . . .* (Hartford, 1809) [B]

Weems, Mason L., *The Life of Benjamin Franklin* . . . (Philadelphia, 1829) [B]

―――――, *The Life of Gen. Francis Marion* . . . (Philadelphia, 1822) [B]

―――――, *The Life of George Washington* . . . (Philadelphia, 1809) [B]

Weik, Jesse W., *The Real Lincoln* (Boston and New York, 1922) [L]

White, Charles T., *Lincoln the Athlete and Other Stories* (New York, 1930) [L]

Whitney, Henry C., *Life of Lincoln* (2 volumes. New York, 1908) [L]

Wilson, George R., *Early Indiana Trails and Surveys* (Indiana Historical Society *Publications,* VI, No. 3, Indianapolis, 1919) [O]

―――――, Historical Notes, comprising 25 volumes, in possession of Miss Margaret Wilson, Jasper, Indiana [MS]

―――――, *History of Dubois County from Its Primitive Days to 1910* . . . (Jasper, Ind., 1910) [B]

Wisconsin, State Historical Society of, Madison
Draper Collection [MS]

Index

[The genealogical system employed in this index to indicate relationship and generation within the Lincoln family is that used by Waldo Lincoln in his *History of the Lincoln Family* (1923). The first American progenitor, Samuel Lincoln, is letter *a*. His children are letters *aa, ab, ac,* etc. The children of his oldest child are *aaa, aab, aac,* etc.; and those of his second oldest child are *aba, abb, abc,* etc., through the succeeding generations.]

Beech Fork community (Ky.), 8, 9.
Beecher, Henry Ward, 170.
Berry, Rachel Shipley (Mrs. Richard, Sr.), 7.
Berry, Richard, Sr., 7–8.
Berry, Richard, Jr., 9, 218.
Berry, William, 126.
Beveridge, Albert J., on water supply on Lincoln farm, 221; no Bible in Lincoln home until 1819, p. 223; on Abraham's relationship with his father, 235.
Bible, Lincoln family, 30–32, 216, 223–24; read by and influence on Abraham, 30–32, 59, 115, 117, 212, 223–24; best gift of God, 223.
Big Bones, Shawnee Indian, 35.
Bingham, Caleb, The American Preceptor, 167.
Birds, of southern Indiana, 37–38. See also Wild turkeys.
Bixby, Widow Lydia, letter to, 237.
Blacksmith shop, 193.
Blair, James, Lincoln neighbor, 98.
Bleakley (Robert) & Montgomery (William), Elizabethtown merchants, 76, 125; Thomas Lincoln's transactions with, 5–6, 9; Daniel Johnston indebted to, 61; Daybook and Ledger, 217.
Boats, docked at New Orleans, 185. See also Flatboats, Steamboats.
Books, read by Abraham and their influence, 211–12, 213; strong religious and moral tone of, 28, 46–47, 66–67, 88, 93, 95, 106–8, 110, 213; illustrations, 30, 36, 91; fallacy of "fifty-mile radius" story, 164; available in and around Little Pigeon Creek community, 165; Æsop's Fables, 46–48, 59, 227, 228; Arabian Nights, 69–70; Bible, 30–32, 115, 212, 223, 224; Bunyan, Pilgrim's Progress, 48–51, 228; Columbian Class Book, 166; Daboll, Schoolmaster's Assistant, 130, 243–44; Defoe, Robinson Crusoe, 67–69, 232; dictionaries, 167–68, 256; Dilworth, Schoolmaster's Assistant, 130, 244; Dilworth, Spelling-Book, 28–30, 80, 106; Franklin's autobiography, 87–91, 94–95, 236; The Kentucky Preceptor, 166, 167, 255; Murray, English Reader, 103–6, 239; Pike, Arithmetick, 128–29, 130, 243; Quin's Jests, 195, 263; Ramsay, Life of George Washington, 162–64, 255; Revised Laws of Indiana (1824), 201–2, 265; Riley, Narrative, 109–11, 239–40; Scott, Lessons in Elocution, 76–80, 106, 234; Webster, American Spelling Book, 66–67, 106, 232, Weems's biographies of Franklin and Gen. Francis Marion, 166, 255; Weems, Washington, 91–95, 236–37, 255.
Boon, Ratliff, 191–92.
Boone, Daniel, 12.
Bowers, Mary and Joseph, attacked by panther, 41.
Brackenridge, Isabella McCullough (Mrs. John A.), 197.
Brackenridge, John A., lawyer, 197–99, 263, 264; alleged to have lent books to Abraham, 201.
Breckinridge, ——, Kentucky lawyer, 198, 263.
Breckinridge, John K., 262.
Bristow, Lavina, 112.
Bristow, Rev. Samuel, minister, Little Pigeon Church, 112, 114, 118, 240.
Brookville (Ind.), 264.
Brooner, Allen, 229.
Brooner, Henry, friend of Abraham's, 45, 171; recalls Abraham's remarkable memory, 80.
Brooner, Peter, Lincoln neighbor, 55, 98; famous hunter 39; death of wife, 54, 55.
Brooner, Mrs. Peter, death, 54, 55.
Browning, Mrs. O. H., 255.
Brumfield, Nancy Lincoln (adaaa e) (Mrs. William), 5, 8, 217, 227.
Brumfield, William, 5, 8, 217.
Buchanon, Joseph, 238.
Bunyan, John, The Pilgrim's Progress, read by Abraham, 48–51, 228.
Burkheart, George, 126.
Bush, Christopher, father of Sally, 60, 125; sheriff, Hardin County, 190; will, 230–31.

284

by Thomas Lincoln, 248, 254; "Old Bluenose," 254; sawpit, 254.
Crawford, William H., 190.
Crume, Mary Lincoln (*adaaa c*) (Mrs. Ralph), 217, 227.
Crume, Ralph, 64, 217.
Crutcher, James, 231.
Culley, Matthew W., 63.
Cumberland Gap, 4.
Cummings, Rev. Uriah, 121.
Cupboards, made by Thomas Lincoln, 140, 248.

Daboll, Nathan, *Schoolmaster's Assistant*, 130, 243–44.
Daniel, Vivian, 148.
Darlington (Ind.), 99.
Davis, William, 193.
Defeated Camp (Ky.), 7, 33.
Defoe, Daniel, *Robinson Crusoe,* read by Abraham, 67–69, 232–33.
Deming, Henry C., 268–69.
Democratic party, 191.
Devin, Rev. Alexander, 114, 119.
Dill, John T., 146.
Dill, Len, 146.
Dilworth, Thomas, *The Schoolmaster's Assistant,* 130, 244.
Dilworth, Thomas, *Spelling-Book,* studied by Abraham, 11, 28–30, 80, 223.
Distillery, Abraham employed in, 171.
Dorsey, Azel, 99.
Dorsey, Azel W., sketch of, 125–27; guardian of James and Charlott Swaney, 99, 126; schoolmaster, 81, 125, 127–28, 238, 239; recalls Abraham as a student, 128, 234; recalled by Lincoln, 242; in Illinois, 243, 244.
Dorsey, Eleanor Spriggs (Mrs. Azel W.), 125.
Dorsey, Greenberry, 125, 126, 242–43.
Dorsey, Sarah, *see* Shipley, Sarah Dorsey (Mrs. Robert, Jr.).
Douglas, Stephen A., Lincoln debates with, 219–20, 233; vote received in Spencer County, 1860, p. 262.
Downs, Rev. Thomas, 112, 113, 118.

Downs, Rev. William, 113–14, 117, 118.
Dupuy, Starke, *Hymns and Spiritual Songs,* 115–16.
Duschene, Madame, 184.
Dutton, John, Lincoln neighbor, 99; operates distillery, 171.

Education, Lincoln on importance of, 268–69. *See also* Schools.
Elizabethtown (Ky.), 4, 5; Thomas and Nancy Lincoln make home in, 9, 10; Sally Lincoln's house and lot in, 63, 204; stories of, 73; specimens of Thomas Lincoln's carpentry and cabinetmaking in, 139.
Elizabethtown (Ky.) Academy, 10–11.
Elizabethtown (Ky.) Woman's Club, 232.
Elkin, Rev. David, delivers sermon at Nancy Lincoln's grave, 55–56; anti-slavery minister, 117.
Emancipation Proclamation, 228.
Enlow, David, 221.
Evans, Julia, 157–58.

Farm implements, 141.
Farmer, Rev. Aaron, 170, 256.
Ferguson, Col. W. D., 261.
Ferries, across Ohio at mouth of Anderson River, 19, 20, 146; at mouth of Crooked Creek, 221; across Anderson River, 145; duties of keepers of, 249.
Fight, between William Grigsby and John D. Johnston, 196–97.
Fitch, John, 148, 250.
Flatboats, construction and description of, 177–78, 259–60; cargos of, 178; described by Col. Baillie, 179; names of, 260.
Flowers, cultivated by pioneer women, 160.
Forests, of southern Indiana, 26–28.
Forsythe, William, 259.
Fortune, William, 194–95.
Franklin, Benjamin, autobiography, read by Abraham, 87–91, 94–95, 236; biography by Weems, 166.
Friend, Charles, 252.

loneliness, 58; affection for Abraham, 59, 150; assumes household tasks, 59; welcomes stepmother and her children, 65, 71–72; engagement and marriage, 150–53; descriptions of, 150, 152–53, 250; joins church, 151; probable dowry, 152; friendship with Elizabeth Crawford, 160, 161; domestic in Crawford home, 161, 254; dies in childbirth, 173–74; grave, 174, 258.

Grigsby, William, fight with John D. Johnston, 196–97.

Grinnell, Josiah B., 227.

Grolier Club, 87–88, 91.

Gulliver, Rev. John P., on Lincoln's way of "putting things," 245.

Gunterman, Henry, Lincoln neighbor, 98.

Half-face camp, erected on Lincoln homesite, 16, 21, 203; not lived in, by Lincoln family, 222.

Hall, Elizabeth, see Hanks, Elizabeth Hall (Mrs. William).

Hall, James, children of, 251.

Hall, Levi, 251.

Hall, Matilda Johnston (Mrs. Squire), death of father, 62; member of Lincoln household, 71; cut by Abraham's axe, 152–53; friendship with Abraham, 152, 156–57, 253; marriage, 153, 154; moves to Illinois, 209; memento of, 252.

Hall, Nancy Hanks (Mrs. Levi), mother of Dennis Hanks, 252.

Hall, Shadrach, 207.

Hall, Squire, helps operate woodyard, 144; marriage to Matilda Johnston, 153, 154; moves to Illinois, 204, 209, 266; memento of, 252; genealogy, 252.

Hall, Wesley, 87, 207.

Hammond tannery, 193, 263.

Hanks, Dennis, comes to Indiana, 51; member of Lincoln household, 58; marriage, 84, 154; helps operate woodyard, 144; moves to Illinois, 204, 209, 266; Indiana property, 205, 252; genealogy, 252; recollections of Nancy Lincoln, 54, 57; on Sarah's loneliness after mother's death, 58; on Abraham's interest in *The Arabian Nights*, 69–70; recollections of Thomas Lincoln, 85, 140, 193; on Abraham's interest in clothes, 154; identifies "story-telling" blacksmith, 193; on water supply on Lincoln farm, 221; on Sally Lincoln's trap to get Thomas to join church, 240; claims that he bought paper for Abraham's copybook, 244; on Thomas Lincoln's landholdings, 253–54; doubts story of Abraham helping drunk, 257; on school at New Harmony, 257.

Hanks, Elizabeth, see Sparrow, Elizabeth Hanks (Mrs. Thomas).

Hanks, Elizabeth Hall (Mrs. William), 252.

Hanks, Elizabeth Johnston (Mrs. Dennis), death of father, 62; member of Lincoln household, 71; marriage, 84, 154; moves to Illinois, 209.

Hanks, James, father of Nancy, 6, 217, 252.

Hanks, John, recalls Thomas Lincoln, 85; on Abraham's speechmaking, 80; describes both Nancy and Sally Lincoln's cooking, 96; recollection of Sarah Lincoln Grigsby, 150; on Abraham's attitude toward girls, 155; on Abraham's politics, 189; on Abraham's honesty, 214; on Nancy Lincoln, 230; urges migration to Illinois, 204.

Hanks, Joseph, Jr., in Indiana, 44.

Hanks, Lucy (Shipley), see Sparrow, Lucy Shipley Hanks (Mrs. Henry).

Hanks, Mary, see Friend, Mary Hanks (Mrs. Jesse).

Hanks, Nancy, see Lincoln, Nancy Hanks.

Hanks, William, 252.

Hargrove, Elizabeth, see Crawford, Elizabeth Hargrove (Mrs. Andrew).

Harmonie (Ind.), terminus of mail route, 43; Rappite community, 122–24. See also New Harmony.

83, 115, 142, 145, 193–96, 211;
jobs, as axeman and railsplitter, 26–
27, 142–44, 248–49; helps father
on meetinghouse, 87; on farm,
141; as day laborer, 142; helps
operate woodyard, 144; as ferryman, 145–46; helps in distillery,
171, 257; helps take flatboat to
New Orleans, 175–85; clerk,
187; builds new cabin, 203–4;
melancholy and depression, causes
of, 174–75, 183, 258; shooting
wild turkey, 36, 174; death of
mother, 58, 59; madness of Matthew Gentry, 134, 174–75, 245–
47; death of sister, 173, 174, 175;
native ability and intellectual and
moral growth, 25, 80, 132–33,
133–34, 135–36, 210–11, 212,
214–15, 245, 267;
political influences, 188–93;
physical growth and appearance,
25, 26, 75, 96, 128, 134–36, 144,
154, 210, 267;
religious influences, of home, 24,
115, 212; of Bible reading, 30–
32, 59, 115, 117, 223; of preachers, 116–21; question of church
membership, 213, 268–69;
speaking and writing, Biblical influence on, 32, 211; Weems's influence on, 237; character of,
228, 232, 268; practices oratory,
80, 121, 211; early journalistic
efforts, 169; essay on kindness to
animals, 169; on temperance,
170;

verbatim quotes: on father's childhood, 4; on murder of grandfather, 33; shooting wild turkey, 36;
kicked by horse, 45; on teachers' requirements, 82; on meaning
of American Revolution, 94; on
wielding the axe, 142; "large for
his age," 210; "never in college or
Academy," 210; "on our own good
soil of Indiana," 215; entries in
family Bible, 216; on migration
from slave to free state, 219–20;
on wilderness that was Spencer

County, 222–23; comparison of
passing of Revolutionary soldiers
with trees struck by hurricane, 223;
on Bible as best gift of God to man,
223; in debate with Douglas, "old
serpent's tail just drawing out of
view," 233; "Major Generalships
. . . not as plenty as blackberries,"
233; lists Franklin as ardently
antislavery, 236; reference to
Weems's *Washington,* 236, 236–
37; on meaning of American Revolution, 237; war, a just retribution
for slavery, 238; on schools attended in Indiana, 238; eulogy on
death of Gen. Zachary Taylor, 237;
on Washington, before Springfield
Washingtonians, 237; "rock on
which you split," 239; paraphrase
of Matthew 12:30, p. 241; declares
antislavery stand, 241; recalls Dorsey, 242; "raised to farm work,"
248; on wanting to work, 248;
"spoken to by but one woman," 253;
on price of public lands, 253; "firm
as the surge repelling rock," 255;
on death of Thomas Jefferson and
John Adams, 256; on temperance,
257; "did work . . . in a small still
house," 257; on trip to New
Orleans, 259, 260; on residence in
Spencer County, 259; "Spanish
moss . . . a drapery of the forest,"
260; "always a whig in politics,"
261; admiration for Clay, 262, 269;
"from the most humble walks of
life," 262; letter to David Turnham, 264–65; speech in Independence Hall, 265; on migration to
Indiana, 267; on education, 267–
68; poems: on the bear hunt, 39–
41, 226–27; inspired by Matthew
Gentry's madness, 246–47; after
visit to old home, 269–70;

quotations and stories attributed to:
on difficulty of traveling from ferry
to homesite, 20; on slowness of
horse mill, 45; story of Bud and
Shedrach, Meshach, and Abed-
nego, 83; potatoes "mighty poor

292

Lincoln, Thomas, brother of Samuel (*a*), 3.

Lincoln, Thomas (*adaaa d*), father of Abraham (*adaaa db*), birth and early life, 4–5, 216; with Uncle Isaac, 5; Kentucky farms, 5, 10; loss of, 12–13; transactions with Bleakley & Montgomery, 5–6, 9; trip to New Orleans, 5, 61, 176; helps build mill race, 6; marriage to Nancy Hanks, 6, 8–9; birth of children, 9–10; interest in Abraham's education, 10, 24, 81, 128, 133, 243; decision to migrate to Indiana, 11–14, 219; opposition to slavery, 13–14; Indiana homesite, 16, 20–21, 42–43; moves family to Indiana, 16–20; construction of cabin, 21–23, witnesses murder of father by Indians, 33; patroller, 34, 60, 190; as hunter, 38; Indiana landholdings, 41–42, 158, 159; relatives in Indiana, 44; death and burial of first wife, 54–55; marriage to Sally Bush Johnston, 59, 63–64, 232; transports Johnston family to Indiana, 64–65; close relationship with Abraham, 84–85, 214, 235; helps construct Little Pigeon meetinghouse, 86–87; garden, 97; Pigeon Creek neighbors, 97–101; joins Little Pigeon Church, 114, 115, 240; grace asked at table, 115, 212; church trustee, 121, 258; carpenter and cabinetmaker, 139–41, 232, 248, 254; as farmer, 141; dowry for daughter, 152; assists Josiah Crawford in building home, 161; builds wagon for James Gentry, 178; Whig in politics, 189–90; new cabin, 203; moves to Illinois, 204, 209; sells farm, 205–6; economic status on departure for Illinois, 206; charges brought against, as church member, settled, 206–7; tombstone record, 216; settles in Coles County (Ill.), 266; "poverty myth," 217; sense of humor and talent for story telling, 34, 85, 193–94, 224; descriptions and estimates of, 85–86, 96, 115, 212, 214.

Lincoln, Thomas (*adaaa dc*), 10, 18.

Lincoln, Thomas (Tad, *adaaa dbd*), 225.

Lincoln and Green, New Orleans merchants, 185.

Little Mount Separate Baptist Church (Ky.), 11, 13, 115.

Little Pigeon Association of United Baptists, 114.

Little Pigeon Baptist Church, construction of meetinghouse, 86–87; established, 112; articles of faith, 113; "Regular Baptist," 112, 114; joins Little Pigeon Association, 114; Thomas and Sally Lincoln join, 114–15, 240; restriction on preaching in, 121; Abraham serves as sexton of, 121–22, 242; school held in, 127, 234; Sarah Lincoln joins, 151; burying ground, 174; Abraham never member of, 213.

Little Pigeon Creek Community, families comprising, 97–99; map of, 100–1; schools, 81, 127, 234–35; libraries in and near, 165; politics of, 192, 193.

Livestock, owned by Thomas Lincoln, 18, 141, 205, 206; cattle poisoned by snakeroot, 53.

Livingston, Robert, 148.

Lockwood, John M., 137.

Logan, Stephen T., 268.

Louisville (Ky.), 43.

Lowe, A. T., compiler of *The Columbian Class Book*, 166.

Lukins, Sarah, 157.

McClellan, Gen. John B., 262.

McCullough, Isabella, *see* Brackenridge, Isabella McCullough (Mrs. John A.).

McDaniel, James, 148.

Macdonald, Donald, on Rappite service, 124.

Madison, James, 15.

Mail route, Harmonie to Louisville, 43; Corydon to Elizabethtown, 43–44.

Maple sugar, 73, 97.

Marion, Gen. Francis, biography by Weems, 166.

Decatur
Site of first
Lincoln home
in Illinois

KASKASKIA RIVER

EMBARRASS RIVER

Terre Haute

Palestine

Vandalia .

ILLINOIS

Lawrenceville . Vincennes

WABASH RIVER

WHITE RIV

Princeton

New
Harmony

Evansville .

Mount Vernon